AF409247

ANGLO-CATHOLIC CLASSICS

Writings produced, re-published or edited by the Oxford fathers (or their disciples) that underwrite the Anglo-Catholic tradition.

NASHOTAH HOUSE PRESS

Nashotah House Theological Seminary
2777 Mission Road
Nashotah, WI 53058

www.nashotah.edu

This work is in the public domain. It is a facsimile copy of the original, except that the title page and the pagination have been altered.

The digitization was created by GoogleBooks.

Cover design by Ben Jefferies

Printed 2022

A
COMPENDIOUS
Ecclesiastical History,

FROM THE

EARLIEST PERIOD TO THE PRESENT TIME.

BY THE

REV. WILLIAM PALMER, M.A.

OF WORCESTER COLLEGE, OXFORD.

A NEW EDITION, ENLARGED.

LONDON:

JAMES BURNS, 17 PORTMAN STREET,

PORTMAN SQUARE.

M.DCCC.XL.

CONTENTS.

CONTENTS.

CHAPTER VIII.

CHAPTER IX.

CHAPTER X.

CHAPTER XI.

CHAPTER XII.

CHAPTER XIII.

CHAPTER XIV.

CHAPTER XV.

CHAPTER XVI.

CHAPTER XVII.

CHAPTER XXVII.

CHAPTER XXVIII.

A COMPENDIOUS

Ecclesiastical History.

CHAPTER I.

INTRODUCTION.

THE history of the world impresses the reflecting mind with the universal tendency of human institutions to decay and dissolution. Whether we contemplate the fate of man himself, or of illustrious empires raised by virtue, cemented by wisdom, but destroyed by luxury and sin, we trace in all the operation of that sentence of death which once passed on all men, and to which all that is merely human must bow.

But in the history of the Church we view not only the working of the law of death, but the counteracting tendency of the Spirit of life, sustaining man amidst his infirmities, elevating him above all that is carnal and terrestrial, and impressing on his actions and his destinies the stamp of eternity. Empires, superstitions, and philosophies, have faded away, but true religion continues always to exist; and as it came in the beginning from above, so at the end of all things it shall return thither again. The patriarchs and the prophets, the law and the gospel, preached to mankind the same religion, which was expanded and developed as the fulness of time drew on. We now behold the fulfilment of what the patriarchs desired to see; we enjoy the reality of those things which the law of Moses foreshadowed; we worship the God of Abel and of Abraham, and serve him with their faith.

And as the true religion has always been essentially the same, so has it ever had to contend with the same inclination of the human heart. That inclination was awfully exemplified in the days of Noah, when "all flesh had corrupted his way upon the earth;" and that patriarch's family were alone found just. It was still more wonderfully manifested in the rebellions and backslidings of the children of Israel. It is again seen in the description which Scripture gives of the fallen state of Jew and Gentile, when the Son of God came to save a perishing world (Rom. i. 1). And who, that reflects on the exhortations and predictions addressed to Christians by the Lord and his disciples, can fail to perceive that the same evil tendency of the human heart was always to remain, even in the state of grace, and to form the chief danger and trial of the Church of God?

The life of a true Christian, as described in Scripture, consists of self-denial, of warfare against the inclinations of nature, of prayer and watchfulness under the deepest consciousness of infirmity, of labour to walk under the guidance of the Spirit of God, with objects, tastes, and desires, altogether different from those of the natural man. It was the sovereign will of God, that those who are saved should be fitted for their glorious inheritance by the discipline of this rough and narrow way; but few, even of the best men, have passed through it without many grievous failures; all have come short of the glory of God, and all have need of serious and frequent repentance. Many, who profess to be disciples, have altogether turned away to the broad and beaten track; and, as our Lord teaches that some should hear the word with joy, but in time of temptation should fall away; that others should permit it to be snatched from them by the assaults of the devil, or to be choked beneath the cares of this world and the deceitfulness of riches; he adds, that in that day many shall begin to say, "We have eaten and drunk in thy presence, and thou hast taught in our streets;" and that his reply shall be, "I know you not whence ye are: depart from me, all ye workers of iniquity."[1]   The kingdom or Church of Christ is, indeed, compared to a field in which tares grow with the wheat,[2] and to a net which was let down into the sea, and gathered of all kinds both bad and good.[3] Such was to be the mingled state of the Christian Church, comprising not only evil men, but good men, subject to infirmities, errors, and sins.

Nor was the Church only to be tried by inward failings; it was to pass through the furnace of affliction and persecution from without.   The saints in heaven are described as "they that came out of great tribulation;"[4] and as the Captain of our salvation was made perfect through sufferings,[5] so it was fitting that the Church, which is his body,[6] should be baptised with the baptism of his afflictions; and accordingly his promise was, "In the world ye shall have tribulation: but be of good cheer; I have overcome the world."[7]

[1] Luke xiii. 26, 27.   [2] Matt. xiii. 24-30, 37-43.
[3] Matt. xiii. 47-50.   [4] Rev. vii 14.   [5] Heb. ii. 10.
[6] Col. i. 24.   [7] John xvi. 33.

There was still a subtler danger in store for the Church, connected indeed with the desires of the natural man, but raised and stimulated by the Author of evil. False Christs and false prophets were to arise, and to shew great signs; insomuch that, if it were possible, they should deceive the very elect.[1] Damnable heresies were to be secretly introduced;[2] false teachers and antichrists, carried away by the desire of a godless pre-eminence, were to subvert the faith of the unstable.[3] As the apostle said, "There must be heresies among you, that they which are approved may be made manifest among you."[4]

Such were to be the infirmities, such the dangers of the Church; and had she been left alone and un-aided amidst them all, "the waters had overwhelmed her, the stream had gone over her soul."[5] Nothing but the Spirit of God within her could have saved her from speedy destruction. But it had been de-creed of old, that in the seed of Abraham "all the nations of the earth should be blessed."[6] It had been foretold by the Spirit, that He "should be for salvation to the end of the earth;"[7] that He "should have dominion from sea to sea, and from the river to the ends of the earth."[8] It had been declared that his kingdom should endure "for ever,"[9] and that "of the increase of his government and peace there should be no end."[10] And therefore when the Son of God came into the world, he said unto his disciples, "On this rock I will build my Church, and the gates of hell shall not prevail against it:"[11] and therefore did he console them in the prospect of his departure; "I will not leave you comfortless, I will come unto you:"[12] "I will pray the Father, and he

---

[1] Matt. xxiii. 24.   [2] 2 Pet. ii. 1.
[3] Acts xx. 30; 1 Tim. iv. 1; 2 Tim. iii.; 1 John ii. 18, iv. 3.
[4] 1 Cor. xi. 19.   [5] Ps. cxxiv. 4.   [6] Gen. xxii. 18.
[7] Is. xlix. 6.   [8] Ps. lxxii. 8.   [9] Daniel ii. 44.
[10] Isaiah ix. 7.   [11] Matt. xvi. 18.   [12] John xiv. 18.

shall give you another Comforter, that he may abide with you for ever, even the Spirit of truth."[1] And when about to ascend up on high, he left to them that encouraging and blessed promise, "Lo, I am with you always, even to the end of the world."[2]

The history of the Church, then, is not like other histories, in which the progress and fate of human enterprises is described; it is the fulfilment of God's will for the salvation of man, the accomplishment of prophecies, the triumph of grace over the imperfection and sins of nature. The perpetuity of the Church; its propagation in all nations; the succession of the true faith; the manifestations of the Holy Spirit's assistance in the lives of Christians; the calamities, errors, afflictions, which, in all ages, beset it,—afford new proofs of the truth of Christianity itself, and inspire the devout mind with humility and faith.

The principal periods of ecclesiastical history may be arranged under the following divisions:— First, the ages of persecution, which terminated with the accession of the Emperor Constantine to universal empire, in A.D. 320, and during which the Church was purest. Secondly, the ages (A.D. 320- 680,) when heresies invaded the Church, and were repelled by the six holy œcumenical synods; and when the ravages of barbarians and heathens were counterbalanced by the conversion of many nations. Thirdly, the period (680-1054) in which ignorance, worldliness, and superstition, began to fall thickly upon the Church, though an earnest spirit of piety still continued to produce evangelists, saints, and martyrs, and to add wide regions to the Church of Christ. Fourthly, the times (1054-1517) when the East and West were estranged by the ambition of

---

[1] John xiv. 16.   [2] Matt. xxviii. 20.

the Roman pontiffs; when those bishops, elevated to the summit of temporal and spiritual power in the West, introduced numberless corruptions and innovations; and when their power began to fade away. Fifthly, the epoch (1517-1839) when a reformation being called for, was resisted by those who ought to have promoted it; when the Western Church became divided; and at length infidelity came to threaten universal destruction.

CHAPTER II.

ON THE EARLY PROGRESS OF CHRISTIANITY.

A.D. 30-320.

HEREUNTO shall we liken the kingdom of God? or with what comparison shall we compare it?—said our Lord. "It is like a grain of mustard-seed, which, when it is sown in the earth, is less than all the seeds that be in the earth. But when it is sown, it groweth up, and becometh greater than all herbs, and shooteth out great branches; so that the fowls of the air may lodge under the shadow of it."[1] The Holy Spirit, by the mouth of the prophet Daniel, had many ages before predicted the same wonderful origin and diffusion of the kingdom of Christ, under the figure of "the stone cut out of the mountain without hands," which "became a great mountain, and filled the whole earth."[2] Thus was Christianity destined to spring from a small and obscure beginning, and to overspread the earth in the luxuriance of its growth. And so it came to pass. From Judæa, the least of

---

[1] Mark iv. 30-32.   [2] Dan. ii. 35, 44, 45.

the nations of the earth, and from twelve of its poorest and most illiterate children, a " sound went into all the earth, and words unto the ends of the world."[1]   The Son of God, when about to depart, had given to them that lofty commission : " All power is given to me in heaven and on earth. Go ye, therefore, and teach all nations, baptising them in the name of the Father, and of the Son, and of the Holy Ghost, teaching them to observe all things that I have commanded you :" and they "went forth and preached every where, the Lord working with them, and confirming the word with signs following."

The number of the disciples assembled in the upper room at Jerusalem, after our Lord's ascension, was only a hundred and twenty ; but the miracles of the day of Pentecost, and the sermon of St. Peter, added three thousand souls ; and ere long, " the Lord adding to the Church daily such as should be saved," the number of the men was five thousand.[2] In vain did the priests and their adherents endeavour to prevent the progress of true religion, by inflicting punishments on its preachers.   The next account is, that " the word of God increased ; and the number of the disciples multiplied in Jerusalem greatly ; and a great company of the priests was obedient to the faith."

The Gospel was, as yet, preached at Jerusalem only—in one city of a remote and obscure province of the Roman empire. What mere worldly calculation could then have imagined the triumphs which were in store for it ? Who could then have expected that philosophies, idolatries, and superstitions, the growth of so many long ages, were to be prostrated and annihilated before it, and that the kingdoms of the earth were to bow beneath its dominion ?

[1] Rom. x. 18.   [2] Acts ii. 47.

The destruction which Satan meditated against the Church in its infancy, was made the means of disseminating it more widely. The great persecution at Jerusalem, A.D. 37, and in which the first martyr, St. Stephen, afforded so noble an instance of the power of faith, dispersed abroad the disciples, who preached throughout Judæa, Samaria, Phœnicia, Cyprus, and Syria. The apostles alone remained at Jerusalem, where they probably continued to preach for several years after this time. Samaria, convinced by the miracles and the doctrine of Philip, with one accord embraced the Gospel: even the sorcerer Simon, deserted by his followers, and amazed at the gifts of the Holy Spirit, received baptism, in the vain hope of obtaining powers so far superior to his own. Tyre and Sidon now stretched forth their hands to the Lord; and at Antioch was a great multitude of believers.

Thus was the first great impulse to the dissemination of Christianity given by the persecution at Jerusalem. The next arose from the preaching of the apostle Paul to the Gentiles, which commenced about A.D. 44, fourteen years after our Lord's ascension. The result of his first mission with Barnabas was the establishment of Churches in Pamphylia, Pisidia, Lycaonia, and Cilicia, constituting the southern portion of Asia Minor. His next circuit, A.D. 49-52, had the effect of extending the Church in Phrygia, Galatia, and Troas, or the centre of Asia Minor; and in Macedonia and Greece. Another journey added the coasts of Asia towards Greece; and the Church of Ephesus was formed, over which St. Paul presided for several years. Carried to Rome, about A.D. 59, he found Christianity already existing in several parts of Italy; and the Roman Church, which had lately been edified by his epistle, was now rapidly extended by his preaching. Released from prison

at Rome, he seems to have revisited Ephesus, where
he left Timothy to exercise the episcopal office; to
have preached in Crete, where Titus was invested
with similar powers; and to have passed through
Macedonia, and even into Spain; whence returning
to Rome, he suffered for Christ about A.D. 68.

The other apostles also preached the Gospel
among the heathen; though St. Paul declared that
" he laboured more abundantly than they all." The
north of Asia Minor, or Cappadocia, Pontus, and
Bithynia (addressed by St. Peter in his epistle), probably received the Gospel from that apostle some
time after A.D. 52; for St. Paul intended in that
year to preach in Bithynia,[1] which he would not
have done, had St. Peter already evangelised that
province, as his rule was, never to build on another's
foundation.[2]   The date of St. Peter's epistle from
Babylon suggests the probability of his having
preached in Chaldæa; and St. Thaddæus is said
to have taught at Edessa and in Mesopotamia.   In
Egypt the Church was founded by St. Mark, who
constituted Anianus the first bishop of Alexandria.
There are also traditions, that Persia, Arabia, Ethiopia, and Britain, were visited by some of the apostles.

Thus, in about thirty years, that little grain of
mustard-seed had grown into a mighty tree, the
roots of which had struck themselves deep in all
parts of the civilised world; and already it extended
" from the river (Euphrates) to the ends of the
earth."   Nor was the success of its propagation in
each locality inferior to the wideness of its dissemination throughout the world. We have seen examples of its rapid increase at Jerusalem, at Samaria,
and Antioch. The heathen historian Tacitus, in
describing the persecution which Christians suffered

---

[1] Acts xvi. 7.   [2] Rom. xv. 20.

at Rome in the time of Nero, A.D. 64-68, says, " At first, those only were apprehended who confessed themselves of that sect; afterwards, a *vast multitude* discovered by them, all of whom were condemned." It appears from a letter of Pliny, the Roman governor of Pontus and Bithynia, about A.D. 107, that Christianity had nearly caused the heathen worship in those countries to be deserted. Consulting the Emperor Trajan as to the mode of dealing with Christians, he says, " Therefore, suspending all judicial proceedings, I have recourse to you for advice; for it has appeared to me a matter highly deserving consideration, especially upon account of the great numbers of persons who are in danger of suffering; for many of all ages and every rank, of both sexes likewise, are accused, and will be accused. Nor has the contagion of this superstition seized cities only, but the lesser towns also, and the open country. Nevertheless it seems to me that it may be restrained and corrected. It is certain, that the (heathen) temples, which were almost forsaken, begin to be more frequented; and the sacred solemnities, after a long remission, are revived. Victims (for the sacrifices) likewise are every where brought up, whereas for some time there were few purchasers." It appears from this remarkable testimony, that Christianity had, in the course of about fifty years, almost subverted idolatry in those provinces.

Little is known of the progress of Christianity for some years after the death of the apostles. The Church was probably engaged chiefly in the labour of converting the population more immediately around it; and we hear little of new missions to the heathen; yet Justin Martyr, about A.D. 150, wrote in his Apology, that "there is no race of men, whether barbarian or Greek, or by whatever other name they be designated, whether they wander in waggons, or

dwell in tents, amongst whom prayers and thanks-
givings are not offered to the Father and Creator of
all, in the name of the crucified Jesus."   We learn
from Irenæus, bishop of Lyons, about A.D. 178, that
the light of the Gospel had, at that time, been received in Germany, France, Spain, and in Libya:
and Tertullian, a few years later, declares that Par-
thia, Media, Armenia, the Getuli and Moors in
Africa, all the borders of Spain, many nations of
Gaul, those parts of Britain which were inaccessible
to the Romans, the Sarmatians, Dacians, Germans,
Scythians, and other nations and islands innumerable, were then subject to the dominion of Christ.
" We are but of yesterday," he said; " yet we have
filled your empire, your cities, your islands, your
castles, your corporate towns, your assemblies, your
very camps, your tribes, your companies, your palace,
your senate, your forum; your temples alone are
left to you."   " We constitute," he elsewhere says,
" almost the majority in every town."

In the succeeding century new nations were
gathered within the fold of Christ.   The assiduous
labours of Origen converted many of the Arabs to
Christianity.   The Goths of Mysia and Thrace
followed their example; and a number of pious
missionaries successfully disseminated the Gospel
throughout Gaul, and founded several Churches in
Germany.

So great was the progress of religion, notwithstanding the violent and cruel persecutions to which
it was continually exposed, that it became no less the
interest than the duty of the first Christian emperor,
Constantine the Great, to relieve the Church from
persecution, to act as the defender of its faith, and to
distinguish it ministers and members by marks of
his favour and generosity.

CHAPTER III.

ON THE FAITH OF THE CHURCH.

A.D. 30-320.

UR Lord's promises to his disciples, that the Spirit of truth should lead them into all truth and abide with them for ever, that the gates of hell should not prevail against his Church, and that he would himself be always with his disciples,—imply that the faith revealed by Jesus Christ should, in every age, continue to purify and sanctify the hearts and lives of his real followers ; and we may hence infer, that the belief which has, in *all ages*, been derived by the Church from holy Scripture; the great truths which Christians have always unanimously held to be essential to the Christian profession, which have supported them under the tortures of martyrdom, and transformed them from sin to righteousness,—that such doctrines are, without doubt, the very same which God himself revealed for the salvation of man.

What, then, was the belief received by all Christians from the beginning ? Let the martyr Irenæus, the friend of St. John's disciple Polycarp, reply : " The Church," he says, " though disseminated throughout the whole world, even unto the ends of the earth, hath received from the apostles the belief in one God, the Father almighty, who made heaven and earth, and the seas and all that in them is ; and in one Christ Jesus, the Son of God, who was made man for our salvation ; and in the Holy Spirit, who, through the prophets, announced the dispensations (of God), the advent of the beloved Christ Jesus our Lord, his birth of a virgin, his suffering, resurrection from the dead, and bodily ascension into heaven, and his coming (again) from the heavens in the glory of the Father, to gather together all things in one, and to raise up all flesh of mankind, in order that, according to the invisible Father's will, every knee of things in heaven, and things in earth, and things under the earth, may bow to Christ Jesus our Lord, our God, our Saviour, and our King, and every tongue confess unto him; and that he may exercise righteous judgment on all—may send spiritual wickedness, and the angels that transgressed and became apostate, and the impious, unrighteous, wicked, and blasphemous among men, into eternal fire; and bestow life and immortality and eternal glory on the righteous, the pious, and those who observe his commandments, and continue in his love, either from the beginning, or from the time of their repentance.

" This preaching, and this faith (as we have said), the Church, though disseminated throughout the whole world, guards as carefully as if she dwelt in one house ; believes as if she had but one soul ; and proclaims, teaches and delivers, as if she possessed but one mouth."

Such was the universal belief of Christians in the second century, as it still continues in the nineteenth. We here find the most plain assertions of the Godhead of the Father, the Son, and the Holy Ghost ; the incarnation and satisfaction of our Lord ; the resurrection and future judgment; and the necessity of obedience and the love of God.   That Christians worshipped our Lord Jesus Christ as God, is attested even by the heathen writer Pliny, A.D. 107.   " They affirmed," he says, " that the whole of their fault lay in this, that they were wont to meet together on a stated day, before it was light, and sing among themselves, alternately, an *hymn to Christ as God*."

The condemnation of heresies in these ages affords an additional illustration of the belief of the

Church. When Theodotus and Artemon, heretics, taught at Rome that our Lord Jesus Christ was not God, but a mere man, they were expelled from communion by Victor, bishop of Rome, and by the Roman Church; and they were universally rejected and abhorred by all Christians. When Paul of Samosata, bishop of Antioch, endeavoured to revive this error, a council or meeting of seventy bishops, from all parts of the East, assembled at Antioch, A.D. 270, and expelled him from the Church. In their epistle, addressed to all the bishops, priests, and deacons, throughout the whole world, and still extant, they declared that " he refused to confess with them that the Son of God came down from heaven;" that he said, " that Jesus Christ is of the earth ; and that he had thus " abjured the faith, and gloried in the *accursed* heresy of Artemon." Nothing can more plainly shew the belief of the Church. The error of Praxeas, Noëtus, and Sabellius, in the third century, who affirmed that the Father, the Son, and the Holy Ghost, are but one person, thus virtually denying that the Son, or the Holy Ghost, could have been " sent" by the Father,[1] or " come from,"[2] or " be with,"[3] or " intercede with,"[4] the Father, were also universally rejected by the Church, as contrary to the Christian faith. The belief of Christians in the incarnation and real bodily existence of Jesus Christ was manifested in their opposition to the Gnostics and Manichæans, who held that our Lord's body was not real, but a mere phantom, and that he did not die on the cross: errors destructive at once of the truth of the Gospel-history, of the atonement of Christ, and of the great miracle of his resurrection from the dead.

Few things, perhaps, can more remarkably ex-

[1] John v. 23.   [2] John xv. 26, xvi. 28.
[3] John i. 1.   [4] Heb. vii. 25.

emplify the tendency of the human heart to evil, than those subterfuges which it devises in order to avoid obedience to the will of a pure and all-wise God.   For what are heresies, but so many efforts to escape from the obligation of an unreserved submission of our understandings and wills to the revelations of infinite and unfathomable Wisdom, under the pretence of a more strict conformity with the doctrine of revelation itself?   All the various heresies which have arisen have alleged the word of God as a sanction for their errors: that sacred and unchangeable truth has been distorted and perverted, in order that the pride of man may be released from the hated necessity of obeying from the heart that form of doctrine which descended from the God of truth, and which ought to be received with childlike humility and affection by every rational and responsible being.   Hence it is that so many new interpretations are invented,—that the Scriptures themselves are corrupted or mutilated,—that one part of God's word is wilfully forgotten, while another is unduly exalted and exclusively dwelt on. Hence conclusions are drawn from particular passages of Scripture, which are in direct contradiction to the general spirit and object of the word of God. And whence does all this proceed, except from the sinful heart of man, and from the temptations of that Spirit of pride and falsehood, that ancient enemy of mankind, who seeks in this way to make the Gospel itself subservient to the destruction of human souls?   To such men the words of Scripture are peculiarly addressed, "What hast thou to do to declare my statutes, or that thou shouldst take my covenant in thy mouth; seeing thou hatest instruction, and castest my words behind thee?" or, in the words of our Saviour, "Why call ye me Lord, Lord, and do not the things which I say?" The awful condemnation of such offenders is pronounced by the apostle Paul, " If any man preach any other gospel unto you than that ye have received, let him be anathema."

But to those who know the purity of the gospel of Jesus Christ, and its utter aversion from sin ; to those who believe that the sins of men brought down the Son of God from infinite glory and blessedness to the bitter death of the cross, in order that the guilt of sin might be washed away by the efficacy of his most awful sufferings; to those who know that the object of his mission on earth was to seek and save that which was lost through sin, to " purify unto himself a peculiar people zealous of good works," and thus to " make them meet to be par- takers of the inheritance of the saints in light ;" to those who have read his lessons, inculcating the most exalted holiness and purity, a severance from the very thoughts, and much more from the desires, the vices, and the sins of the world and the flesh,— how strange is it to reflect, that even from the ear- liest times, Satan has succeeded in deceiving some wicked men into a persuasion, that the disciples of Him who came to condemn sin, and to terminate its dominion, might *continue in sin !*

When the holy apostles shewed that the law of rites and ceremonies given by Moses to the Jews was not binding on the Gentiles; and that even in respect of the Jews, its obligation had been termi- nated by the manifestation of that Redeemer, whom the law of Moses and all its sacrifices prefigured and foreshadowed; and when, advancing still further, they shewed to both Jew and Gentile, that fallen man could not, by his own righteousness or works, deserve remission of sin and become acceptable to the pure and holy God; that the salvation of man was only the work of God's mercy and grace extended to those who were ready to perish; and that man's true righteousness is that firm belief in God and God's word, which God himself alone can give, and which is a fountain of holiness springing up in the heart, and converting man from carnal things, and from the deadness of nature, to the blessing of a new and spiritual life in Christ Jesus;—when the apostles thus taught man to humble himself before his Creator, and to look only to his mercy for pardon and salvation, the enemies of the Gospel argued that the apostles themselves regarded good works and holiness of life as unnecessary; and that a mere dry and barren belief in Christ, unaccompanied by any fruits of holiness, was sufficient to obtain salvation.   St. Paul himself, and St. James, abundantly refuted such errors, and they were always afterwards rejected as heresies by the Church of Christ.   The following passage from the epistle of St. Clement, bishop of Rome, written in the name of the Roman Church to the Church of Corinth, some time before the end of the first century, will suffice to shew what was the doctrine of the early Church on this subject.

"Let us then lay hold of God's blessing, and let us consider what are the ways by which we may attain unto it.   Let us look back upon those things that have happened from the beginning. Wherefore was our father Abraham blessed? Was it not because that, through faith, he wrought righteousness and truth? Isaac, being fully persuaded of what he knew was to come, cheerfully yielded himself up for a sacrifice.   Jacob with humility departed out of his own country, fleeing from his brother, and went unto Laban, and served him; and so the sceptre of the twelve tribes of Israel was given unto him.   Now, what the greatness of this gift was, will plainly appear, if we will take the pains distinctly to consider all the parts of it.   For from him (Jacob) came our Lord Jesus Christ according to the flesh; from him came the kings, and princes, and rulers in Judah. Nor were the rest of his tribes in any small glory, God having provided that 'thy seed (saith he) shall be as the stars of heaven.'

" They were all therefore glorified, not for their own sake, or for their own works, or for the righteousness that they themselves wrought, but through His will. And we also, being called by the same will in Christ Jesus, are not justified by ourselves, neither by our own wisdom, or knowledge, or piety, or the works we have done in the holiness of our hearts; but by that faith, by which Almighty God has justified all men from the beginning: to whom be glory for ever and ever, amen.

" What shall we do, therefore, brethren? Shall we be slothful in well-doing, and lay aside our charity? God forbid that any such thing should be done by us. But rather let us hasten, with all earnestness and readiness of mind, to perfect every good work. We see how all righteous men have been adorned with good works: wherefore even the Lord himself, having adorned himself with his good works, rejoiced. Having therefore such an example, let us without delay fulfil his will; and with all our strength work the work of righteousness.

" The good workman with confidence receives the bread of his labour; but the sluggish and lazy cannot look him in the face that set him to work. We must therefore be ready and forward in well-doing: for from Him (God) are all things. And thus he foretells us, ' Behold, the Lord cometh, and his reward is with him, even before his face, to render to every one according to his work.' He warned us therefore beforehand, with all his heart, to this end, that we should not be slothful and negligent in well-doing. Let our boasting, therefore, and our confidence be in God. Let us submit ourselves to his

will. Let us consider the whole multitude of his
angels, how ready they stand to minister to his will;
as the Scripture saith, ' Thousands of thousands
stand before him, and ten thousand minister unto
him.   And they cried, saying, Holy, holy, holy is
the Lord of Sabaoth: the whole earth is full of his
glory.' Wherefore let us also, being conscientiously
gathered together in concord with one another, as it
were with one mouth, cry earnestly unto him, that
he would make us partakers of his great and glorious promises.   For he saith, ' Eye hath not seen,
nor ear heard, neither have entered into the heart of
man, the things which God has prepared for them
that wait for him.' "

Thus did this venerable and apostolical man urge
the necessity of Christian holiness and obedience to
the Divine will.   The doctrine taught by St. Ignatius, who had been made bishop of Antioch by the
apostles, was in perfect harmony with that of St. Clement.   Writing to the Church of the Ephesians
shortly before his martyrdom, he urges on them the
obligation of united worship and of harmony. " Nothing," he says, " is better than peace; by which all
war, both spiritual and earthly, is abolished.   Of all
which nothing is hid from you, if ye have perfect
faith and charity in Jesus Christ, which are the beginning and end of life: for the beginning is faith,
the end charity.   And these two, joined together,
are of God: but all other things which concern a
holy life are the consequences of these.   No man
professing a true faith sinneth; neither does he who
has charity hate any one.   ' The tree is made manifest by its fruits.'   So they who profess themselves
to be Christians are known by what they do.   For
Christianity is not an outward profession; but shews
itself in the power of faith, if a man be found faithful unto the end.   It is better for a man to hold his

peace, and *be;* than to say 'he is a Christian,' and *not to be.* It is good to teach; if what he says, he does likewise."

CHAPTER IV.

FRUITS OF FAITH EXEMPLIFIED IN THE MARTYRS.

A.D. 30-320.

AVING seen the belief which was unanimously received by the primitive Church, let us now proceed to observe its fruits. The power of true faith has never been more wonderfully exhibited than in the patience, the courage, and magnanimity of the martyrs. Animated by the promises of their Saviour, " whosoever shall confess me before men, him will I confess before my Father in heaven—he that loseth his life for my sake shall find it—rejoice and be exceeding glad, for so persecuted they the prophets which were before you,"—they believed, and triumphed in the belief, that their short affliction was to work for them a far more exceeding and eternal weight of glory.

But the afflictions which they suffered were enough to have broken down the strongest heart. Every thing that malice and ingenuity could devise was employed to shake their resolution. The rage and insolence of a brutal populace, the scourges and tortures of legal barbarity, and the more subtle torment of promises and entreaties to save their lives by compliance in idolatrous rites, were the portion of innumerable disciples of Christ. The Jews had been the earliest enemies of the Christian faith; but their hatred was soon forgotten, in the persecutions which, for three centuries, were inflicted by the Roman emperors.   To Nero, a tyrant whose name became proverbial, even with the heathen, for all that was abominable in impurity and fearful in cruelty, belongs the evil pre-eminence of being the first great persecutor of the Church.   Accused by the popular rumour of having caused a dreadful fire, which had nearly consumed Rome, in order that he might have the honour of rebuilding it with greater magnificence, Nero expended large sums of money in conciliating the populace, in adorning the city, and in sacrifices to his gods.   "But," adds the heathen historian Tacitus, "neither human assistance, nor the gifts of the emperor, nor the atonements offered to the gods, availed: the infamy of that horrible transaction still adhered to him.   To repress, if possible, this common rumour, Nero procured others to be accused, and punished with exquisite tortures a race of men detested for their evil practices, who were commonly known by the name of Christians.   The author of that sect was Christus, who, in the reign of Tiberius, was punished with death, as a criminal, by the procurator Pontius Pilate.   But this pestilent superstition, though checked for a while, broke out afresh, not only in Judæa, where the evil first originated, but even in the city (Rome), the common sink into which every thing filthy and abominable flows from all quarters of the world.   At first, those only were apprehended who confessed themselves of that sect; afterwards, a vast multitude discovered by them; all of whom were condemned, not so much for the crime of burning the city, as for their enmity to mankind. Their executions were so contrived as to expose them to derision and contempt.   Some were covered over with the skins of wild beasts, that they might be torn to pieces by dogs; some were crucified; while others, having been daubed over with combustible materials, were set up as lights in the night-time, and thus burned to death. For these spectacles, Nero gave his own gardens; and at the same time exhibited there the diversions of the circus; sometimes standing in the crowd as a spectator, in the habit of a charioteer, and at other times driving a chariot himself: until at length these men, though really criminal, and deserving exemplary punishment, began to be commiserated as people who were destroyed, not out of regard to the public welfare, but only to gratify the cruelty of one man."

Such was the dreadful commencement of persecution—such the torments under which Christians steadfastly continued in their profession of Christ. The heathen regarded this steadfastness as obstinacy and insanity. The rejection of all the gods of the heathen, and all their worship, was stigmatised as atheism and impiety. Abstinence from the vices, the corruptions, and the vile pleasures of the world, was treated as the result of a sour and unsocial temper. But though "hated of all men" for the name of Christ, true religion only multiplied and increased under persecution. St. Paul was at this time beheaded at Rome, and St. Peter was crucified with his head downwards.

The next persecution was under Domitian, A.D. 93, during which the apostle John was immersed in a cauldron of boiling oil, at Rome, and miraculously escaping without hurt, was banished to the isle of Patmos, where he beheld the visions of the Apocalypse; and from whence he went to Ephesus, and presided over the Churches of Asia. The reigns of Trajan, Aurelius, Antoninus, Severus, Decius, Valerian, Diocletian, and Maximian, were also stained by persecutions of the Christians. The last of these was also the most severe; it continued for ten successive years, during which innumerable martyrs attested their belief in Jesus Christ.

I shall select, as an illustration of the faith of Christians under persecution, the following account of the martyrdom of St. Polycarp, who had been made bishop of Smyrna by the apostles, and was a disciple of St. John.   The epistle of the Church of Smyrna, in which it occurs, and which was written A.D. 167, commences as follows :—

"The Church of God which is at Smyrna, to that which is at Philomelium, and to all the Churches of the holy Catholic Church, in all parts, mercy, peace, and love, be multiplied from God the Father, and from the Lord Jesus Christ."   Having described the constancy of mind with which many of the martyrs in that city had borne the most dreadful tortures, they proceed thus:—"The admirable Polycarp, when he first heard of these things, remained undisturbed, preserving his calmness and serenity ; and he had resolved to remain in the city, but being persuaded by the entreaties and prayers of his friends, he retired to a village not far off, where he continued with a few others, occupied day and night only in continual prayer, supplicating and beseeching peace for the Churches throughout the world; for this was his continual habit.   And, as he was praying, he saw a vision, three days before he was taken ; and, behold, the pillow under his head seemed to him on fire. Whereupon, turning to those who were with him, he said, prophetically, that he should be burnt alive." He was at length discovered by the persecutors. " Arriving in the evening, they found him resting in an upper chamber, whence he might have escaped with ease into another house, but he would not, saying, ' The will of the Lord be done ;' and, having heard of their arrival, he went down and spoke to them with so joyful and mild a countenance, that they, who knew him not before, thought they beheld somewhat wonderful, when they saw his old age and the gravity and constancy of his demeanour, and they marvelled why such diligence was used to take an aged man like this. He immediately offered to them refreshment, and requested permission from them to pray in freedom for one hour; which being granted, he arose and prayed, being so full of the grace of God, that those who were present, and heard him pray, were amazed, and many of them repented that they had taken so venerable and holy a man.

"When he had ceased his prayer, in which he made mention of all whom he had ever known, whether small or great, eminent or obscure, and of all the Catholic Church throughout the world; the hour of departure being come, he was placed on an ass, and brought into the city, that being the great Sabbath. Here the irenarch Herod, and his father Nicetas, met him, who placed him in their chariot; and seated beside him, persuaded him, saying, 'What is the harm to say, Lord Cæsar, and to sacrifice, and so to save your life?' And he at first answered them not; but when they continued, he said, 'I will not do what you counsel me.' Then having failed to persuade him, they uttered reproaches, and threw him violently down, so that in falling from the chariot he hurt his thigh-bone. Unmoved, and as if he had not thus suffered, he went with alacrity and speed to the amphitheatre, whither he was led. And when the tumult there was so great that few could hear, a voice from heaven came to Polycarp, as he entered the amphitheatre, 'Be strong, and quit thee like a man, Polycarp.' No one beheld the speaker, but many of us heard the voice.

"When, therefore, he was brought forth, there was a great tumult among those who heard that he was taken. Moreover, the proconsul asked, as he approached, if 'he were Polycarp?' and when he had assented, he persuaded him to deny (Christ), saying,

'Have pity on thine old age,' and such other things
as are customary with them; as, 'Swear by the fortune of Cæsar; repent; say, Away with the godless!'
(Christians). Then Polycarp, looking constantly on
all the crowd in the amphitheatre, stretching forth
his hand towards them, groaning, and looking up to
heaven, said, 'Away with the godless!' But when
the proconsul pressed him, and said, 'Swear, and I
will release thee—reproach Christ;' Polycarp replied, 'Eighty and six years do I serve him, and
never hath he injured me; and how can I blaspheme
my King and my Saviour?' When the proconsul
continued to urge him, saying, 'Swear by the fortune of Cæsar;' Polycarp saith, 'Since thou art so
vainly urgent that I should swear by the fortune of
Cæsar, and feignest not to know what I am, hear me
declare it with boldness, I am a Christian. If thou
desirest to hear the reasons for our faith, grant me
a day, and hear them.' The proconsul said, 'Persuade the people.' Polycarp replied, 'Thee I have
thought worthy to hear the reasons for our faith, for
we are taught to render unto powers and authorities
constituted of God the honour which is fitting, and
which is not injurious to us; but for these (people),
I have not thought them worthy to hear my defence.'
The proconsul said, 'I have wild beasts, and will
cast thee unto them, except thou repentest.' He
replied, 'Call them; I cannot change from good to
evil; it is good to change from sin to righteousness.'
The proconsul, 'I will cause thee to be devoured
by fire, since thou despisest the beasts, unless thou
repentest.' Polycarp, 'Thou threatenest fire which
burneth but for a time and is then extinguished, for
thou knowest not the fire of future judgment, and of
eternal punishment reserved for the wicked. But
why tarriest thou? Bring what thou wilt.' Having said this, and much more, he was filled with

courage and joy, and his countenance was full of grace; so that not only he failed not with terror at what was said unto him, but the proconsul was amazed, and sent his crier to proclaim thrice in the midst of the amphitheatre, 'Polycarp has confessed himself a Christian.'

"When this was proclaimed, all the crowd of Gentiles and Jews at Smyrna cried aloud, with irrepressible fury, 'This is the teacher of Asia, the father of the Christians, the destroyer of our gods, who teacheth many not to sacrifice or to worship.' Thus saying, they called out and requested the asiarch Philip to let loose a lion at Polycarp. He said that it was not lawful for him to do so, as the combats of beasts had closed. They then cried out with one accord that Polycarp should be burned alive."

The account proceeds:—" These things were no sooner said than done, the crowd instantly collecting wood and combustibles from the workshops and baths; the Jews, especially, as their manner is, lending their willing assistance. But when the fuel was ready, he laid aside his vesture, and loosing his zone, endeavoured to take off his under-garments. This he had not been accustomed to do, as all the faithful contended who should first touch his skin; for always, even before his old age, he was universally reverenced for his virtue. The materials prepared for the fire were speedily placed around him, and when they would have nailed him to the stake, he said, 'Leave me thus; for He who hath given me power to endure the fire, will grant me also to remain steadfast without your nails;' and they did not do so, but bound him to it. And he, with his hands bound behind him, like a comely ram chosen from the flock to be a whole burnt-offering to God, said, 'Father of thy beloved and blessed Son Jesus Christ, through whom we have received the knowledge of thee; God of angels, and powers, and of all the creation, and of all the generation of the righteous who live in thy presence ; I bless thee because thou hast thought me worthy of this day and this hour, to take part in the number of thy martyrs, in the cup of Christ, to the resurrection of soul and body in the incorruption of the Holy Spirit, to eternal life. Amongst whom may I be received this day into thy presence as a rich and acceptable sacrifice, as thou hast before ordained and hast now fulfilled ; thou, who art without falsehood, the true God. For this, and for all things, I praise thee, I bless thee, I glorify thee ; through the eternal High-priest Jesus Christ, thy beloved Son; through whom be glory to thee with him, in the Holy Spirit, both now and unto all ages to come. Amen.'

" When he had uttered the amen, and finished his prayer, the executioners lighted the fire ; but when a great flame burst forth, we, to whom it was permitted to behold, and who were retained that we might relate it to the rest, beheld a wondrous thing ; for the fire, affording the appearance of a vault, like the sail of a ship filled with the wind, surrounded in a circle the body of the martyr ; and he was in the midst, not like burning flesh, but like gold and silver in the furnace, and we smelt a savour sweet as incense or some other precious perfumes. The wicked, observing that his body could not be consumed by fire, commanded the executioner to approach and pierce him with a sword, which being done, a great quantity of blood came forth, insomuch that the fire was extinguished, and the crowd marvelled because the difference was so great between unbelievers and the elect, of whom, this our apostolic and prophetic teacher, the bishop of the Catholic Church in Smyrna, was the most admirable in these our times."

The narrative adds, that their enemies endeavoured to prevent the Christians from obtaining the remains of the martyr. They urged the proconsul that his body should not be given, " Lest, forsaking the crucified (Jesus), they should begin to adore this man. And this they said by the suggestion and aid of the Jews, who had watched our endeavours to remove him from the fire, being ignorant that we can never forsake Christ, who suffered for the salvation of those who are saved out of all the world, nor adore any other. For him, as being the Son of God, we worship; but the martyrs, as being disciples and imitators of the Lord, we love as they deserve, on account of their unconquerable love to their King and Master."

In the persecution under the Emperor Antoninus, which occurred about A.D. 178, the Christians in all parts of the world were most sorely tried, and tormented with extreme cruelty. A most interesting record of the faith and patience of the martyrs at Lyons and Vienne in France, has been preserved to us, in the epistle addressed by the brethren dwelling in those cities to the Churches of Asia and Phrygia; and in which, after describing the beginning of persecution, the insults of the populace, and the imprisonment of the brethren, who had openly confessed that they were Christians, we find the following history :—

"Those who were worthy were daily apprehended, filling up their number, so that there were taken up from the two Churches all the best men, and those by whom things here were chiefly kept together. There were also taken up some heathen servants belonging to persons amongst our number, since the governor ordered a public inquisition to be made after us all. And they, by advice of Satan, fearing the tortures which they saw the saints endure, the soldiers urging them on, belied us as holding Thyestean feasts,[1] and guilty of impurities like those of Œdipus, and such things as it is not allowed us to mention or even to think of, no, nor to believe that they ever existed among mankind. But when these things were noised abroad, all were infuriated against us; so that, even if any had before shewn moderation on account of connexions, even these were greatly enraged, and stung with malice against us.

"But most eminently did all the rage of the populace, the governor, and the soldiers, light on Sanctus, a deacon of Vienne, and on Maturus, one newly enlightened, but a noble champion, and on Attalus, a Pergamene by birth, who had always been a ' pillar and support' of those in this neighbourhood; and on Blandina, by whom CHRIST shewed that the things which are lowly esteemed among men, and held by them mean and contemptible, are thought worthy of great honour with God, for that love of him, which is shewed forth in power, and does not boast in a vain appearance.

"For whereas all were in fear, and her own mistress according to the flesh (who also herself was one champion among the martyrs,) was in agony for her, lest she should be unable to make even one bold confession, from the weakness of her body; Blandina was filled with such strength, that even those who tortured her by turns, in every possible way, from morning till evening, were wearied and gave it up, themselves confessing that they were conquered, having nothing now that they could do to her. And they wondered at her remaining still alive, her whole body being mangled and pierced in every part; and declared, that any one kind of torture was enough

[1] That is, eating human flesh. The heathens frequently accused the early Christians of eating the flesh and drinking the blood of children; a calumny founded on our faith concerning the reception of Christ's body and blood in the holy eucharist.

to deprive her of life, not to say so many and so severe. But that blessed woman, like a brave wrestler, renewed her strength in confessing; and to her it was recovery, and rest, and ease from her sufferings, to say, 'I am a Christian; and nothing vile is done amongst us.'

"Sanctus also, for his part, enduring exceedingly and above every man all the cruelties of men with a noble patience, when the wicked hoped that, by means of the continuance and severity of the tortures, they should hear something from him that ought not to be uttered, set himself against them with such firmness as not to mention even his own name, nor that of the nation or city whence he was, nor whether he were bond or free; but to all questions he answered, in the Roman tongue, 'I am a Christian.' This he repeatedly declared to be to him instead of a name, instead of a country, and instead of a family; but no other word did the heathen hear from him. Whence also there was great strife both of the governor and torturers against him, so that when they had nothing left that they could do to him, at last they fastened red-hot plates of brass on the tenderest parts of his body. But though his limbs were burning, he remained upright and unshrinking, steadfast to his confession, bathed and strengthened from heaven with that fountain of living water, that springs from the well of Christ. But his body bore witness of what had been done, being one entire wound and bruise, and wrenched and deprived of the external form of man. In whom Christ himself suffering shewed forth great glory, confounding the adversary, and shewing for an example to others, that nothing is terrible where is the love of the Father; nothing painful where is the glory of Christ.

"And then the devil, thinking he had already

swallowed up one woman of the number of those who had denied Christ, named Biblias, led her to the torture, to compel her to say impious things concerning us, as one now easily to be broken, and without courage. But she came to herself under the tortures, and awoke, so to speak, from a deep sleep, being reminded by temporal punishment of the eternal misery of hell; and declared, in contradiction of the blasphemies, 'How should those devour children, with whom it is not allowed even to eat the blood of animals?' And from this time she confessed herself to be a Christian, and was added to the number of the martyrs.

"The blessed Pothinius, who was entrusted with the bishopric of the Church in Lyons, above ninety years of age, and quite worn out in body, scarce able to breathe from his previous infirmity, but renewed in strength by the readiness of his spirit, in his earnest desire of martyrdom, himself also was dragged to the tribunal; his body worn out with age and disease, but his life being still kept in him, that Christ might triumph through it; who, when brought by the soldiers to the tribunal, all the authorities of the city following him, and all the crowd, as though he had been Christ himself, uttering all sorts of cries against him, bore a good testimony. And when asked by the governor who might be the God of the Christians, he said, 'If thou be worthy, thou shalt know.' After this he was dragged about without mercy, and suffered all kinds of buffeting, those who were near him insulting him with their hands and feet, without regard to his age; and those at a distance throwing at him whatever came to hand; and all thinking any one guilty of a great fault and impiety who should be wanting in insolence towards him. For they considered that they should thus avenge their gods. And he was cast, scarce alive, into the prison, and died after two days.

"Maturus and Sanctus again went through, in the amphitheatre, every torture, as if they had absolutely suffered nothing before. Rather, as having now in several combats foiled the adversary, and engaged in the contest for the very crown, they supported again the course of scourging usually inflicted there, and the dragging about by the beasts, and whatever else the mad populace shouted and demanded, on this side or that, to have done to them; and, above all, the iron seat, on which their bodies being scorched, choked them with the smell. Blandina, hung up on a cross, was placed to be devoured by the beasts that were turned in. She thus visibly hanging in the figure of a cross, and engaged in earnest prayer, wrought great readiness in those who underwent the conflict; since they saw in the midst of their sufferings, even with the outward eye, in their sister, Him who was crucified for them, to persuade those who believe in Him, that every one who hath suffered for the glory of Christ, hath for ever communion with the living God. And none of the beasts having at that time touched her, she was taken down from the cross, and carried up again to the prison, to be kept for another conflict."

Under the apprehension of such torments, several persons were so overcome by fear as to deny Christ. We have already seen one instance of recovery from this lamentable failure; but the Christians were now to rejoice at the return of those who had forsaken their Saviour. The account proceeds:—

"But Christ was greatly glorified in those who had denied before, but then confessed, contrary to the expectation of the heathen. For these were even separately examined, as in the idea that they were to be dismissed; but confessing, they were added to the number of the martyrs. And while they were under examination, one Alexander, a Phrygian by birth, and a physician by profession, who had lived many years in the provinces of Gaul, and was known by almost all for his love to God, and boldness in declaring the word (for he was not without a share of the apostolic gift), standing by the tribunal, and encouraging them by signs in their confession, was observed by those who stood round the tribunal, and having acknowledged that he was a Christian, he was condemned to be thrown to the wild beasts. The next day he and Attalus were put to death in the amphitheatre; Alexander without uttering a groan or syllable, but conversing in his heart with God. But Attalus, when he was placed on the iron seat and scorched, when the vapour went up from his body, said to the crowd, in the Roman tongue, 'Behold, this is man-eating, which yourselves do; but we neither eat men, nor do any other evil thing.' And when asked what name God hath, he answered, 'God hath not a name as a man hath.'"

Blandina was last brought in, with a boy from Pontus, only fifteen years of age, whom she encouraged, in the midst of most dreadful and lingering tortures, to confess the name of Christ; and thus, "having stirred up her children, and sent them forward victorious to the KING; and having herself gone through all the same conflicts with her children, she hastened after them, rejoicing and exulting in her departure, as if called to a marriage-supper, instead of being thrown to wild beasts. And after the scourging, after the wild beasts, after the scorching, at last she was placed in a basket, and thrown to a bull, and died, after having been much tossed about by the animal, having no feeling of her sufferings, through her hope and hold of those things which she believed, and her converse with Christ."

Space will not permit me to cite similar examples
of faith and Christian heroism from the martyrdoms
of the blessed Simeon, bishop of Jerusalem; St.
Ignatius, bishop of Antioch; Justin Martyr; Per-
petua and Felicitas; St. Cyprian, bishop of Carthage; and others innumerable.

CHAPTER V.

FRUITS OF FAITH EXEMPLIFIED IN THE LIVES OF CHRISTIANS.

A.D. 30-320.

N these ages the profession of Chris-
tianity was attended with such dangers,
and involved so perfect a renunciation
of this world, that worldly, sinful, in-
sincere, and even irresolute men, were
rarely found in the communion of the Church. The
mass of Christians were thoroughly in earnest, full of
zeal, and concentrating their hopes and their labours
in the service of their Creator and Redeemer. If
the Church in later ages seem less pure and bright,
it should be remembered that the world had then
ceased to persecute; that it had even attached itself
externally to religion; and thus, that a large number of professing Christians were not in reality followers of our Lord.   For what the apostle says—
" He is not a Jew which is one outwardly; neither
is that circumcision which is outward in the flesh;
but he is a Jew which is one inwardly; and circumcision is that of the heart"[1]—may be applied equally
to the case of Christians.   The number of the real
disciples of Christ, who constitute the soul of the

[1] Rom. ii. 28, 29.

Church, its vital and undying members, has perhaps not been less in later ages than in the times of persecution; but the number of false brethren, and the multitude of scandals, has been greatly increased.

The lives of Christians during the first three centuries exhibited striking evidence of the power of faith, and fulfilled the divine precept, "Let your light so shine before men, that they may see your good works, and glorify your Father which is in heaven." To the morality and virtue of their conduct, frequent appeal was made by the Christian apologists. "We," says Justin Martyr, "who formerly rejoiced in licentiousness, now embrace discretion and chastity; we who resorted to magical arts, now devote ourselves to the unbegotten God, the God of goodness; we who set our affections on wealth and possessions, now bring to the common stock all our property, and share it with the indigent; we who, owing to diversity of customs, would not share the same hearth with a different race, now, since the appearance of Christ, live together, and pray for our enemies, and endeavour to persuade those who unjustly hate us, that by leading a life conformed to the excellent precepts of Christianity, they may be filled with the good hope of obtaining like happiness with ourselves from that God who is Lord above all things." There were many instances in those times of persons selling their goods, and giving them to the poor, though the practice was not general. It was customary for all Christians to receive the sacrament of the eucharist every Sunday; in some churches, indeed, especially in time of persecution, it was administered every day; and it was considered a grievous offence to forsake the table of the Lord. The manners and duties of Christians are described by Tertullian in his argument, that Christian women ought only to marry believers like themselves.   A Christian marriage, he says, " is made by the Church, confirmed by the eucharist, sealed by the blessing, carried by angels to the heavenly Father, and ratified by him.   Two believers bear the same yoke; they are but one flesh and one spirit; they pray together, kneel together, fast together, instruct and exhort each other.   They are together in the Church, and at the table of God; in persecution and in consolation.   They do not conceal their actions from each other, nor inconvenience each other.   They may visit the sick, and be present at the sacrifice of prayer without inquietude.   They sing psalms and hymns together, and excite one another to praise God."

Amongst the most illustrious saints and eminent men who adorned the Church in the first century, we may name St. Clement, who was made bishop of Rome by the apostles, and who sent to the Church of Corinth an epistle exhorting them to mutual love and harmony, which is still extant, and from which some extracts have been already given.   St. Ignatius had also been constituted bishop of Antioch by the apostles; and on his being carried to Rome, A.D. 107, to suffer martyrdom, he addressed many pious epistles to the Christian Churches, exhorting them to confess the true faith, and to remain united to their bishops, priests, and deacons.

St. Justin Martyr, one of the earliest and most celebrated writers in defence of the Christian religion against heathens and Jews, was a native of Syria; and having vainly sought wisdom, and happiness, and the knowledge of God, amongst the various sects of heathen philosophy, he happened one day to meet an aged Christian of a sweet and grave demeanour, who entered into discourse with Justin, and having quietly reproved him for his preference of knowledge to practice, he proceeded to shew " that all the heathen philosophers had erred in principles, that they were ignorant of God; and that the only real sages were the prophets, whom God himself had inspired, as plainly appeared by their predictions and their miracles." He added, " that those prophets had instructed us concerning God the Father and Author of all things, and his Son Jesus Christ whom he had sent; and that it was necessary that God should open the gates of light to us, and cause us to know the truth." From this discourse Justin was led, by Divine grace, to an exceeding desire and love for the holy Scriptures, and he was soon convinced that the doctrine of our Saviour was the only sure and certain truth. He then perceived the utter falsehood of the calumnies against Christians: " I understood," he says, " that it was impossible they should live in vice and in the love of pleasure. For, said I, where is the voluptuous or intemperate man, who even partakes of human flesh, that would seek death, and thus deprive himself of his pleasures? And who is there that would not rather live always in this world, and conceal himself from the magistrates, far from denouncing himself and being put to death?" Justin now became a Christian indeed; and about A.D. 148 he composed an Apology for the Christians, which he dedicated to the emperor Antoninus, and which furnishes an invaluable record of the faith and practice of the Christian Church. This holy man wrote several other books in defence of the truth; and at length testified his faith in Jesus Christ in the presence of all the people, and having been scourged by order of the Roman prefect, he was beheaded.

Of St. Polycarp, bishop of Smyrna, and disciple of St. John, some account has already been given. In his time some differences having arisen between the Asiatic and other Churches about the time of celebrating Easter, the venerable Polycarp came from the east to Rome, to confer with Anicetus, bishop of that Church, on the matters in dispute. The conference resulted in an agreement that mutual charity and peace ought not to be broken on account of this difference. Nevertheless Anicetus could not prevail on Polycarp to forsake the Asiatic custom of observing Easter-day at the same time as the Jews; nor could Polycarp prevail on Anicetus to follow that custom; for each party believed themselves bound to continue the same ordinances which had descended to them from their forefathers. These holy bishops received the communion together; and Anicetus, to do honour to Polycarp, requested him to consecrate the eucharist in his church. When St. Polycarp was at Rome, he met the heretic Marcion, (who denied that God was the Creator of the world, and affirmed that the Old Testament was the work of the devil); and when asked by Marcion, " whether he knew him," he replied, " I know thee for the first-born of Satan." St. Polycarp wrote an epistle to the Church of the Philippians, full of pious exhortations, which is still extant; and suffered martyrdom as we have already seen.

St. Irenæus, a most learned and illustrious bishop, was in his early youth a disciple of Polycarp, bishop of Smyrna, and afterwards went to France, where he became a presbyter of the Church of Lyons, and was in this office when the dreadful persecution, which has been before described, arose in the time of Antoninus. After the death of Pothinus, he succeeded to the vacant bishopric; and he has obtained immortal fame by his great work " against heresies," in which he proves most triumphantly, against the Gnostics, that there is but one true God, the Creator of the world; and that his Son, our Lord Jesus Christ, was truly both God and man. St. Irenæus was zealous in his endeavours to preserve the peace of the Church,

which was endangered about A.D. 198 by the attempt
of Victor, bishop of Rome, to oblige the Asiatic
Churches to forsake their rule concerning Easter;
and having assembled a synod[1] of clergy in France,
he wrote to Victor exhorting him not to separate the
brethren of Asia from his communion for such a
cause as mere attachment to their own customs.
" This dispute," he says, " relates not only to the
day of Easter, but to the manner of fasting also.
For some believe that they ought not to fast above
one day (before Easter), others two, others more;
some reckon for their fast forty hours, day and night
included.   And this difference of observances has
not begun in our times; it has existed long under
our predecessors, who seem not to have transmitted
to posterity customs introduced by simplicity or
ignorance.   Nevertheless they have all preserved
peace, and we continue to keep it amongst us; so
that the difference of fasting confirms the unity of
faith."   St. Irenæus was diligent in spreading the
gospel in France; and at length his great services
to the Church were crowned by martyrdom.

CLEMENT, a most learned presbyter of the Church
of Alexandria, flourished about A.D. 194.   He was a
disciple of Patænus, a man of eminent piety and
learning, who presided over the Christian school
at Alexandria, and preached to the heathens in
India.   Clement became the successor of Patænus,
and composed many works in defence of Christianity, and on the duties of believers, which shew the
vast extent of his knowledge, and the sincerity of his
devotion.   Clement pointed out to believers the duty
of moderation in all things, especially in the indulgence of the appetites.   He wished them to eat only
what was necessary for health, to sleep but sparingly,

----

[1] Assembly.

to abstain from gay and expensive clothing, to be bountiful to the poor.   He forbad all luxury, expensive furniture, perfumes, attendance on public exhibitions and theatres.   His object was to model Christians after the likeness of Christ, dead to this world, and devoted only to the duties, the hopes, and the pleasures of spiritual religion.

TERTULLIAN, a presbyter of the Church at Carthage in Africa, was contemporary with Clement of Alexandria, and had been originally a pagan, but after his baptism he devoted himself to the service of the Church, and wrote many useful books on the duties of Christians, and in defence of the truth against pagans and heretics.   He addressed a book to his wife, in which he pointed out the duty of Christians not to contract marriages with unbelievers. But it is lamentable to add, that after many and great services to the cause of religion, he was at length deceived by the imposture of Montanus, who had professed himself to be " the Comforter" promised by our Lord to his disciples.   Tertullian now fell away from the Church, and died in separation from its communion.

Amongst the most remarkable men in the Church after this time was ORIGEN, who having succeeded Clement in the government of the school of Alexandria, made himself renowned in the Christian Church by his commentaries on Scripture, and his versions and editions of the sacred volume.   He also defended the Christian faith against the objections of the heathen Celsus, and converted many unbelievers to Christianity.   NARCISSUS and GREGORY, bishops of Jerusalem and Cæsarea, are said to have. had the gift of miracles; and Origen says that many miracles continued to be wrought in his time for the conversion of the heathen.

ST. CYPRIAN, bishop of Carthage, was a native of

Africa; and having applied himself to the study of philosophy and eloquence, he became eminently distinguished among his contemporaries. He was still a pagan, and the self-denial and purity exacted by the law of Christ appeared to him difficult, if not impossible. "It appeared to me extremely hard," he said, " to be born again to a new life, and to become another man, still keeping the same body. How can one at once get rid of rooted and hardened habits, which arise either from nature itself, or from long custom? How can one learn frugality, when accustomed to an abundant and delicate table? How shall he who has been clothed in rich garments, shining with gold and purple, humble himself to a simple and plain attire? When one is accustomed to dignities, honours, and a crowd of friends and clients, it is impossible to resolve on living in privacy; one regards solitude as a punishment. I often held converse thus with myself; but when the life-giving water (baptism) had washed away the sins of my past life, and my cleansed heart had received light from on high and the heavenly Spirit, I was amazed how my doubts vanished away; all was open; all was clear; and I found easy what had appeared to me impossible; so as to acknowledge, that whatsoever is born according to the flesh, and lives in crime, is of the earth; and that whatsoever is enlivened by the Holy Spirit, cometh from God." The conversion of St. Cyprian to the Christian religion, was a subject of great annoyance to the pagans, and his exhaustless zeal soon drew down on him a storm of persecution, which terminated in his martyrdom. His first act was to sell all his goods and distribute them among the poor; thus at once manifesting his little value for the things of this world, and shewing that mercy which God preferred even before sacrifice. He was presently made a presbyter of the Church of

Carthage, and soon after, on the death of Donatus in 248, he was elected bishop. His great desire was now to exhort the brethren to holiness of life; and he availed himself of all the examples of piety in the Holy Scriptures, to urge on his people the imitation of such virtues. He would point out to them the example of Job, " who cared so little for his temporal possessions, and made such advances in piety, that even his calamities made no change in it: neither want nor pain overcame him; the persuasions of his wife, the bitter pains of his body, did not subdue him. Virtue and deeply-rooted devotion remained fixed in their seat, nor yielded to the violence of the devil's temptations, so that even in his adversity he blessed his God." Such were the examples which the holy Cyprian in those days of persecution and affliction held out to the brethren. He had a particular friendship with Cæcilius, an aged presbyter and a just man, who had brought him from the errors of false religion to the knowledge of Jesus Christ. Cyprian always honoured, venerated, and loved this presbyter, not merely as an ordinary friend, but as a parent, from whom he had derived new life; and when the time was near in which Cæcilius was to be called away from this world, he commended to Cyprian the care of his wife and children; and thus made him the heir of his affection, whom he had formerly made partaker of the communion of his Church.

Cyprian had been exceedingly reluctant to undertake the sacred and responsible office of a bishop, considering himself unworthy of so great an honour, but was overcome at last by the entreaties of the people. Some persons had opposed his election; but he dealt with them with such gentleness, patience, and benevolence, that, to the surprise of many, they became some of the most attached and closest of his friends. " Who," says his affectionate deacon, Pontius, " who can sufficiently describe his conduct — what piety, what vigour, what mercy, what discipline! So much sanctity and grace was resplendent in his countenance, that they who beheld him were amazed. His look was at once serious and joyful, neither severely sad, nor overmuch mild and gentle, but a mingling together of both; so that one might have doubted whether he were more to be loved or feared, had he not deserved to be both one and the other. His dress was not unsuitable to his countenance, moderate and temperate. No worldly pride inflated him: nor did any affected penury in dress render his appearance mean; for this sort of clothing, no less than an ostentatious and ambitious frugality, arises from vain-glory." St. Cyprian devoted himself especially to the care of the poor.

While Cyprian was thus engaged, the persecution under the Emperor Decius commenced with great severity in Africa, as well as in all other parts of the Roman empire. The heathen populace at Carthage cried out in the theatre, demanding that Cyprian should be thrown to the lions. It was essential for his safety to retire into the country, which he did for a time. During his absence, a discontented presbyter, named Novatus, formed a party in the Church of Carthage, and after a time separated from its communion. A similar calamity occurred to the Roman Church after Cyprian had returned to Carthage; — for, when Cornelius had been lawfully constituted bishop of Rome, Novatian caused himself to be ordained as a rival bishop, and established a distinct sect. Cyprian, full of charity and zeal, wrote a treatise on the Unity of the Church, in which he exposed the wickedness of those who separated from the communion of the bishop, and caused division in the Church where nothing but charity and love ought to exist. A difference afterwards arose between Stephen, bishop of Rome, and St. Cyprian, in which the latter evinced the utmost firmness in maintaining the custom of the African and Asiatic Churches against that of the Roman. This difference related to the mode of receiving converts from heresies, who had been baptised in their own sects; and the African Churches, considering that the grace of God could not accompany any acts performed in a state of separation from Jesus Christ and his Church, were in the habit of baptising converts from heresy, as if they had not received any Christian baptism before: on the other hand, the Roman Churches had been accustomed to admit heretics to communion by the imposition of hands; thus, as it were, completing what had been deficient in their former state. Stephen, a proud and violent man, endeavoured to intimidate the African bishops into submission by excommunicating them; but they resisted this irregular proceeding with Christian firmness; and Firmilian, bishop of Cæsarea, in Cappadocia, observed that such unjust excommunications could only separate their authors from the Catholic Church.

A most terrible pestilence at one time raged in Carthage, and so great a terror had seized the people, that the sick were left unaided in their extremity; all the natural affections seemed to be extinguished, and multitudes of dead bodies were cast into the streets, and lay neglected there. St. Cyprian assembled the believers, and exhorted them to works of piety by the examples set forth in holy Scripture. He then allotted to each person his share in the holy work of charity; the poor contributed their labour, and the rich their wealth, and thus an abundant relief was afforded, not only to the Christians, but to the heathen. St. Cyprian at this time wrote a book, encouraging his people, and exhorting them to remember, that death ought to be to the true believer rather a subject of joy and triumph, than of despondency and fear.

"The kingdom of God, most beloved brethren," said he, "is at hand. The reward of life, the joy of everlasting salvation, perpetual happiness, the possession of paradise once lost, are now drawing near, while the world is passing away. Great and heavenly things are now succeeding to earthly things; small and perishing concerns are giving way to Eternity. What room is there here for anxiety and care? Who, under such circumstances, is sad and trembling, but that man who is devoid of faith and hope? It is only for that man to fear death who is unwilling to depart to Christ. It is for him to be reluctant to go to Christ, who does not believe that he shall reign with him. It is written that the just shall ' live by faith.' If thou art just, and livest by faith, why, when thou art to be with Christ, and art secure by the promise of God—why dost thou not embrace that call unto Christ, and rejoice to be delivered from the devil? When it was revealed from heaven unto Simeon, that truly just man, who by faith kept all the commands of God, that he should not depart before he beheld Christ, and when the child Christ had come with his mother into the temple, he felt in his spirit that Christ, who had been foretold to him, was now born, and when he had seen him, he knew that he should quickly die; and yet, rejoicing at his death so near at hand, and secure that he should soon be called away, he took the child in his hands, and blessing the Lord, he exclaimed and said, ' Lord, now lettest thou thy servant depart in peace according to thy word, for mine eyes have seen thy salvation.'

"The servants of God possess peace and tranquil

rest, when, delivered from the storms of this world, we arrive at the haven of eternal rest and safety; when, after this death is no more, we attain to immortality.   That indeed is true peace; that is real tranquillity; that is lasting and perpetual joy.   But what is there in the world save daily contest against the devil, warfare and continual conflict against his arms and weapons? We have to contend with avarice, with immodesty, with anger, with ambition. We have continual and grievous wrestling with the vices of the flesh and the allurements of the world. The mind of man, besieged and encompassed by the assaults of Satan, can scarcely meet, scarcely resist them all. If avarice be overthrown, evil desire arises: if that be subdued, ambition succeeds. If ambition be contemned, wrath exasperates us, pride inflates, excess invites, envy breaketh concord, and jealousy destroyeth friendship. Such are the persecutions which thy mind each day endures—such the dangers by which thy heart is assailed: and is it then thy pleasure to remain long here, exposed as thou art to all the weapons of the devil, when thou oughtest rather to wish and desire, by the speedy assistance of death, to hasten away unto Christ; who himself teaches us, saying, ‘ Verily, verily, I say unto you, that ye shall weep and lament, but the world shall rejoice; ye shall be sorrowful, but your sorrow shall be turned into joy?’ Who would not wish to lose sorrow? Who would not hasten to attain joy? Now the Lord himself declares *when* our sorrow shall be turned into joy, saying, ‘ I will see you again, and your heart shall rejoice, and your joy no man taketh from you.’

“ Since, then, it is joy to see Christ, nor can our joy exist except when we see him; what blindness or madness is it, to love the burdens, the punishments, the terrors of the world; and not rather to hasten unto that joy which can never be taken away?" " The reason of this is, my beloved brethren, a want of faith, because no one believes in the truth of the promises of that God who is TRUE, whose word is firm and eternal to them that believe. If a grave and worthy man should promise thee any thing, thou wouldst rely on his promise, nor believe that one whom thou knewest to be constant in his words and actions, would fail or deceive thee. Now GOD speaks with thee, and dost thou waver in unbelief? God promises to thee, departing from this world, immortality and eternity, and dost thou doubt? This is, not to know God ; this is, to offend Christ with the sin of unbelief, who is the master of believers only ; this is, to have in the Church, in the house of faith, no settled faith.

" Let us consider, most beloved brethren, and continually reflect, that we have renounced the world, and that we only abide here as strangers and pilgrims. Let us embrace that time which gives to each one his home, which, delivering us from this world, and loosing us from worldly snares, restores us to paradise and the kingdom. Who that is placed in a foreign land would not hasten to return to his own country? Who that saileth towards his own, would not eagerly desire a prosperous wind, to bring him swiftly to the embrace of those he loves? Our country we believe to be paradise : the patriarchs we esteem our parents. Why then do we not speed and run, that we may behold our country, and salute our parents? There a great multitude of those who are dear to us await us ; a numerous and abundant crowd of parents, brethren, children, already secure of their own salvation, yet still anxious for ours, desire us. How great a joy for them and us in common, to behold and embrace them ! What pleasure of celestial kingdoms is there, without fear-of death, and with eternal life what great and perpetual happiness! There is the glorious choir of the apostles; there the number of the rejoicing prophets; there an innumerable people of martyrs, crowned for the victory of their contest and sufferings; triumphant virgins, who have subdued the desires of the flesh and body by the strength of continence; the merciful rewarded, who have performed works of righteousness in nourishing and bestowing alms on the poor, who, observing the commandments of the Lord, have transferred their earthly possessions to the treasury of heaven. To these, beloved brethren, let us with eager desire hasten; and let us wish that we may quickly be with them, quickly come to Christ. May God behold this thought in us. May the Lord Christ observe this purpose of mind and faith in us, Who shall give his greatest rewards of glory to those whose desires are greatest towards himself."

Such were the exhortations of the holy Cyprian. He was a few years afterwards called to bear witness to the faith of Jesus Christ in the face of torment and death, and he did not shrink from the path which he had so often pointed out to his brethren, but laid down his life for the Gospel, A.D. 258.

CHAPTER VI.

ON THE COMMUNION, RITES, AND DISCIPLINE OF THE CHURCH.

A.D. 30-320.

O precept is more frequently inculcated in sacred Scripture than that of mutual love and charity between all Christians. "By this," said our Lord, "shall all men know that ye are my disciples, if ye have love one to another."[1] By their relation to God as their heavenly Father, they are made brethren to one another; and therefore the apostolical command is, " Love as brethren." Such is the duty of Christians; they are bound to regard all their brethren as members of the same spiritual body as themselves; and hence results the obligation of holding communion in all possible respects with all members of the Church of Christ. Our Lord prayed that his disciples might be " one;" the apostles exhorted them to permit no schisms, no contentions among them,[2] and to avoid those who caused divisions,[3] whom they characterised as " sensual, not having the Spirit."[4]

This communion of all particular Churches with each other, as parts and members of the one great spiritual body or society of believers, existed for some ages in much more perfection than it subsequently did, when earthly ambition and unchristian feelings were engendered by prosperity, and the tares began to grow thickly among the good wheat. In the time of the apostles it was manifested by the reception and admission to religious communion of Christians who came from other countries; by contributions for the relief of distressed believers in all parts; and by the exchange of letters and advice. The same practices continued for many ages to be general. Each bishop then could give to any member of his Church who might visit foreign countries, commendatory letters, which, on being presented to the most remote Churches, secured his immediate admission to all the privileges of Christian fellowship, and, in case of necessity, to the kind offices of Christian benevolence. We have in the epistle of

---

[1] John xiii. 15.   [2] 1 Cor. i. 10-12.
[3] Rom. xvi. 17, 18.   [4] Jude 19.

St. Clement, bishop of Rome, and the Roman Church, addressed to the Church of Corinth, before the end of the first century, on occasion of a schism in the latter Church, an instance of the same fraternal intercourse and solicitude; and in the following centuries, the epistles of Dionysius, bishop of Corinth, to many Churches in Pontus, Crete, &c., and that of the council of Antioch (A.D. 270) to all the Churches, are further examples of the same practice. We learn from Dionysius, that even in the second century, the Church of Rome was remarkable for the extent of its charities to the distressed and persecuted Christians at Corinth and in the East; and Dionysius of Alexandria, in the following century, attests that the same truly Christian conduct was still in full exercise, and that its benefits were felt even in the remote regions of Arabia.

But, notwithstanding the obligations of Christians to cultivate brotherly love, the harmony of the Church has but too often been interrupted. Even in the time of St. Paul, the Church of Corinth was full of parties and division, as it afterwards was in the time of St. Clement. Paul and Barnabas themselves separated and departed asunder from each other. In the second century a serious division arose between the Roman and the Asiatic Churches; for when the latter persisted in retaining their ancient custom of celebrating Easter rather on the same day with the Jews, than with the rest of the Catholic Church, Victor, bishop of Rome, proceeded to the extent of separating them from his communion; an act which was disapproved by St. Irenæus and the greater part of the Church.

In the following century (A.D. 250) a difference arose between Stephen, bishop of Rome, and the African Churches. The latter, as we have seen in Cyprian's life, maintained that baptisms performed by sectarians and heretics were null and void, and that all converts to the Church ought to be baptised; while the Roman Church did not reiterate baptism when it had been administered by heretics with the proper external form, but received converts into the Church by the imposition of hands in confirmation. Stephen insisted that the custom of the Roman Church should be adopted, and separated the African Churches, on their refusal, from his communion. This act, however, was not approved or recognised by the majority of bishops.

These dissensions between independent Churches were of a very different character from formal schisms. The former consisted in a temporary withdrawal of the usual marks of intercourse between different Churches; the latter were separations from the Church, the establishment of rival worship, rival ministers, different communions in the same place. In the one case charity was chilled; in the other it was entirely destroyed. Novatian, disappointed of the bishopric of Rome, rebelled against his bishop, Cornelius, and established a rival community at Rome, of which he was constituted the bishop; but when the case was known, he was condemned by the whole body of the Church throughout the world, and his sect was rejected as schismatical. In the following century, the bishops of Numidia, enraged at the election of Cæcilianus to the see of Carthage in their absence, pretended that he had been ordained by apostates, and having ordained rival bishops at Carthage and elsewhere in Africa, separated from the communion of the universal Church (which supported Cæcilianus), declaring it apostate. They denied that its members were Christian, that its baptism was valid, or its clergy lawfully ordained; and refused to hold communion with them. These sectarians, called Donatists, were, after full examina-

tion of their cause by councils of bishops, and by the
emperor Constantine, universally rejected and condemned.   They continued, however, for two or three
centuries to disturb and persecute the Church in
Africa.   Separations like these, where rival worship
was established, were in those ages regarded as most
heinous sins, and destructive of salvation.

I now proceed to the consideration of the sacraments and rites of the Church.   One of the fullest
and most interesting details of the celebration of
Baptism and the Lord's supper in those days which
has been preserved, occurs in the writings of Justin
Martyr.   "We shall relate," he says " the manner
in which those who are renewed through Christ
dedicate themselves to God."   " As many as are
persuaded and believe what is taught and said by us
(Christians), and promise that they will live accordingly, are instructed with prayer and fasting to beseech from God the remission of their sins ; we also
fasting and praying along with them.   Then we
bring them to a place where there is water, and they
are regenerated in the same mode of regeneration as
that with which we were ourselves regenerated ; for
then they are washed in water, in the name of God
the Father and Lord of all, and of our Saviour Jesus
Christ, and of the Holy Ghost ; for Christ himself
said, Except ye be regenerated, ye cannot enter into
the kingdom of heaven."   This was the manner in
which all converts from heathenism were admitted
into the Christian Church, and made partakers of
all its blessed promises and privileges.   When infants were baptised, the parents or godfathers made
the same engagements in their name.   The practice
of infant baptism was generally established before
the time of Irenæus (A.D. 178) ; and in that of
Cyprian (A.D. 250), the question was only whether
they ought to be baptised before the eighth day after

their birth. As infants had been admitted by circumcision into covenant with God under the older dispensation ; and as our Lord had shewn his favour to them by taking them in his arms, blessing them, and saying, that " of such is the kingdom of heaven ;" and as it is related that the apostles baptised whole households of their converts,—the Church always believed that the children of Christians ought not to be left in the condition of heathens, but received at once into the Christian body by holy baptism, and instructed to walk worthy of the high gifts which they had received.

The rite of Confirmation followed that of baptism. The apostles had laid their hands on those who were baptised, in order that they might receive additional gifts of the Holy Ghost ; and we find from Tertullian that this custom was still observed by the bishops, the successors of the apostles, as it has always continued to be from that age to the present. Confirmation was generally administered soon after baptism ; and it does not seem that for many centuries the discipline of the Church separated those rites by such an interval as is now customary ; but it must be remembered, that in the first ages baptism was rarely administered except by the bishop, and at the great festivals of Easter and Pentecost, when numbers of converts from heathenism, who had been for months under catechetical instruction, and the children of Christians, were altogether baptised with great solemnity, and immediately afterwards were confirmed.

" After baptism," says Justin Martyr, " we lead him (the convert) to the place where those who are called brethren are assembled, and prepared to offer earnest prayers both for themselves and for those who have been illuminated (baptised), and for all other people every where, that they may be thought worthy to know the truth, and be found good men, and keepers of the commandments, that they may be saved with an eternal salvation. Having ceased from prayers, we salute each other with a kiss. Then bread, and a cup of wine and water mixed, is brought to the president (bishop) of the brethren, and he, taking them, offers praise and glory to the Father of all, through the name of the Son and of the Holy Spirit, and maketh a very long thanksgiving, because He hath thought us worthy of these gifts; and when he has concluded the prayers and thanksgiving, all the people present approve it with acclamation, saying, Amen. Now 'amen' in the Hebrew tongue signifies 'So be it.'"

"When the president has offered thanksgiving, and all the people responded, those who are called deacons amongst us give to every one present a portion of the bread, and of the wine and water which has been blessed, and carry it to those who are not present. And this food we call the eucharist, of which no one is permitted to partake except he believes in the truth of our doctrine, and has been baptised in the laver for the remission of sins and regeneration, and lives so as Christ has taught: for we do not receive it as common bread or common drink; but as, by the word of God, our Saviour Jesus Christ was incarnate, and had flesh and blood for our salvation, so also we have been instructed, that the food, blessed by the word of prayer which is from him, through which our flesh and blood by a change are nourished, is (spiritually) the flesh and blood of that incarnate Jesus. For the apostles, in the commentaries written by them, which are called Gospels, have informed us that they were commanded to do so by Jesus, who took bread and gave thanks, and after giving thanks said, 'Do this in remembrance of me; this is my body:' and in the same manner took the cup, and having given thanks, said, ' This is my blood,' and distributed it to them only" (*i. e.* only to believers).

"After this," he continues, "we always continually remind each other of these things; and the rich assist the poor, and we are continually with each other. In all our offerings, we bless the Creator of all things, through his Son Jesus Christ, and through the Holy Spirit. And on the day called Sunday, all who dwell in the city or the country assemble in one place, and the memorials of the apostles, and the writings of the prophets, are read as the time permits. Then, when the reader ceases, the president in a discourse exhorts and admonishes to the imitation of these excellent precepts. We then all rise together, and send up prayers; and, as we have said, when the prayers cease, bread is offered, and wine and water."

"But those who are wealthy and so disposed contribute each as he pleases; and the collection is deposited with the president, who assists the orphans and widows, and those who are in want, through sickness or some other cause, also those who are in prison, and guests who are foreigners; and, in short, he is the guardian of all who are in distress. And on the Sunday we all assemble together, because it is the first day, on which God, changing darkness and matter, created the world, and Jesus Christ our Saviour on the same day rose from the dead."

In those early times the creed was used, as it still is, as a confession of faith preparatory to receiving the sacrament of baptism. When the Ethiopian eunuch desired to be baptised, Philip said to him, " If thou believest with all thine heart, thou mayest." And he answered and said, " I believe that Jesus Christ is the Son of God." Here is an instance of a creed, or profession of faith, even in the time of the apostles. Indeed, as our Lord had required faith in his doctrines, as well as baptism, in order to salvation, the Church was bound to ascertain as far as possible that those who desired baptism were believers, and therefore to require from them a profession of their faith. Creeds in this point of view, as summaries of the Gospel, are as old as the time of the apostles; their length and fulness varied in different Churches, and sometimes new articles were added, in order to assert the truth in opposition to prevalent heresies. The apostles' creed was the ancient baptismal creed of the Roman and Italian Churches; the Nicene creed was founded on the ancient creeds of the Eastern Churches by the holy synod of 318 bishops at Nice (A.D. 325), and was adopted as the rule of faith by the universal Church in all subsequent times. This creed was introduced into the liturgy or service of the eucharist in the fifth and sixth centuries.

What has been said of the apostolical antiquity of creeds applies also to liturgies. It appears that, in the fourth century, there were four forms of administering the eucharist in existence, which had continued in different parts of the universal Church from the remotest antiquity. These forms agreed in all their principal parts: their variety consisted chiefly in the different *order* in which those parts were arranged. One form prevailed in Judæa, Syria, Asia Minor, Macedonia, Greece; and, in the fifth century, was ascribed by the Church of Jerusalem to James the apostle. Another, which was established by St. Mark, prevailed in Egypt and Ethiopia. A third, which has been attributed, with some probability, to St. John the apostle, was used in Ephesus, and afterwards in France, Spain, and probably Britain. A fourth apostolical form existed in Rome, Italy, and Africa. Every Church had and exercised the power of improving its liturgy by the addition of new rites and prayers; but all adhered to the general order and substance delivered from the beginning. The liturgy or service for the holy communion now used in England resembles the ancient Gallican in the most essential points.

Penitence was regarded as the remedy for sin committed after baptism. It was generally taught that confession of secret sins to God, with a truly contrite heart and changed life, were sufficient to obtain remission of sins. In the case of sins, however, which were public and caused scandal, a different method was pursued. St. Paul had commanded the Corinthian Church to expel from its communion a person who had committed a grievous and scandalous sin, and had enjoined them to receive him again on his sincere repentance. The Church, acting on this principle, excommunicated any of its members who fell into grievous sin, unless they voluntarily submitted to a lengthened course of penitence. Penitence for seven, ten, fifteen, or even twenty years, was required for some sins, in proportion to their enormity or scandal. During this period, the penitent first stood outside the church while divine service was proceeding; then, in process of time, was admitted into the church, but obliged to assume the humblest attitude, and forbidden to partake of the eucharist. During all this time, he was obliged further to manifest his grief by fasting, weeping, mourning, wearing sackcloth, and imploring the prayers of the brethren for his soul. Such was the severity of the ancient discipline; but the bishop had the power of diminishing the time, in cases where repentance was deep and manifest. The Church was at length fully satisfied, and the penitent was then solemnly absolved and blessed, and admitted to the full privileges of Christian fellowship. The same sort of penitence was required from those who had been excommunicated for their sins, and desired to return to the Church.

Those who committed great sins in secret were recommended to disclose their guilt to discreet and judicious ministers of God, and receive from them directions for the course of private penitence which they ought to pursue. In the latter part of the third century, a penitentiary was appointed in most churches, whose duty it was to hear such voluntary confessions, and to offer spiritual advice to penitents. About a century afterwards, this office was discontinued by Nectarius, bishop of Constantinople, on occasion of the scandal caused by an imprudent publication of a crime, through the indiscretion of the penitentiary of that Church; and from this time, private penitents in the eastern Churches approached the Lord's table at their own discretion.

The ministry of the Church instituted by the apostles consisted of bishops, priests, and deacons. The apostles retained the government of all Churches in their own hands at first, only appointing deacons and bishops, or presbyters (for these two names are indiscriminately used in holy Scripture); but when about to depart from this world, they constituted bishops or chief presbyters " in their own place," as we learn from St. Irenæus. Thus Timothy was placed at Ephesus, Titus at Crete, Dionysius the Areopagite at Athens, Linus at Rome, Anianus at Alexandria, as James had been long before appointed bishop at Jerusalem. Even the opponents of episcopacy admit, that by the middle of the second century all Churches were governed by bishops; and, in fact, no instance of any Church not under episcopal superintendence has ever been pointed out in the course of fifteen centuries after Christ. Amongst Churches, some had pre-eminent distinction from their opulence and magnitude, or the civil distinctions which their cities enjoyed; and thus, in the second and third centuries, the Churches of the principal cities, such as Rome, Alexandria, Antioch, Jerusalem, and Carthage, were much honoured. All bishops and Churches, however, were regarded as perfectly equal in the sight of God; and all regulated their own affairs, and exercised discipline with perfect freedom.

The rules for the appointment of bishops and clergy were various. In some Churches, the people united with the clergy in electing their bishop; in others, the clergy alone appointed him. Ordination followed, in which a priest received imposition of hands from one bishop, while a bishop was ordained by several. Each bishop was aided in his ministry by presbyters, or priests, and deacons, whom he generally consulted in important matters. The administration of the revenues of the Church was under his direction, and the deacons were his almoners.

Those who were departing from this life were strengthened by receiving the holy communion, which the great council of Nice, A.D. 325, commanded not to be refused to any Christian, who might desire it in his last hour.

CHAPTER VII.

THE FAITH OF THE CHURCH DEFENDED BY THE SIX ŒCUMENICAL SYNODS.

A.D. 320-680.

N the period of the Church's history on which we now enter, temptations of a different sort assailed her faith. The times of persecution for the name of Christ had now passed away; but the watchful enemy of man seized the moment when prosperity began to lull the Church into security, to introduce errors which were destructive of all true faith, and which led to persecutions, divisions, and innumerable calamities.

Religion had tasted the sweets of peace for a few years after the persecution of Diocletian had ceased, and her borders had been enlarged by the conversion of the king and people of Armenia by St. Gregory the illuminator, when the most formidable heresy by which she has ever been afflicted made its appearance. The evil doctrine of Arius, presbyter of Alexandria, disturbed the Christian world for fifty years. Several Roman emperors, deceived by the arts of one of the most crafty and unprincipled parties that ever existed, threw the whole weight of their authority into its scale; and sometimes it seemed for a moment triumphant. The doctrine of the Arians was, that our Lord Jesus Christ had been created, like all other things, by God; that he was not truly God, but a creature liable to fall into vice and sin; and that there was a time when he did not exist. To terminate the disputes excited by these blasphemies, the FIRST ŒCUMENICAL SYNOD, consisting of three hundred and eighteen holy bishops, many of whom had been confessors and exiles in the time of heathen persecution, assembled at Nice in Bithynia, by order of the Emperor Constantine the Great, A.D. 325, when Arius was heard before all the bishops; and his doctrine having been fully examined and universally condemned as impious, he was driven from the communion of the Church; and the Christian faith was declared in that celebrated Nicene creed, which has ever since been received as the rule of faith by all Christian Churches. In this creed it was professed that Christ is " of the same substance " (homoüsion) with the Father, *i. e.* of the same *real Godhead.*

This judgment was immediately approved and acted on by the whole Church dispersed throughout the world; and even the Arian party in the synod, not daring to utter any thing in opposition to the true faith, returned to their Churches acquiescing in the decree. Arius himself at last professed to believe in the Nicene faith; and it was not till A.D. 341, that the Arians ventured to compose a new creed. In the meantime, Eusebius of Nicomedia, and other leaders of the Arians, concealing their real sentiments, proceeded, by the aid of unjust accusations, false witnesses, and violence, to depose and persecute the principal champions of orthodoxy. St. Athanasius, who, when a deacon at the synod of Nice, had distinguished himself in opposition to Arius, and who had been soon after ordained patriarch of Alexandria, became the chief object of their hostility. The Emperor Constantine, deceived by Eusebius of Nicomedia, required the re-admission of Arius to the communion of the Church at Alexandria; and on the firm refusal of Athanasius, the Arians accused him to the emperor of causing division, and of other offences. Athanasius shewed that his accusers were unworthy of belief. The Arians then excited the Meletians (another sect which had separated itself from the Church) to charge him with imposing a tax in Egypt by his own authority; and, on the failure of this accusation, to allege that he had broken a sacred chalice, and put to death one of his clergy. But, on inquiry, this person was found to be still alive, having secreted himself in consequence of some offence which he had committed. The Emperor Constantine then wrote to Athanasius, expressing his approbation and confidence in him.

His enemies, however, were not discouraged. They at length prevailed on the emperor to assemble a synod at Tyre (A.D. 334), where the Arian bishops alone were present: and when Athanasius had proved that the witnesses against him were unworthy of credit, and demanded time to bring additional proofs of his innocence, the Arians became so violent, that the imperial officers who were present privately removed him, lest his life should fall a sacrifice to their fury; and he was then condemned, and deprived of his bishopric in his absence. Athanasius besought the emperor to examine the case; and he accordingly wrote to the bishops of the synod, but was at last persuaded by Eusebius of Nicomedia to banish Athanasius to Treves, in Gaul. When Arius was about to be admitted to communion at Constantinople, by command of the emperor, he died in a sudden and terrible manner; and Constantine himself dying in 337, was succeeded by his sons.

Shortly after the death of the emperor, his son Constantine, who ruled in Gaul, permitted Athanasius to return to Alexandria, and wrote to the Church of that city, commending their bishop in the highest terms. But Athanasius was ere long again expelled by the Emperor Constantius, at the request of the Arian synod of Antioch, A.D. 341; and Gregory, an Arian, was appointed bishop in his place. A large body of troops accompanied the intruding bishop to Alexandria, to secure his peaceful entrance into the city, and to expel Athanasius. That holy bishop feared lest the people should suffer on his account; but he commanded divine service to be performed in the church that evening; and when the soldiers had entered the church to make him a prisoner, he commanded a psalm to be sung; and as the soldiers waited till the psalm was ended, Athanasius in the mean while escaped through the crowd of singers, and hid himself. For a long time he lived in a dark cavern of the earth, which had formerly been a reservoir for water. His habitation was known only to those with whom he dwelt, and to a maid who was thought worthy to minister to him; but she was tempted by the promises of the Arians, and Athanasius was about to fall into their hands, when God warned him of his danger, and he escaped. He then went to Rome, where he appealed to the bishop, Julius; and his cause having been examined in a synod at Rome, he was pronounced innocent, and acknowledged as the lawful bishop of Alexandria. This judgment was soon after renewed by the great synod of Sardica, A.D. 347, which at the same time approved the Nicene faith, and condemned the Arian party, who had withdrawn from it on perceiving the sentiments of the majority. The cause of orthodoxy now obtained a temporary triumph. The Emperor Constans, who ruled in the West, threatened to declare war against Constantius, if Athanasius was not restored to his see; and accordingly that bishop, with several other of the persecuted orthodox bishops of the East, were restored to their flocks. Athanasius returned in triumph, with letters of the highest recommendation, from Julius of Rome, from the Emperor Constantius, from Maximus of Jerusalem, and the bishops of Palestine. Even the Arian bishops Valens and Ursacius, who had been most active in procuring his condemnation, acknowledged that all their charges had been false, deplored their wickedness, and sought his communion.

The eastern Church, however, was still troubled by the presence of Arian bishops, though many prelates, and the people generally, held the true faith. The western Church was generally orthodox; and for some time after the synod of Sardica, the western and eastern Churches were separated from communion on account of St. Athanasius. The favourable prospects of true religion became speedily overclouded again. The Arians continued their machinations, under the authority of the Emperor Constantius; and, in 353 and 355, caused synods to be assembled at Arles and at Milan, in which, by force and fraud, the condemnation of St. Athanasius and other orthodox bishops was again obtained. The emperor had twice sent messengers to bring him to Milan; but the people of Alexandria would not permit him to leave the city, well knowing the dangers which awaited him there. Troops were then marched from Egypt and Libya to seize him; but when they had surrounded the church in which he was, he again disappeared, and was not to be found. An Arian, named George, was ordained bishop in his place.

It was at this time, perhaps, that St. Athanasius again had a remarkable escape from his enemies. While he was sailing up the Nile into the interior of Egypt, his persecutors, hearing of it, followed him; but he, being admonished of God, informed his companions of their danger, and commanded them to return to Alexandria. They accordingly turned about, and coming with the stream, passed the pursuing ship, arrived safe in the city, and remained unobserved in the crowd. On account of these wonderful escapes, he was accused by the Arians and Gentiles of practising magic.

When the great object of their dread had been thus removed, the Arians began more openly to attempt the destruction of the Nicene faith. They had already composed several creeds more or less unsound, and capable of Arian interpretations; but they now framed a new formula, in which the Divinity of Christ was apparently asserted strongly, while it really admitted of an interpretation favourable to Arian views; and having induced the emperor to assemble the bishops of the West, to the number of four hundred, at Ariminum in Italy, A.D. 359, they proposed it for their adoption. The synod,

however, immediately required the Arian bishops to
subscribe the Nicene creed, and deposed those who
refused to do so; and it was only after they had
been wearied out by a delay of many months, inti-
midated by the threats of the emperor, and solemnly
assured by the Arians that they received the creed
in the orthodox sense, that the bishops at last gave
way, and, in hopes of securing peace, permitted the
omission of the term *homoüsion* ("of the same substance"), which occurred in the Nicene creed. The
majority of the bishops, too, either deceived or inti-
midated, subscribed the new creed; but the decep-
tion was soon discovered. The Arians proclaimed
every where that the Nicene faith was condemned,
and announced their own interpretation of the creed
lately adopted. But though heresy seemed for a
moment triumphant, it was soon to be overthrown.
France and Italy, roused by the celebrated Hilary,
bishop of Poictiers, who returned from his exile in
the East A.D. 360, declared their adherence to the
true faith, annulled the proceedings at Ariminum,
expelled the Arians from communion, and transmitted their resolutions to the orthodox bishops of
the East. Egypt was already proclaiming its agreement with their faith; for on the death of Constantius, A.D. 361, Athanasius re-appeared suddenly in
the church of Alexandria, after having entirely disappeared for seven years, during which he had dwelt
among the monks in Upper Egypt. When he thus,
beyond all expectation, appeared again, the people of
Alexandria rejoiced with exceeding joy, and delivered
all the churches to him, expelling the Arians. At
the same time, Lucifer, bishop of Cagliari, and Eusebius of Vercellæ, returned from the Upper Thebais,
where Constantius had condemned them to perpetual
exile for their faith; and Eusebius was present in
the synod of Alexandria, held by Athanasius to con-

firm the Nicene creed. When the emperor, Julian the Apostate, heard that St. Athanasius was again in Alexandria, and that he was converting many of the heathen to Christianity, he commanded him to leave the city. When departing from his see, and beholding the people weeping around him, he said, " Take courage ; this is but a little cloud, which shall quickly pass away." And so indeed it proved : for on the accession of Jovian, in 363, Athanasius was restored to his see, and testified to that orthodox emperor, that the true faith was then received in all the Churches of Spain, Britain, Gaul, Italy, Dalmatia, Dacia, Mysia, Macedonia, Greece, Africa, Sardinia, Cyprus, Crete, Pamphylia, Syria, Isauria, Egypt, Libya, Pontus, Cappadocia, and in all the East. Many councils of bishops successively confirmed the orthodox faith ; and even those bishops of the East who were called Semi-Arians from their not adopting the word *homoüsion,* and who had been deceived by the real Arians, but whose faith differed not from that of the Catholic Church, now united in the universal acceptance of the Nicene faith. Thus the Arian heresy, when it seemed most prosperous, suddenly fell ; and, after lingering for a time under the protection of the Emperor Valens, and afterwards amongst the barbarous nations beyond the Roman empire, it disappeared from the face of the earth.

The protection vouchsafed by God to the true faith was never more wonderfully exemplified than in the existence and final triumph of the Nicene creed. Craft and violence alike failed to overthrow the belief of the Church. The truth is, that this heresy had never been able to take deep root in the Church. Arian bishops in the East governed a people whose pious simplicity was unable to detect errors veiled under the guise of orthodox language ; but when, at length, the real tenets of the Arians began

to be more openly developed, and when the multi-
plication of creeds, and their internal divisions, had
shewn the uncertainty of their faith, and when the
patronage of the state was withdrawn from their
cause, they fell at once.

While the Arian impiety was falling, the enemy
of man was engaged in drawing forth from it a new
temptation for the faith of the Church.   All Christians had hitherto believed that the Holy Ghost was
truly the Spirit of God; but the Arian Macedonius
taught that the Holy Ghost was merely a creature
made by the Son, contrary to the words of Christ,
who described him as the "Spirit of truth, which
proceedeth from the Father."   This doctrine was
condemned as anti-Christian by many councils in
Europe and Asia, but especially by the council of
one hundred and fifty bishops at Constantinople,
assembled by the Emperor Theodosius in A.D. 381,
and which, having been ever since universally approved by the Church, has been termed THE SECOND
ŒCUMENICAL SYNOD.   On this occasion the Nicene
creed was enlarged, in order to express the belief of
Christians that the Holy Ghost is truly God.

The Macedonian heresy had not many adherents,
and did not long continue to trouble the Church;
but the disputatious and proud spirit of Arianism
had engendered a brood of errors.   Sabellianism re-
appeared in the person of Photinus; while Apolli-
naris denied that our Lord possessed a human reasonable soul.   These errors were universally condemned, and their authors were numbered with the
heretics.

Though religion was suffering so grievously from
the disturbances excited by heresies, it continued to
expand itself among the heathen.   Ethiopia was now
converted by Frumentius, who was consecrated the
first bishop of the Ethiopians by St. Athanasius.

The natives of Georgia, of Iberia, and the Goths of Thrace, Mœsia, and Dacia, also received the light of the Gospel. St. Martin, bishop of Tours, completed the conversion of the Gauls, and is said to have had the gift of miracles. Thus did that grain of mustard-seed sown by Christ continue to increase.

The Church was now threatened with new afflictions and adversities, in the decay of the Roman empire. Attracted by the prospect of an easy spoil, the barbarian nations of the Goths, Heruli, Vandals, Huns, Franks, Saxons, precipitated themselves successively on a luxurious and unwarlike population; and scenes of the most dreadful carnage and destruction overspread every province of the falling empire. The greatest portion of its possessions in the West became the prey of the invaders; and the Churches of Britain, Germany, Italy, Spain, and Africa, groaned beneath the yoke of heathen or Arian conquerors. In Africa, the Vandals, who were Arians, endeavoured to extirpate the true faith by most cruelly persecuting its defenders, and by prohibiting all ordinations to the sacred ministry. These savage invaders were gradually converted from their errors; but the destruction of learning which they caused exercised a permanently evil influence on Christianity. Ignorant themselves, and despising all literature, they were devoted only to war and to the chase; and even their conversion to Christianity effected no alteration in the national character and tastes. Hence education was despised, the most ordinary literary attainments neglected, and, as a sure result, superstitions were gradually introduced, and found too ready an acceptance.

While Christianity was suffering grievous afflictions and persecutions from the barbarians, the torch of discord was again lighted by the heretic Pelagius, at the end of the fourth century. Pelagius denied

that human nature is inclined to evil, or that man
needs the assistance of Divine grace to lead and
assist him to perform good works.   This doctrine
was most strenuously opposed by the illustrious St.
Augustine, bishop of Hippo in Africa, and was condemned by many councils in the East and West, especially by a council of two hundred bishops at Carthage in 417, the decrees of which were generally
approved by the Church.   This council excommunicated all those who taught that Adam was naturally
mortal, so that death was not the punishment of sin;
or that it is unnecessary to baptise infants; or that
they do not derive from Adam any original sin which
needs to be expiated by regeneration; or that the
words of St. John, "If we say that we have no sin,
we deceive ourselves," are merely to be understood
as an expression of humility, not as the declaration
of a real fact: for, as the decree adds, "the following
words of the apostle, 'But if we confess our sins,
He is faithful and just to forgive us our sins, and
to cleanse us from all unrighteousness,' shew sufficiently that they were not mere expressions of humility, but of truth."   The heresy of Pelagius was
finally condemned in the third œcumenical synod,
of which I am about to speak.

Nestorius, a vain and arrogant man, being ordained to the patriarchal see of Constantinople, declaimed violently against the title of Theotokos,
applied by ancient piety to the Virgin Mary, signi-
fying that she was the mother of our God and
Saviour Jesus Christ,—and taught that God the
Word and the man Christ Jesus were different persons under the same appearance.   This was contrary
to the Scripture, which said that "the Word was
made flesh," and that God "purchased the Church
with his own blood;" implying evidently that *one*
and the same person, who was both God and man,

had died for the sins of the world. A council of two hundred bishops at Ephesus, and which the Church reckons as the THIRD ŒCUMENICAL SYNOD, condemned the errors of Nestorius; and the decision, though disputed for a short time by the bishops of Syria, under some feelings of jealousy, was speedily adopted by the whole Christian world. ST. CYRIL of Alexandria had the honour of being the principal opponent of this heresy. The adherents of Nestorius, being banished from the Roman empire, obtained an establishment from the king of Persia, and have continued to exist as a distinct sect even to the present day.

In opposing the errors of Nestorius, some persons fell into the opposite error of confounding the divine and human natures of our Lord. Eutyches, an abbot at Constantinople, taught that in Jesus Christ was but *one nature*, compounded of the divine and human natures; so that, according to his doctrine, our Lord was not properly either God or man, but a sort of third Being between the two, of a mixed and compounded nature. Deposed for this heresy by many bishops at Constantinople, he was irregularly restored by a synod at Ephesus, which, under the direction of Dioscorus, bishop of Alexandria, acted with the most savage violence against the defenders of orthodoxy. THE FOURTH ŒCUMENICAL SYNOD of Chalcedon, consisting of six hundred and thirty bishops, finally judged in this cause, A.D. 451; and having condemned Dioscorus and Eutyches, established the true and sound doctrine of the Church, derived from holy Scripture, and taught by ST. LEO, bishop of Rome, in his celebrated epistle,—*i. e.* that in our Lord Jesus Christ there are two perfect and distinct natures, the godhead and manhood, united in one person, without mixture, change, or confusion. This doctrine was immediately approved and accepted by the great body of Christians throughout the world, and has so continued to the present day. The adherents of Dioscorus, called Monophysites (*i.e.* upholders of the *one nature*), or Jacobites, abounded in Egypt and Syria, and their sect has survived in those countries till the present day.

The Church was consoled under these various afflictions by the conversion of several heathen nations. The natives of Libanus and of a portion of Arabia were converted by the persuasions and authority of St. Simeon Stylites. The apostolical labours of St. PATRICK were rewarded by the conversion of the Irish nation to Christianity. Palladius had been previously ordained to the same mission by Cœlestinus, bishop of Rome; but dying soon, was succeeded by St. Patrick in A.D. 432. The Gospel had indeed already some adherents in that country, but Christianity now became general, and for the next four or five centuries learning and religion shed a bright lustre on that remote island, when barbarism and ignorance prevailed over the rest of Europe. The Church of Ireland during these ages remained independent, and was not subject to the papal jurisdiction. Clovis, king of the Franks, and founder of the French monarchy, received baptism, with many of his people, from Remigius, bishop of Rheims, A.D. 496.

The East still remained troubled by the remains of the Eutychian heresy, and the West was subject to the dominion of savage nations, who either rejected Christianity, or were imbued with the Arian heresy,—when a controversy arose in the East concerning certain writings of Theodorus, Ibas, and Theodoret, which supported the Nestorian heresy, and which were used by its adherents to promote their views. A council of one hundred and sixty bishops, assembled at Constantinople by the Emperor

Justinian, A.D. 553, and which the Church acknowledges as THE FIFTH ŒCUMENICAL SYNOD, condemned these writings and various errors of the Nestorians, and approved all the doctrine of the four preceding œcumenical synods. This synod was thus a sort of supplement to the third œcumenical synod. It was immediately received by the great body of the Church, though some bishops in Africa and Italy for a time did not acknowledge it; as they supposed, through mistake, that the writings of Theodore and Theodoret had been approved by the synod of Chalcedon.

Britain had now been for many years subject to the Saxons, who gradually subdued the Christian inhabitants, and formed settlements among them. These invaders, however, still remained in their heathenism, when ST. GREGORY the Great, bishop of Rome, commiserating their condition, sent ST. AUGUSTINE and other pious brethren to preach the Gospel in this country. Arriving about 590, he founded several Christian churches; but the conversion of the Saxons to the faith was chiefly due to several holy bishops and missionaries from Ireland in the following century. The ancient churches of the Britons which still continued, as well as the Irish churches, were not subject to the jurisdiction of the bishop of Rome; nor was the Anglo-Saxon Church for several centuries, though much reverence was felt for the ancient and celebrated Church of Rome, and much assistance derived from it in the earlier stages of their existence.

In the seventh century, a heresy began to be advocated, which, like the Eutychian, endangered the doctrine of the perfect divinity and perfect humanity of our Lord: for it was now asserted, that, after the incarnation, there was but one *will* in our Lord,—that of the incarnate God. But it is plain, that if we admit the doctrine of *two* perfect *natures,*

each possessed of all its distinctive capacities and
faculties, the doctrine of *two wills*, the divine and
human, immediately follows. If this latter doctrine
be denied, then the doctrine of two natures cannot
be maintained; so that the Monothelites (believers
in *one* will), who *did* deny that two wills, perfectly
united and harmonious, exist in our Lord, were only
a branch of the Eutychians.

The controversies which so long disturbed the
Church on this occasion were caused by a very
injudicious attempt of the Emperor Heraclius to
re-unite the Eutychians to the Church. This sovereign, desirous of strengthening the eastern empire,
conferred with the leaders of the Eutychians, or
Monophysite sect, and was assured by them, that
they would willingly unite themselves to the Church,
provided it were declared, that in Christ there was
but " one will and one operation." On this the emperor published an edict in favour of that doctrine,
which was received by Sergius patriarch of Constantinople, by Cyrus of Alexandria, and by the
patriarch of Antioch; and in consequence, many of
the Monophysites were received into the communion of the eastern Churches, where they still retained their errors. Honorius, bishop of Rome,
approved of this scandalous compromise of the
truth, and accepted the communion of the heretics.
Sophronius, patriarch of Jerusalem, alone, amongst
the chief bishops of the Church, resisted the Monothelites, and headed the orthodox. But, although
religion was thus betrayed by those who ought to
have been foremost in its defence, and although the
power of the state was arrayed in maintenance of
false principles, the promises of God to his Church
prevented the perpetuation of so great an evil. It
was in vain that Honorius of Rome sanctioned the
Monothelite heresy; it was in vain that the Empe-

ror Heraclius and Constans issued new edicts, commanding silence on the controversy, and endeavoured to stifle the voice of the orthodox believers. The truth prevailed; and after a struggle, which continued for upwards of half a century, the Monothelite heresy, and its supporters, Theodore of Pharan, Sergius, Pyrrhus, Paul and Peter of Constantinople, Honorius bishop of Rome, Cyrus of Alexandria, and others, were condemned in the SIXTH ŒCUMENICAL SYNOD of one hundred and seventy bishops, held at Constantinople by order of the Emperor Constantine Pogonatus in 680.

The circumstance of Honorius of Rome's condemnation for heresy by this synod, which has been clearly established by Bossuet, and many other of the most eminent Romish controversialists, affords an irresistible proof that the bishops of Rome were not infallible in faith, and that the universal Church has never acknowledged them to be so. It is also worthy of remark, that the sixth œcumenical synod was the last which could justly claim the title of universal, or pretend to represent the judgment of the whole Church. The succeeding synods, which are styled universal by Romanists, have never been acknowledged by the whole eastern and western Church, as the early synods were.[1] The seventh synod, as it is called, remained rejected by the western Church up to the fourteenth century. The eighth and following synods have been always rejected by the eastern Churches, even to the present day.

Whilst the Monothelite heresy was disturbing the Church, the false prophet Mahomet and his followers were conquering the Asiatic possessions of the eastern empire, and extending their triumphs

---

[1] See Palmer's Treatise on the Church, vol. ii. p. 200-249.

through Egypt, and along the northern coast of Africa.

Mahomet was an impostor whose pretensions would have sunk into immediate obscurity, like those of many other pretended prophets, had they not been sustained by force of arms and vast military success. Born of a noble but indigent family in Arabia, he repaired his fortunes by marriage with a rich widow, and early in the seventh century conceived the design of assuming the character of a prophet. With this view he assumed an appearance of great sanctity, retiring frequently to a cave for the purpose of private meditation; and at length he announced that he had been favoured with a new revelation from God. During the first two years of his mission, however, he made very few converts; but in A.D. 622 he was invited to the city of Medina by the inhabitants of that place, who hoped, by establishing Mahomet as their sovereign, to put an end to a long train of divisions and factions which had afflicted them. Thus invested with sovereign power, Mahomet assumed a new tone, and declared that a divine commission had been given to him to establish the true religion by force of arms, and to destroy idolatry. The state of Arabia was at that time peculiarly favourable to his designs. A number of different sects and religions existed in that country, none of which was sufficiently strong to check the career of the impostor. He strenuously inculcated the doctrine of the unity of God, and other points which were held in common by large classes of his countrymen. He admitted that the Jewish and the Christian revelations were divine; but he pretended that they were only introductory to his own: and while he denounced eternal damnation to those who should refuse to receive it, he forced them, at the point of the sword, to take the alternative of slavery or death. It is not wonderful that such pretensions, coupled with such power, should have speedily rendered the impostor and his religion triumphant in Arabia. From thence he issued forth upon the provinces of the eastern empire, which, swayed by a feeble government, and rent by divisions and heresies, were unable to offer any opposition. Mahomet died in the midst of military triumphs; but his successors followed his example, and the greater portion of the East and of Africa became their prey.

In Egypt and the East the invaders were assisted by the Eutychian and Nestorian heretics, and their religion consequently received a degree of favour which was denied to that of the Church. Persecution at length assailed the faith of Christians; and the result was, that in Africa, after four or five centuries, we hear no more of those five hundred episcopal sees which had formerly shed light on that region. In the East, Christianity slowly declined under oppression and persecution; but it was always preserved; and after the lapse of twelve hundred years, there are still many churches in Asia Minor, Syria, Palestine, and Egypt, though they bear but a small proportion to the eight hundred episcopal churches which, in the fifth century, existed in those countries.

It would be in vain for us to attempt to fathom the profound depths of those divine counsels which permitted so large a portion of Christianity to pine away and perish beneath the yoke of Mahommedan infidelity. What may be the final ends and objects of this visitation are at present concealed from our view; but some lessons it does distinctly convey. The Nestorians and Eutychians of the East had revolted against the truth of the Gospel, and arrogantly despised the united judgments of the whole

Christian world. The Donatists in Africa had separated from their Christian brethren, and by violence and bloodshed had established their human church. In all those countries which Mahommedanism permanently subjugated, schism and heresy had struck deep roots and obtained many adherents. The separatists made common cause with the infidels, and rejoiced to see the Church oppressed; but they brought destruction on themselves. All were involved in a common ruin; and those who had rejected the truth, as well as those who retained it, were delivered over to the tyranny and the degradation of the infidel dominion. How great must have been those offences, and how odious in the sight of God, which brought down so terrible a punishment on these nations, involving even the Church of God in their calamities! And may we not most justly fear, lest nations in which similar offences extensively and long prevail, may be delivered over to judgments equally awful, and deprived of those means of grace, and that way of salvation, which so many of them have despised and rejected? Such examples should furnish new arguments against voluntary separations from the Church of Christ; arguments addressed as much to those who love peace and order, and the welfare of their country, as to those who are fearful of incurring the displeasure of that God, who is not the Author of turbulence and disorder under the pretence of religion, but of meekness, humbleness, brotherly love, and unity.

The decline of Christianity in the East and Africa was, however, very gradual, and the Church beheld the spread of the Gospel amongst many other nations. Christianity was now subduing the remnants of paganism in England, and exciting there and in Ireland a spirit of apostolical zeal, which disseminated the light of truth among many barbarous nations in the west of Europe. The Suevi, Boii, and Franks of Germany, were converted by St. Columbanus, in the early part of the seventh century. St. Gallus became the apostle of Switzerland; St. Kilianus, of the eastern Franks; and St. Willibrord and his companions, of Batavia, Friesland, and Westphalia. These holy missionaries were all natives of Ireland, except the last, who was an Anglo-Saxon.

CHAPTER VIII,

FRUITS OF FAITH EXEMPLIFIED IN THE SAINTS AND MARTYRS.

A.D. 320-680.

WE have now seen the promises of our Saviour verified in the continual existence of his true Church, amidst the terrors of persecution and the temptations of heresy. We have seen it expanding itself "from the river to the ends of the earth;" and though in some branches "minished and brought low," yet containing a principle of vitality which enabled it to repair its losses by new and vigorous shoots. We have seen those great truths which Scripture teaches unanimously and firmly maintained during this period. Let us now contemplate the fruits which that faith continued to produce.

The holy men of this period may be divided into two classes: those who spent their time in a private religious life, and those who were engaged in the ministry of the Church. I shall mention some of the most remarkable men in each class successively.

Many of the most truly pious and holy men whom these ages produced, were among those who lived retired from the world, and who were engaged solely in the service of God. A life entirely devoted to religion, and separated from all domestic cares, pleasures, and occupations, had been the characteristic of the ascetics and sacred virgins even from the time of the apostles; but the monastic or solitary life was first exhibited on a broad scale by Antony and his disciples in Egypt, at the latter end of the third and beginning of the fourth century.

In the present age it is, perhaps, difficult to appreciate justly the religious character of ascetic religion in the early Church. The monastic system of later ages, with its wealth, its indolence, the spirit of superstition or of worldly intrigue, which have too frequently disgraced it, not to speak of still more unworthy and degrading faults, has but too justly excited the strongest feelings of disapprobation. But we should do an injustice to the Christian Church generally, if we imagined that such corruptions originally prevailed; or that the saints and martyrs lent their countenance to institutions, which were either in contradiction to the holy Scripture, or injurious to Christian piety, charity, and devotion.

The Christian who best knows his own heart will most deeply feel the continual tendency of the world, with all its busy thoughts and interests, to deaden his sense of religion, and to withdraw him from the love and service of his Creator. He will feel that even the best and purest sympathies of life require the chastening influence of solemn recollections and self-denial, to prevent their becoming hinderances in the way of his salvation. Our Lord has said, " He that loveth father or mother more than me is not worthy of me; and he that loveth son or daughter more than me is not worthy of me. And he that taketh not up his cross and followeth after me is not worthy of me."

It was this that, in those early ages, led many earnest Christians, who felt their own infirmities, and sought for salvation, to relinquish the world, its wealth, its pleasures, its business and temptations, and to retire into quiet places, far from the noise of cities and the ordinary haunts of men, where the labour of their own hands procured for them the simplest food on which human life could be sustained, and garments proportioned at once to their poverty and the humility of their spirit. Thus having fulfilled the apostolic precept, to "work," and content with food and raiment, the simple objects to which Christ limited his disciples' earthly wishes, they devoted their lives to repentance, to rigorous self-examination, to prayer and psalmody, to the study of God's word, to the continual reception of the sacrament of Christ's body and blood, to works of charity towards the sick and afflicted, in a word, to all the parts of a life entirely religious, and to continual preparation for death. They literally followed the advice of our Lord to his disciples, " Sell that ye have, and give to the poor;" and after the example of our Lord and of his apostle St. Paul, and in accordance with their advice to those who were " able to bear it," they refrained from the permitted and honourable state of marriage, that they might " care for the things of the Lord; that they might be holy both in body and in spirit."[1] And who can be so cold and so uncharitable as to feel no sympathy with this holy zeal, this self-denying love of

---

[1] 1 Cor. vii. 34.

God? The contemplation of such instances of earnest religion ought rather to provoke us to a godly jealousy, to induce contrition for our own want of zeal, and to stimulate our faith. Those deeds of Christian devotion, the recital of which so deeply affected the eloquent and profound St. Augustine, and which were made the immediate instrument of his conversion, cannot be unworthy the attention of Christians in any age. It may not be difficult to point out instances of enthusiasm, of excessive mortifications, of superstition, and of errors, amongst some of the ancient solitaries; but it would be hard indeed to rival their religious zeal, their love of God, their ardent pursuit of salvation, and their resolution in casting aside every weight that could detain them in their Christian course.

The monastic life was for ages strictly voluntary. Those who devoted themselves to it took no vows of chastity, poverty, or obedience. They were retained only by the love of God, and the desire of salvation, in their state of separation from the world. Instances were to be met with of persons who, after they had entered on the monastic life, found themselves unequal to its privations, and returned to the usual condition of Christians. Such instances were, however, looked on with dissatisfaction, as evincing a levity and changeableness which were calculated to cause scandal to the brethren, and to hold out an example of want of resolution in the service of God; and with such views, the Church imposed a certain time of penance on those who forsook the monastic state and contracted marriage; but nothing further was done. No anathemas were denounced against them; no one attempted to dissolve their marriages, or force them back again into a mode of life which was unsuited to them, and which, unless voluntary, was altogether vain and unprofitable. These were abuses, which, with monastic vows, grew up in times long subsequent to those which are now before us, and when the spirit which animated an Antony and a Benedict had become extinct.

ANTONY was born in Egypt, A.D. 251; and being left an orphan at an early age, he gave his paternal lands to the inhabitants of the place where he resided, and, having sold the rest of his possessions, he distributed them among the poor. Then, associating himself with those who were zealous in religion, he emulated all their virtues; and finding a religious life delightful in practice, though difficult at the commencement, he continually devised new methods of devotion, self-denial, and temperance. His food was bread and salt, and water for drink; and he frequently remained fasting for two or three entire days. He sometimes passed the night without sleep, engaged in continual prayer, in which a large part of the night was always spent. His couch was a mat, or more commonly the bare ground. After fifteen years thus spent, he retired to a ruined castle in the desert, where he remained in perfect solitude for twenty years, and where his existence was known only by those of his friends who approached and heard him singing psalms. At length he was prevailed on to come forth from his retreat, and it was then seen that he was indeed a holy man. His soul was calm, unshaken by sadness or joy; he was neither troubled to see the multitudes who came to visit him, nor pleased with their applause. He was exceedingly meek, most benevolent, agreeable, and inoffensive, to those whom he met and conversed with, even though they should differ from him. The sanctity of his life influenced many persons to follow his example, and place themselves under his guidance; and thus the monastic institution commenced in Egypt. St.

Antony died in 356, at the age of 105. Amongst other instructions, he advised those who were desirous of avoiding sin, to occupy themselves with some employment; "and let each of us," he said, "remark and write down the actions and movements of his soul, as if we ought to render an account of ourselves to each other. Be assured, that the shame of being *known*, will cause us to cease from sin, and from evil thoughts: our own writing will supply the place of our brethren's eyes." St. Antony is said to have cured many sick persons by his prayers. His humility and reverence for the clergy was very great. He was so humble, that he bowed himself before bishops and presbyters; and when consulted by deacons, he gave them his advice, but did not offer prayer before them. He knew no other language but the Egyptian, and was not able to read; but, by continual attention, he had perfectly learned the Scriptures. He was never ashamed to learn,—listened to every one,—and if any person made a useful remark, he acknowledged his obligation. His countenance was so pure and calm, so undisturbed by any passion, and so full of a holy joy, that they who had never seen him were able immediately to distinguish him amongst many other brethren. St. Antony supported himself by the labour of his hands, and whatever he possessed beyond his immediate necessities he gave to the poor. He rarely left his retirement, except to plead the cause of those who were oppressed; for many persons brought their complaints to him, and urged his intercession in their favour with the magistrates. St. Athanasius was on terms of friendship with this venerable man; he induced him to come to Alexandria, for the purpose of declaring publicly his condemnation of the Arian heresy; a circumstance which was of very great service to the cause of orthodoxy. When about to depart from this life, he called his disciples, and said, " I enter, as it is written, the path of my fathers; for I see that the Lord calleth me." Then recommending them to abstain from all communion with the Arians, and not to permit his body to be carried into Egypt, lest it should be embalmed and preserved in houses, he continued, " Bury it yourselves, and cover it with earth, in some place known only to you. At the day of resurrection, I shall receive it incorruptible from the hands of the Saviour. Farewell, my children; Antony departs, and is no more with you." Having thus spoken, and embraced them, he died.

Next to Antony, the chief founders of monasteries in Egypt were Ammon and Pachomius. By the rule of the latter, his disciples were permitted to eat, drink, labour, and fast, as they pleased ; but those who eat more abundantly were expected to perform more laborious works. On the first and last days of the week, all received the holy eucharist. They prayed twelve times in the day ; and when about to take food, they sang psalms.

Ecclesiastical history has preserved several interesting anecdotes of these virtuous men. Pior was accustomed to take his food walking about.; and when asked wherefore he did so, he said, " I wish not to regard my eating as a serious occupation, but as a superfluity." To another person, who made the same inquiry, he said, " It was in order that he might not be affected by any bodily enjoyment, even in eating." Pambos, not knowing letters, went to some one to be taught a psalm; but having heard the first verse of the thirty-ninth psalm (" I said, I will take heed unto my ways, that I offend not with my tongue"), he would not hear the second verse, but departed, saying, that this one verse was sufficient for him, if he could learn it practically. And

when he who taught him the verse afterwards reproved him, because he had not for some months
visited him, Pambos replied, that he had not yet
learned the verse practically: and many years after,
being asked by an acquaintance whether he had yet
learned that verse, " In nineteen years," he said, " I
have scarcely learned to practise it."   Pambos, by
the invitation of St. Athanasius, came from the desert to Alexandria, and seeing there a public dancer,
who was a sinner, he wept. When asked wherefore
he wept, he said, " Two things have moved me;
first, the end of that woman; the other, that I do
not use such diligence to please God, as she does to
please wicked men." Another brother, named Pi-
tirus, was skilled in the physical sciences, and continually explained various scientific questions to
those who met him, but with each of his explana-
tions he offered up prayer. A certain disciple was
informed of the death of his father, but he said to
the messenger, " Cease to blaspheme, for my Father
is immortal." One of the brethren being possessed
of nothing but the book of the Gospels, sold it, and
gave the money to feed the poor, saying, " I have
sold that same word, which saith, Sell all that ye
have, and give to the poor."

Hilarion was the great founder of the monastic
state in Syria; and St. Basil carried this discipline
into Pontus. It also spread rapidly in Persia, Asia
Minor, Mesopotamia, and all the East. It was introduced at Milan by St. Ambrose; in Africa, by St.
Augustine; in France, by St. Martin. The number
of such religious men and virgins in the fourth and
fifth centuries was exceedingly great. The spirit of
earnest religion in those days very commonly took
this form. The worship of God and self-discipline
were not their only employments. Manual labour
was strictly enforced, and all the offices of Christian

charity were discharged. In particular, the instruction of the ignorant, and the conversion of the heathen, occupied their attention. Valentinus was at the head of a great congregation in Cœlesyria, where he, with many of his brethren, lived to a very old age; and " it appears to me," says an ancient historian, " that God prolonged the lives of these men for the benefit of religion; for they brought over the Syrians in general, and many of the Saracens and Persians, from heathenism to Christianity."

The principles of self-denial received in the monastic fraternities, however laudable when taught and practised in moderation, were occasionally pushed to excess and error. Eustathius, bishop of Sebaste in Armenia, gave rules to the societies in that country; but he is said, through too great strictness, to have fallen into strange observances and practices, contrary to the laws of the Church. His disciples blamed marriage; refused to pray in the houses of married persons; despised the married clergy; fasted even on the Lord's day; held meetings for worship in private houses in opposition to the Church; and condemned those who eat flesh. For this reason, the neighbouring bishops assembled at Gangra, A.D. 370, and declared them separated from the Catholic Church, unless they should forsake their errors.

An example of want of moderation in self-denial and mortifications is frequently pointed out in the case of ST. SIMEON STYLITES, who lived in the fifth century. Yet it is impossible not to admit that, with some excesses in these respects, there was much to admire and venerate in his piety. He was, at first, a monk in Syria, where he became so remarkable by his extreme austerity, that his superiors and companions judged it excessive, and he was obliged to leave the society. He then established himself as an anchorite, or perfect solitary, on a mountain near Antioch, where he is said to have fasted forty days and forty nights, and to have used a degree of mortification which some of the bishops blamed. But the fame of his sanctity spreading far and wide, he was followed by so great a multitude of people from Arabia, Persia, Armenia, and all the East and West, who came to him to see him and touch his garments, that, in order to avoid their importunity, he constructed a pillar, on the top of which he remained for many years, even till his death. He was engaged in perpetual prayer and fasting ; he believed himself to be the last and lowest of men ; was humble, obliging, and kind to all who approached him ; and his exhortations were not unblessed by God, for he converted a great number of unbelieving Iberians, Armenians, Persians, and Arabians, who came to see him in troops of two or three hundred, or even a thousand, renounced their idols, received baptism, and learned Christianity from his mouth. Theodoret, bishop of Cyrus, speaks of this as an eye-witness of the fact. His piety was held in much reverence by the king and queen of Persia, and by the emperors Theodosius and Marcian ; the latter of whom went to visit him in disguise. St. Simeon was a firm and resolute defender of the orthodox faith against the Eutychian heresy, and died A.D. 461.

I now turn to the other class of holy men who adorned the Church in these ages. I have already spoken of St. Athanasius, the most renowned champion of the true faith against Arianism. He was supported by many holy confessors, especially by Hilary, bishop of Poictiers, in France, and Eusebius, of Vercellæ in Italy, who both suffered exile and bonds for their faith ; as did Lucifer, bishop of Cagliari, who, however, afterwards shewed an unreasonable degree of severity in refusing pardon to those who had fallen in the time of the Arian persecution; and even went so far as to separate from the communion of the Church, which generally adopted a milder course. The learned EUSEBIUS, bishop of Cæsarea, though at first connected with the Arian party, condemned their errors, and collected the history of the Church. St. CYRIL, bishop of Jerusalem, and MELETIUS of Antioch, though ordained by the Arians, confessed and suffered for the true faith.

MELETIUS had been appointed bishop of Sebaste in Armenia, and had become remarkable for piety and virtue; when the see of Antioch becoming vacant, he was unanimously chosen, A.D. 360, to fill that important office. Antioch had now for many years been subject to bishops who were more or less tinged with Arianism; and the orthodox believers, who were termed Eustathians, were separated from their communion. St. Athanasius was now in exile. The Council of Ariminum had reeently decided in the manner which the Arians wished, and the bishops of the East had followed their example. In short, heresy seemed for a moment triumphant. The Arians themselves, supported by the emperor, selected Meletius to preside over the see of Antioch; and the believers of that city might have looked forward with despondency to the future. But the prayers and alms of Meletius, like those of the centurion, " had come up for a memorial before God;" and the errors which he had imbibed from his early instructors had been in secret replaced by that strength and purity of faith which the Holy Spirit can alone inspire. The gentleness, humility, and meekness, which had always characterised him, were now to lend additional power to the display of still higher virtues. The emperor and the Arian bishops were assembled in the great church of Antioch, with a vast multitude of people, to witness the enthronement of Meletius; and the text on which the bishops were to preach had been selected by the emperor himself. It was one of those which the heretics perverted to establish their blasphemies. On this text several of their bishops in succession discoursed, and preached their errors. Meletius then spoke; and having commenced his sermon with expressions of the utmost humility and charity, he proceeded to shew, that the passage under consideration was perfectly consistent with the doctrine of the real Godhead of our Saviour Christ; and then, to the astonishment and dismay of many of his audience, he boldly preached that truth, which they had so long denied and persecuted. The Arian archdeacon ran up to Meletius, and prevented his speaking by placing his hand on his mouth; but when Meletius found his lips closed, he continued still to make his belief known to the people, by thrusting out his hand and raising *three* fingers, then withdrawing them and shewing *one*. When the archdeacon seized his hand, Meletius with a loud voice exhorted all his hearers to hold the Nicene belief; and testified that those who held the contrary doctrine had erred from the truth. At this noble and courageous testimony the orthodox believers, who were present in numbers, shouted and leaped for joy, while the Arians were proportionably dispirited. Meletius entered with vigour on his sacred office; taught, admonished, and corrected his people; cut off from the Church those who denied the truth; confirmed the weak, encouraged the believing; and though soon driven into exile by his persecutors, he left the Church of Antioch established and immovable in the faith. After a time he was restored to his see, and beheld the triumph of the orthodox doctrine throughout the world.

St. Martin, bishop of Tours, was at first a soldier, and was so remarkable for his charity, that once, in the midst of winter, when the severity of the cold was so extreme that many persons died of it, having met a poor man at the gate of the city, and having nothing else to bestow, he divided his cloak with his sword, and gave half of it to the beggar. But the next night he saw in a dream his Saviour arrayed in the half of his garment, and surrounded by the angels; and he was so deeply impressed by his dream, that he gave up the military life and was baptised. When he was returning to his native land, he was taken prisoner by robbers in the Alps; but in the midst of the greatest dangers, he evinced such magnanimity, and so piously exhorted the lawless men by whom he was surrounded, that one of them believed, and besought Martin to pray for him, and afterwards became a religious man. In his own country, Illyria, he so strongly opposed the Arians, that he was beaten with rods, and compelled to escape. He then fled to the island of Gallinaria, on the coast of Italy, with a religious presbyter, where they lived for some time on herbs. He was a friend of St. Hilary of Poictiers; and passing into France, founded a monastery near Poictiers, but was afterwards made bishop of Tours by the unanimous choice of the people, though he was most reluctant to undertake the office. After his consecration, he still retained the same habits of life, the same humility of heart, and the same poverty of attire, which had always distinguished him; but to this was united all the authority and gravity of a bishop. He for some time lived in a little cell attached to the church; but being disturbed by the number of visitors, he founded a monastery two miles off, in a desert place, where he lived like all the other monks.   The employment of the younger brethren in this society consisted in transcribing books; the elders were devoted only to prayer and meditation.   St. Martin obtained so powerful an ascendency over the minds of the people, that he was enabled to overthrow the heathen temples, and build churches in their place.   When he was invited by the Emperor Maximus to dine at his table, he refused, saying that he could not partake of the table of a man who had deprived one emperor of his throne, and another of his life.   When the emperor excused himself, alleging that he had been compelled to receive the crown, and that he had not done so voluntarily, Martin accepted his invitation; but, to the surprise of every one, he gave the cup to his presbyter to drink before the emperor and his relatives.   The empress, sitting at his feet, listened day and night to his discourses; and having obtained the emperor's permission to entertain him at her own house, she attended him at table, performed the humblest offices, and preserved the very crumbs which he had left as precious relics.   St. Martin is said to have been enabled to work miracles for the conversion of the heathen; but many of those which are recorded of him are merely fabulous.   He attained to the age of more than eighty years, and knew that his end was drawing near.   Having gone to visit a remote part of his diocese for the purpose of reconciling the clergy of a church who were at variance, his strength suddenly failed, and he called together his disciples, and informed them that he was about to depart this life.   Then they began with one accord to say to him, weeping: "My father, why dost thou leave us?   Rapacious wolves will seize on thy flock, and who shall deliver them when the shepherd is smitten? We knew that thou longest for Jesus Christ, but thy reward is certain. Have pity, then, on us whom thou leavest." Touched by their tears he also wept, and replied: " O Lord, if I be still needful to thy people, I do not refuse to labour. Thy will be done." He was in a fever for some days, but he passed all his time in prayer, lying in sackcloth and ashes; and when his brethren wished to place some straw beneath him, he said that " it became a Christian to die on ashes;" and as they sought to turn him on his side to relieve his pains, he said to them: " Let me, my brethren, behold the heaven rather than the earth, that when my spirit departs to God, it may enter at once upon its way." When tempted by the devil, he exclaimed, " Thou hast nothing in me. I shall go to Abraham's bosom." Thus speaking, he expired.

St. Basil of Cæsarea, and St. Gregory of Nazianzum, were united by intimate friendship in their youth, whilst they studied at Athens under the most celebrated teachers of the age; and when their studies were completed, Basil returned to Cæsarea, and from thence went to the monasteries of Egypt, Mesopotamia, and Syria, in order to see the religious life in its perfection, and to derive spiritual instruction from the pious men who dwelt there. Returning to Pontus, he retired to the desert to practise the religious life. Here he was soon joined by his friend Gregory Nazianzen; and they continued there for a long time, engaged in prayer, and the study of the holy Scripture, which they read with the assistance of ancient commentators, especially Origen. They also laboured with their hands, carrying wood, cutting stones, planting and watering trees, and cultivating their garden. Nevertheless, they lived in the utmost poverty, and on the hardest fare. A great number of other persons imitated their exam-

ple, amongst whom was Gregory, afterwards bishop
of Nyssa, brother of Basil; and Basil gave rules for
the monastic life, which are still followed by the
monks of the order of St. Basil, in the eastern
Church.   About A.D. 362, Basil and Gregory Nazianzen were ordained priests, but still continued to
reside in the desert till 370, when Basil came forth
to assist Eusebius, bishop of Cæsarea, against the
heretics; and being skilled in the writings of Origen,
he and Gregory confuted the Arians, who adduced
those writings in proof of their errors: and though
they, with their leader Eunomius, had been famed
for learning, they appeared perfectly ignorant when
they encountered these champions of the truth.
Basil was soon after elected bishop of Cæsarea, in
Cappadocia; and fearing lest heresy should prevail
in Pontus, he passed through the Churches, preaching the true faith, and confirming the wavering.
When this came to the ears of the Arian emperor
Valens, he caused Basil to be brought before the
tribunal of the prefect Modestus; and when the
latter demanded why he did not embrace the creed
of the emperor, Basil boldly reproved the Arian
heresy; and when the prefect threatened death, he
replied, " Death will be a favour to me, since it will
send me unto God, for whom I live, and whom I
have long sought."   The emperor was at last overcome by his firmness, and Basil was released.   This
holy man was eminent for his works of charity towards the poor and afflicted.   He built near Cæsarea
an immense hospital, which was supported by lands
given by the emperor to the Church of that city.   A
refuge was there afforded to all who were in sickness and distress, especially to the lepers, who had
formerly lived in various parts of the town, and
caused horror by their appearance.   In this hospital
were apartments for the physicians, servants, and

tradesmen requisite for so great an establishment. St. Basil himself frequently went there to instruct and comfort the poor and infirm; and he would even touch and embrace the lepers, to set an example of charity to others. Gregory Nazianzen was, against his will, ordained bishop of Sasima by Basil. He continued, however, to govern the Church of Nazianzum during the lifetime of his father, who was the bishop of that see; and, like Basil, he went through the cities and strengthened those who were feeble in the faith. Afterwards he resided at Constantinople, where the Arians were in great force and possessed the churches; and by his eloquence he raised the Church there to great prosperity. St. Gregory was not only celebrated for his eloquence, but for the power and wisdom with which he refuted the arguments of those who denied the Godhead of our Lord Jesus Christ. He preached repeatedly on the subject, to the delight and edification of believers; and wrote many books in vindication of the truth, which gained for him the title of THEOLOGIAN, by which he has ever since been known. He was at length installed bishop of Constantinople by the second œcumenical synod; but soon after resigned his see, in consequence of some divisions which had arisen, and retired to Cappadocia, where he died in A.D. 391, at the age of more than ninety years. St. Basil had died in 379, reverenced by all the Christian world.

Amongst the most illustrious defenders of the true faith at this time was AMBROSE, archbishop of Milan. He had been made governor of that city by the emperor Valentinian; when, the see becoming vacant in 374, by the death of an Arian bishop, and the people being violently disturbed as to the choice of a successor, Ambrose exhorted them to peace and concord, when all demanded at once that he should

be their bishop.   He in vain resisted, and attempted
to fly.   The emperor's commands arrived, and he
was consecrated bishop.   He sold all his goods and
gave them to the poor, and applied with the utmost
diligence to the study of holy Scripture.   In order
to redeem captives from the hands of the Goths, he
even sold the plate of the church, merely reserving
what was absolutely necessary.   His firmness was
soon evinced by his resistance to the will of the
Empress Justina, mother of Valentinian, who prevailed on the emperor to demand one of the churches
in Milan for the Arians.   St. Ambrose firmly and
successfully opposed this attempt, though at the
peril of his life.   The Emperor Theodosius having
cruelly put to death a great multitude of people at
Thessalonica, in consequence of a tumult having
arisen, in which one of his officers was killed, Ambrose had the courage to reprove the emperor for
an act so unworthy of the Christian religion.   When
Theodosius came to Milan, Ambrose had retired
from that city, and had addressed to the emperor a
letter, representing with all the respect of a subject,
but all the seriousness and earnestness of a pastor,
the grievous nature of his crime, and urging him to
contrition and penitence.   When Ambrose returned
to Milan, Theodosius presented himself at the door
of the church, and was about to enter, but the holy
bishop refused to permit his entrance; and when
the emperor observed to him, that even David had
committed adultery and homicide, Ambrose replied,
" Since thou hast imitated his fault, imitate also his
repentance."   The emperor felt the force of this
appeal: he retired, and after several months of sorrow, was at length restored to communion, when he
had consented to submit to public penance in the
church, and to make a law commanding that the
execution of all criminals should be deferred for

thirty days after their condemnation. Happy indeed were those days, when bishops dared to admonish sovereigns of their duty to God and to His Church; and still more happy, when emperors were not ashamed to acknowledge their sins, and to manifest their contrition in the sight of all the world. The great Theodosius was thenceforward the friend of St. Ambrose; and when he felt himself about to depart from this life, he sent for that venerable bishop, and placed his children in his hands. St. Ambrose composed many eloquent and pious books, and died A.D. 397.

St. John, called Chrysostom (the golden-mouthed) for his eloquence, was originally intended for the bar; but forsaking the path of worldly honour, he retired from the world to devote himself to prayer and the study of Scripture; and afterwards, being appointed presbyter of Antioch, he became the most celebrated preacher of his age; so that in 397, when the see of Constantinople was vacant, the Emperor Honorius sent for him, and caused him to be ordained bishop by a great synod of bishops. The sanctity and severity of doctrine and practice which had made him so remarkable at Antioch, led him to exercise a vigilant and unpopular strictness of discipline in the imperial city; and his zeal displayed itself further in visiting the neighbouring province, and removing unworthy bishops. The people of Constantinople heard his sermons eagerly and insatiably; and the crowds were so great that their lives were endangered by the multitude, all endeavouring to press nearer to him, that they might hear more accurately; while he himself, sitting in the midst of the church, taught them from the desk of the reader. But the severity of his discipline, and his condemnation of vice, raised against him many enemies; and having taken the part of some monks who had been oppressed by Theophilus, bishop of Alexandria, that prelate, availing himself of the assistance of the empress, whom Chrysostom had offended by a sermon, in which he spoke of women with but little respect, came to Constantinople and held a synod, in which Chrysostom was deposed by his enemies. But when the people heard it, they assembled in the church, required a larger synod to be held, resisted the imperial officers who were sent to take their bishop into exile; and when, at length, he was removed, they broke into insurrection, and surrounded the palace with cries and lamentations, demanding the recall of Chrysostom, which the emperor was obliged to grant. Restored to his see by a synod of sixty bishops, Chrysostom again, ere long, fell under the imperial displeasure in consequence of his objections to the erection of a statue of the Empress Eudoxia. He was then driven forth into exile in Armenia, where he died in 407; and the eastern and western Churches were for some time divided on his account, as the former maintained the lawfulness of his expulsion, while the latter regarded him as a saint.

St. Jerome and St. Augustine, the most learned of all the fathers, now adorned the Church. The former spent the greater part of his life in the monastic state, in Palestine, and died in 420. St. Augustine was born in Africa, and in his early life fell into vices, and adopted the Manichæan heresy; but being at Milan, he became an attendant on the ministry of Ambrose, while his pious mother Monica prayed continually for his conversion. One day, a Christian, named Pontitian, coming to visit him, saw on his table the epistles of St. Paul, and learned, to his great joy, that Augustine devoted much of his time to the study of Scripture. The conversation gradually turned on the life of St. Antony and the

Egyptian and eastern monks, of whom Augustine had never heard before. When Pontitian had described all their piety, and self-denial, and zeal, and also mentioned the effect which the recital had produced on two officers of the emperor at Treves, who, on hearing it, had forsaken the world, and embraced a religious life, St. Augustine was deeply moved by the comparison of his own life and conduct with what he had heard, and went forth into the garden in the greatest agitation and compunction, where, having wept a long time, and prayed to God, he heard from a neighbouring house the voice of a child often repeating these words,—" Take—read ;" and regarding it as a sort of heavenly admonition, he returned to the house, and took up the epistles of St. Paul, when the first verse he read was, " Let us walk honestly, as in the day; not in rioting and drunkenness, not in chambering and wantonness, not in strife and envying. But put ye on the Lord Jesus Christ, and make not provision for the flesh, to fulfil the lusts thereof." His mind was now completely changed: he received baptism from St. Ambrose, and returned to Africa, where he gave himself up to retirement, prayer, meditation, and the composition of books against the Manichæan heresy. He sold all his possessions and gave· them to the poor, and was made presbyter, and afterwards bishop of Hippo, where he lived in the monastic state. His life was devoted to the maintenance of the truth against heathens, heretics, and schismatics, especially against the Pelagians and the Donatists; and his various writings made him celebrated in all parts of the world. When seized with fever, and lying on his death-bed, this eminent saint caused the seven penitential psalms to be recited; and having desired them to be fixed up before him, he read them continually with many tears. He commanded that he should never be disturbed, and spent his whole remaining time in prayer, until at length he calmly and peacefully expired, in the presence of all his friends, A.D. 430.

I have already spoken of St. Cyril of Alexandria, and St. Leo the Great, bishop of Rome, as the great opponents of the Nestorian and Eutychian heresies in the fifth century: both of these eminent prelates left many writings, which are still extant. St. Benedict, a man of eminent piety and zeal, in 529 founded the monastery of Mount Casino, in Italy; and his rule was adopted for many centuries by all the monasteries in the western Church; but they very soon relaxed the strictness of its observance, and the conduct of the monks too frequently reflected disgrace on their profession.

CHAPTER IX.

UNITY AND DISCIPLINE OF THE CHURCH.

A.D. 320-680.

AMONG the Christian Churches throughout the world, the Church of the imperial city of Rome had obtained an early distinction. Seated in the capital of the world, abounding in wealth and in numbers, remarkable for a munificence which was felt by the distressed and afflicted in all parts, endowed with a firmness of faith which opposed a steady and formidable resistance to every heresy, and founded by the holy apostles Peter and Paul, the Roman Church stood conspicuous amongst Christian communities; and even in the third century, the neighbouring Churches in Italy, Sicily, and the adjoining islands, placed themselves under its jurisdiction. The first œcumenical synod of Nice approved of this jurisdiction, which constituted the patriarchate of Rome; but the bishop of Rome had no ordinary jurisdiction beyond his patriarchate. The appeals of St. Athanasius and the other orthodox bishops, when persecuted by the Arians, to Julius of Rome, and the support which they received from that bishop, led the great synod of Sardica, in 341, to give the Roman bishop the power of ordering the causes of bishops to be re-heard, in cases where it appeared to him that they were unjustly condemned. This decree was indeed never received in the eastern or the African Church; and only gradually, after the lapse of some centuries, in the western Church; but it laid a foundation, on which the Roman see began to build its pretensions. In the latter part of the fourth century, the spirit of encroachment began to work in that Church; its bishops now extended their jurisdiction beyond the ancient limits approved by the synod of Nice, and invested the bishop of Thessalonica with the title of " Vicar of the Apostolical See" in Illyricum, with the view of bringing, by this means, that province and Greece under their ecclesiastical sway. In the following century, the bishops of Arles and of Seville were declared vicars for Gaul and Spain: in the sixth, Augustine was made vicar for Britain. The principal bishops in each country were thus engaged in the interests of Rome, and were encouraged gradually to make inroads on the liberties of the Churches. These vicars were appointed chiefly under the pretence that the Roman bishop was bound by his station to see that the ancient discipline of the Church, and the law of Christ, were duly observed; and this notion was confirmed, if not cre-

ated, by the habit of many bishops, in all parts of
the world, of consulting the Roman Church on difficult cases of discipline, and frequently adopting
its advice. It is true that they merely sought the
advice of a Church of apostolical antiquity and of
strict discipline; but that advice was often given in
a tone of authority; and the decretal epistles of the
popes, which we possess from the time of Siricius
(the latter part of the fourth century), formed gradually a body of precedents, which led the bishops
of Rome and the western bishops to ascribe to the
former a sort of legislative power in the Church,
which was in the event productive of the most injurious consequences. But, during the period now
before us, the authority of the Roman see, however
encroaching, was almost always virtuously exercised;
and if it excited somewhat of a spirit of ambition
and encroachment on the part of other great sees,
the evil was, in some degree, counterbalanced by
the effective resistance which it was enabled to give
to heresy, and to the ecclesiastical disorders and
corruptions introduced by the invasions of the barbarous nations. Its efforts were chiefly limited to
procure the observation of the canons, or laws of
discipline, made by the œcumenical synods; to encourage the spread of Christianity in heathen nations; and to provide for the necessities and peculiar circumstances of newly-founded Churches.

The Church, however, felt that an authority
which arose in any degree from a spirit of encroachment could not fail to be ultimately injurious; and
accordingly the third œcumenical synod, in 431, ex-
pressly forbad any patriarch to assume jurisdiction
over Churches which had not from the beginning
been subject to his see; lest, as they said, under the
guise of religion, the swelling of worldly pride should
find an entrance, the canons of the fathers be vio-

lated, and we imperceptibly lose that liberty which Christ purchased for us by his blood. According to this canon, it was unlawful for the Roman see to assume any ordinary jurisdiction in Britain; though, when religion had been oppressed by the heathen Saxons in that country, Pope Gregory acted most laudably in sending missionaries there to convert the barbarians. But this was only an act of charity, such as any Christian bishop might have done; and could not give his successors any right of jurisdiction in England, in opposition to the law of the œcumenical synod. Happy indeed had it been for religion, if the Roman Church had adhered to the spirit of this decree, and refrained from adding to its original and lawful jurisdiction.

The rival see of Constantinople now rose suddenly to dignity and power. When Constantine the Great removed the seat of empire from Rome to Constantinople, the bishop of that city soon obtained jurisdiction over the surrounding bishops of Thrace. The second œcumenical synod declared him second in dignity only to the Bishop of Rome; and the fourth made them equal in dignity and authority, while it sanctioned the jurisdiction which St. Chrysostom and his successors had acquired over Asia Minor. The other patriarchs were those of Alexandria, Antioch, and Jerusalem; but the patriarch of Constantinople, who was given the title of " œcumenical, or universal patriarch," by the Roman emperors in the sixth century, became, and has always since continued, the head of the eastern Church.

By the middle of the fifth century, these five patriarchal sees were fully established; and, as they occupy an important place in ecclesiastical history, it may be well, in this place, briefly to consider the extent and nature of their jurisdiction.

I have already spoken of the patriarchate of Rome: it extended over the "suburbicarian" provinces (so called from their vicinity to Rome, the capital of the empire), which included the greater portion of Italy, together with Sicily, Sardinia, and Corsica. In these provinces there were about 240 bishoprics. The patriarchate of Constantinople extended over the whole of Asia Minor, with the exception of the province of Cilicia, as well as over Thrace in Europe, and comprised about 400 bishoprics. The patriarchate of Antioch included the provinces of Cilicia, Mesopotamia, Arabia, and others which intervened between them, and consisted of about 230 bishoprics. The patriarchate of Jerusalem consisted of the three provinces of Palestine, and included 50 bishoprics. The patriarchate of Alexandria extended over the provinces of Egypt, Libya, and Pentapolis, which were divided into 108 episcopal sees.

Besides these provinces, which were subject to patriarchs by custom and the decrees of the œcumenical councils, there were many others which were independent of patriarchs, and governed only by their own metropolitans and provincial synods. Armenia, which is said to have contained about 200 sees, was subject to its own metropolitan, entitled catholic. There were also numerous episcopal sees in Persia, Assyria, Chaldea, Arabia, and India, probably not fewer than 100. The island of Cyprus was also independent of any foreign jurisdiction, and contained 15 bishoprics. The civil diocese of Illyricum, including Dacia, Mœsia, Dalmatia, Epirus, Macedonia, Greece, &c. consisted of about 130 episcopal sees. In the northern part of Italy, about 70 bishoprics existed beyond the Roman patriarchate, and were principally subject to the archbishop of Milan. In ancient Gaul, extend-tending to the Rhine, there were about 122 sees; in Spain, 76; in Britain and Ireland, 60 or 70; and in Africa, nearly 500. The patriarch of Rome gradually usurped jurisdiction over Illyricum from the fourth to the eighth century, when the emperors of the East suppressed his jurisdiction, and transferred those provinces to the patriarch of Constantinople. Gaul, Spain, and Britain, were also usurped by the same see of Rome in subsequent times; but the last of these was restored to its independence in the sixteenth century. From what has been observed above, it appears that in the fifth century the episcopal sees of the Eastern and Western Churches exceeded the number of two thousand.

Let us next consider the powers and privileges of the patriarchs. They were as follows. A patriarch had the right of ordaining the metropolitan, or principal bishop, in each of the provinces subject to his jurisdiction. He might assemble all his metropolitans and bishops in a patriarchal council, to decide questions of doctrine and discipline. Those who conceived themselves unjustly treated by the judgments of metropolitans, might appeal to him for redress. He might censure metropolitans, if they were remiss in their duties; and was consulted by them in all important and difficult cases.

The metropolitan was the bishop of the metropolis of a Roman province. According to the ancient canons, he summoned the provincial synod of all the bishops of the province, in which he presided. Nothing could be enacted in this synod without his consent, which was also to be sought for in every important matter which concerned the whole province. The metropolitan, with all the provincial bishops, confirmed and ordained newly-elected bishops. They also translated bishops, judged bishops accused of heresy or other offences, deposed them from their sees, made canons or laws of discipline for the whole province, and decided controversies in matters of doctrine. Where these provinces were subject to patriarchs, the judgments of their synods might be reversed by the patriarchal synod; but where they were independent, their judgment was ordinarily final.

In the early ages of Christianity, every large town was an episcopal see; and had England and Ireland in those ages been as thickly peopled as Asia Minor, Italy, or Africa, we should have had three or four hundred bishoprics in these countries. Every Church then consisted of laity and clergy; the latter consisting of a bishop, presbyters, and deacons, together with other inferior clerks. The bishop usually administered the eucharist every Sunday at least; preached the Gospel; celebrated baptism, which, except in cases of necessity, was only administered at the feasts of Easter and Pentecost; ordained, confirmed, excommunicated, absolved penitents, and generally performed most of the offices of the sacred ministry. The presbyters were his assistants in these pious works; but did not for a long time preach or administer the sacraments, except in the bishop's absence, or by his desire. The deacons were chiefly, though not solely, engaged in ministering to the poor. They read the Scriptures in church, preserved order in the congregation, were employed by the bishop on missions to other Churches, and catechised the children.

The bishop generally consulted his clergy, and sometimes even the people, in cases of any importance or difficulty. As the country around was converted to Christianity, and lesser Churches were established, the bishop appointed presbyters to minister there; and the laws of the Church required him to visit every Church in his diocese at least once in the year, and institute a most rigorous examination into the state of religion. In very large dioceses, however, which were at first thinly inhabited, but in the course of ages became exceedingly populous, it was altogether impossible for the bishop to fulfil the wishes of the Church unaided. Hence chorepiscopi, or rural bishops and visitors, and afterwards rural deans and archdeacons, were appointed to assist the bishop in the labour of visiting the Churches.

With such arduous duties and responsibilities, it is not to be wondered at that many persons in those ages refused to undertake the episcopal office. The bishops were generally far from rich in the goods of this world ; indeed they commonly considered it their duty to live in great poverty and humility, and to bestow the greater part of their revenues on the poor, and on the building of churches. As soon as Christianity was delivered from persecution, numbers of churches were erected, and adorned with the utmost magnificence. The seats of the presbyters were arranged in a semicircle behind the altar ; the bishop sat on a higher seat in the midst of this semicircle ; the deacons stood before the presbyters. The bishop generally preached from the steps of the altar. The Scriptures were read by the deacons from the ambon, or pulpit ; and the men and women sat at different sides of the church.

The whole body of ecclesiastical laws and discipline of the Church in these ages is comprised in a collection entitled " The Code of Canons of the Primitive Church," which has been published by Justel, Beveridge, and Johnson. This code, which was collected in the fifth century, included the canons or ecclesiastical laws made in the first four œcumenical councils, and in the provincial councils or synods of Ancyra, A.D. 314; Neocæsarea, A.D. 314; Antioch, A.D. 341; Laodicea, A.D. 370; Gangra, A.D. 375. It comprises the rules for the ordination of the clergy, the offices of patriarchs, metropolitans, bishops, presbyters, and deacons, regulations concerning the administration of the sacraments, public penitence, the mode of dealing with heretics, schismatics, and heathens,—in short, every thing which relates to the discipline of the Church. This ancient code, with the addition of some canons made in other synods, is still received by the whole of the Eastern Church.   In the West it became gradually obsolete and forgotten after the twelfth century, when the compilation of Gratian was published, which comprised, indeed, most of the ancient canons, but without accuracy, and which was also crowded with a number of forged canons and decrees calculated to support the papal usurpations.

The communion of Churches received several interruptions during this period. After the council of Sardica, in 341, the eastern and western bishops remained for some years estranged from mutual communion, in consequence of their contentions about St. Athanasius. A similar division was caused in the latter part of the same century by the ordination of two patriarchs of Antioch by different parties, one of whom was recognised by the eastern, and the other by the western Church. This division was healed by the pious care of St. Chrysostom. The deposition of that great man, and the ordination of another in his place to the see of Constantinople, led to a division between the East and West, which continued for many years, until justice was done by the Churches of the East to the memory of that illustrious bishop. Another division arose in 482, when Acacius, bishop of Constantinople, having caused the re-union of the Monophysites to the

Church, on principles which left the authority of the fourth œcumenical synod in doubt, and thus compromised the truth, he was deposed and excommunicated by Felix, bishop of Rome. The great body of the eastern bishops, though orthodox themselves, did not admit the propriety of this act; and the result was, that the eastern and western Churches were again estranged from mutual communion for twenty-five years. In the following century, the Churches of Africa, Tuscany, Illyricum, and some others, refused for a time to admit the fifth œcumenical synod, and were out of communion with the rest of the Church; but on full inquiry, they adopted the general decision. The ancient British and Irish Churches, in the sixth and seventh centuries, were treated as schismatics by the Roman Church, in consequence of their adherence to their ancient customs, and for not submitting to the authority of the papal see; but they were acknowledged as Christians by other Churches.

These divisions, however much they diminished the glory of the Church, did not altogether destroy the principle of Christian charity. It was still universally held that the Church formed but one spiritual fraternity; that all Christians were members of the same body; and that it was their duty to hold communion with each other. When divisions arose, excommunication consisted generally in a simple withdrawal of communion, without any sentence of anathema, or of total separation from Christianity. These withdrawals of communion were intended to procure the reformation of the offending party; and the divided Churches always retained the same principle of veneration for Scripture, as interpreted by the doctrine of the universal Church in all past ages, and sincerely endeavoured to be re-united to their brethren in Christ.

There was a wide distinction between such divisions of Churches, and that which existed between the universal Church and the Donatists and Luciferians. I have already observed, that the former arose from opposition to the appointment of a bishop in Africa. When the Donatists found their proceedings condemned generally in the Church, they declared the universal Church apostate; refused to communicate with it; asserted that Christianity was limited to Africa; denied that baptism, ordination, or any other rites conferred by the Church, were valid; and employed bands of murderers and robbers, called Circumcelliones, to persecute and maltreat all who did not agree with them. Under such circumstances they were most justly considered as schismatics, and as forming no part of the Church of Christ. The Luciferians were a comparatively small sect, who, after the example of Lucifer, bishop of Cagliari, condemned the Church for shewing mercy to those who repented of the Arian heresy, and for permitting them, on easy terms, to re-unite themselves to the Christian community. Lucifer and his followers went so far as to separate from the communion of all Christendom, and to pronounce it fallen from the faith; and they were, in consequence, numbered amongst the schismatics.

CHAPTER X.

ON THE RISE OF ABUSES AND CORRUPTIONS.

A.D. 320-680.

THE strong faith of the early Christians in some instances degenerated into credulity. Accustomed to the contemplation of the miracles recorded in the holy Scriptures, and still continuing to hear of occasional miracles wrought for the conversion of the heathen, they received with too ready a credence many tales of wonders and signs which superstition or imposture spread abroad. In western Europe, the ignorance of a long night of political barbarism and warfare rendered the multitude prone to the reception of such errors. Men of eminent sanctity were supposed to have the power of working miracles by their prayers; and the veneration which attached to their persons when living followed them beyond the grave.

The Church has not always been gifted with a spirit of wisdom and foreknowledge to discern the future abuses of opinions and practices, which it originally permitted without reproof. Could the pious fathers of the fourth century, who in their orations apostrophised the departed saints and martyrs, and called for their prayers to God, have foreseen the abuses to which this practice was to lead; could they have known that these expressions of an ardent, though somewhat unregulated feeling, were to induce others, in process of time, to adopt such invocations as a stated portion of their daily worship—to lead in later ages to actual *prayers* addressed to the saints themselves, and to cause such prayers and invocations almost to supplant the worship of God among the ignorant or superstitious—they would have carefully avoided the introduction of a practice so dangerous to true religion. Yet during the period before us, the invocation of saints, however superfluous and unwise, neither usurped so large a portion of the worship of Christians, nor was in itself so censurable, as it became in after-ages. It consisted simply in addresses to the saints to pray to God for us; nor is there any evidence that it was a universal practice. The invocation of angels was directly prohibited by the council of Laodicea, in the fourth century; yet in the seventh it was introduced into some litanies of the western Church. The invocation of saints then also appeared for the first time in public worship in these formularies.

The same affection, the same veneration, with which the spirits of the saints and martyrs were regarded by the early Christians, attended their earthly remains; and the same credulity of individuals led to the circulation of an opinion that even their inanimate relics could procure blessings for those who touched them with faith, since the dead bones of the prophet Elisha, the hem of our Lord's garment, and the handkerchiefs from St. Paul's body, had wrought miracles. Hence the relics of martyrs and saints were, in the fourth and following centuries, regarded with very great veneration in many parts of the Church; and they gradually even became temptations to the ignorant and enthusiastic, who too willingly received the tales of marvels which they were said to have worked, and sometimes seemed inclined to forget the Author and Giver of all good things, in their admiration of the gifts which they attributed to his creatures. The desire of possessing such relics became so great in the fifth and following centuries, that it led dishonest men to produce a number of spurious relics; so that, after the lapse of some ages, it became almost impossible to distinguish the true from the false. The custom of placing relics in churches, which began in the fourth or fifth century, and became universal in the seventh, also contributed to swell the number of false relics. No one will deny that the remains of martyrs and holy men ought to be treated with honour and respect; but when this assumes the character of superstitious or idolatrous worship, the Church is bound to remove the cause of such abuses. It was this that led the Church of England, in the sixteenth century, to remove the alleged relics of saints,—a measure which was justified by a strong necessity.

It was a pious and natural feeling of love, which led many Christians, in the fourth and following centuries, to make pilgrimages to visit the scenes of our Saviour's life and death, and the tombs of the martyrs and saints whose virtues had adorned Christianity. But this custom led to serious abuses: it led clergy as well as laity to forsake the sphere of their appointed duties, and to consume their time in wandering over the earth. After the period of which I am now speaking, the evil increased much; and St. Boniface, about 750, complained of the disgrace which religion suffered from the sinful lives of many persons who had undertaken such journeys. This practice even became one means by which the ancient penitential discipline was subverted; for it was customary with some bishops, after the period now before us, to commute the lengthened canonical penances, for pilgrimages to Jerusalem or to some other holy place.

The use of pictures or sculptures representing our Saviour, the chief events of sacred history, or the saints, was not unfrequent in the fifth and sixth centuries. These pictures were only intended for ornament, for the information of the ignorant, or to excite pious recollections: all worship to them was forbidden. St. Epiphanius, A.D. 400, tore the vail of a church on which the picture of a saint was embroidered. Serenus, bishop of Marseilles, about 600, destroyed images which the people worshipped ; and Pope Gregory the Great, while he questioned the propriety of the act, yet equally disapproved of the abuse it was designed to prevent.

The evils of which I have been speaking were all engrafted on opinions or practices in themselves blameless or excusable; and it was frequently difficult to distinguish precisely between right and wrong, to trace the boundary between piety and superstition. But as the Scriptures were still understood by many of the people, we have reason to believe that such evils could not yet have been of a very serious character or wide prevalence.

Another evil was slowly growing, at the close of the period now under consideration. When Christianity was first disseminated, the earliest gift of the Holy Spirit was that of tongues, in order that every nation might hear in its own language the wonderful works of God, and that every tongue might confess that Jesus is the Lord. Accordingly, at first, every nation employed its own language in the worship of God; for, as St. Paul said to those who celebrated the eucharist in a language unknown to their hearers, "When thou shalt bless with the spirit, how shall he that occupieth the room of the unlearned say Amen, at thy giving of thanks, seeing he understandeth not what thou sayest?"[1] Guided by these apostolical instructions, the Greeks used their own language in divine service. The Churches of Syria

---

[1] 1 Cor. xiv. 16.

and Mesopotamia used the Syriac language; the native Egyptians Coptic; the Grecian colonies at Alexandria, and in Sicily and Naples, prayed in Greek. The Ethiopic was used in Abyssinia, the Armenian in Armenia, Sclavonic in Russia, and Illyric in Illyria. The Latin was vernacular in Italy, Africa, Spain, Gaul, and was employed in the liturgy of those Churches. Even after the Goths and other barbarous nations had invaded the West, the mass of the Christian population still spoke the Latin language; and for several ages it did not become so corrupted by the admixture of foreign words as to be unintelligible to the people. The same observation may be applied generally to the eastern Churches, in which the language of the liturgy long continued to be more or less understood by the people. The period in which it ceased to be so, must be placed after the ages now under consideration; but an unwisely applied reverence for the ancient liturgies of the Church led, in the sixth and following centuries, to the adoption of Latin services in the newly-founded Churches in England, Germany, and the northern nations; a measure which was certainly much less excusable than the retention of the ancient language in the other parts of the West. It is true, indeed, that the validity of the sacraments was not vitally affected by their being administered in a language understood only by the minister, provided that the recipients were instructed in the meaning of the essential rites and prayers, and taught to unite their supplications with those of the Church; but this could only be an indifferent substitute for that united worship in voice and heart, which the Church had universally received from the apostles; and it had a tendency to cause, in the less-informed part of the community, a blind and superstitious dependence on the effects of the sacraments, to the neglect of all preparation on their own parts, instead of an enlightened and spiritual apprehension of those sacred mysteries and graces which are conveyed by the sacraments only to the penitent and believing soul.

The discipline of the Church with regard to the marriage of the clergy was different in the East and the West. In the earliest ages of the Church, no restriction whatever had been placed on the clergy in this respect. The apostles Peter and Philip, and several others, were married; and St. Paul had included amongst the qualifications of a bishop, his being " the husband of one wife." He also asserted his own right to " lead about a sister, a wife, as well as other apostles," though he preferred to remain unmarried. On the other hand, our Lord himself, when the apostles said to him, "If the case of the man be so with his wife, it is good not to marry," replied, " All men cannot receive this saying—he that is able to receive it, let him receive it." And while he honoured the marriage of Cana with his presence, and delivered so many injunctions concerning the sanctity and inviolability of that state, he himself always continued unmarried. St. Paul wished that all men were even as he was; but "every man hath his proper gift of God." His reason was, " He that is unmarried careth for the things that belong unto the Lord." Such, then, were the rules of the Gospel, affording liberty to all Christians to marry, or to abstain from marriage, as they should judge most conducive to their salvation, and to the glory of God ; but at the same time acknowledging that those who were enabled to refrain from marriage, to devote themselves entirely to God, are to be accounted most happy.

On these principles we find that many of the clergy in the early ages were married. Such as

Valens, a presbyter of Philippi, mentioned by Polycarp; Chæremon, bishop of Nilus, mentioned by
Eusebius; several presbyters of Carthage, in the
time of St. Cyprian; Phileas, bishop of Thmuis;
Demetrianus, bishop of Antioch, Gregory Nazianzen's father; and many others, whose names occur
in ecclesiastical history. Socrates, who wrote in
the fifth century, observes, that many eminent bishops had wives and children; and that those who
remained single, did so by their own free choice,
and not by the obligation of any law. Up to the
year 692, when an eastern synod forbade bishops
to remain with their wives, the contrary practice
existed in several Churches, especially in Africa
and Libya. In Ireland this custom remained to a
very late period: till the twelfth century, the Irish
bishops and clergy were generally married.

The rules of the eastern and western Churches
have been different in some degree since the fifth
century, when the latter in general forbade the
clergy to live in the married state, under the im-
pression that they would thus be enabled to fulfil
more devotedly the office of the sacred ministry.
But the experience of ages shewed that this discipline was very inexpedient, as it was plainly not
enjoined by any Divine command; and from the
tenth to the twelfth century, considerable numbers
of the western clergy were married; but the Roman
pontiffs after that enforced celibacy with extreme
severity. In the eastern Church the presbyters and
inferior clergy have always been married, though
they are not allowed to contract marriage after their
ordination.

The great majority of the early Christians, if we
may judge by the writers of the first four centuries,
held that immediately after this life the righteous
were admitted to a region of peace and happiness:

but as they believed that the soul would be re-united to the body at the last day, before ascending into heaven, and therefore that it was not yet in a state of such perfect blessedness as admitted of no increase; and as it was the opinion of many, that the saints were to rise from the dead before the rest of mankind, and to share in the glory of the millennium, —it was customary in the Church, from the remotest antiquity, to offer prayers for the perfect peace and joy of the departed believers, and for their participation in the first resurrection. It was also the opinion of Origen, and of several other fathers, that at the last day, all believers, without exception, shall pass through some fire, which shall purge away all traces of sin and imperfection, and render them meet for the presence of God. This opinion, however, was not received by Christians as an article of faith. St. Augustine, in the fifth century, regarded it only as " not incredible" that some of the faithful may after this life be saved by a sort of purifying fire. Gregory the Great, A.D. 600, first maintained the doctrine that there is a purgatory fire, before the day of judgment, for slight faults not repented of in this life: this doctrine he founded chiefly on certain alleged visions of souls in torment for their sins. Thus began the doctrine of purgatory, which, however, was never received by the eastern Church, and was only gradually adopted in the west. Even in the twelfth century, as we learn from Otto Frisingensis, it was only held by "some" writers; and it was never declared an article of faith till 1438, in the council of Florence, the authority of which has always been doubtful even among Romanists.

CHAPTER XI.

PROGRESS OF CHRISTIANITY.

A.D. 680-1054.

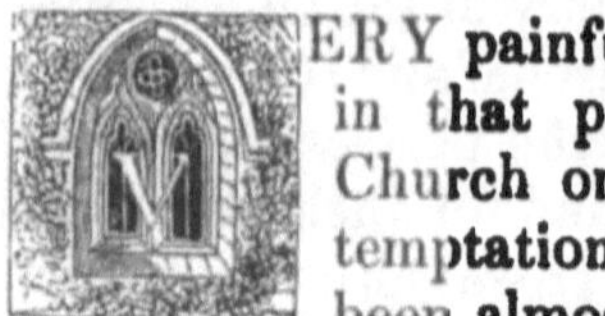

ERY painful features present themselves in that period of the history of the Church on which we now enter. The temptations of heresy had indeed now been almost exhausted; and the human mind, wearied with novelties and dissensions, reposed itself more implicitly on the authority of the Church: but ignorance and barbarism were fast overspreading the traces of ancient civilisation, and religion too often became mingled with superstition. The perpetual state of warfare between rival princes, the feebleness of governments, unable to control their powerful and turbulent subjects, caused a general lawlessness and disorder, destructive of those habits which are most congenial to Christianity. Add to this the incursions and ravages of Saracens, Danes, and Normans, which threw all the west of Europe into confusion; the insurrections and inroads of Saxons, Sclavonians, Hungarians, and Turks, which equally disturbed the East and the North; and we may then see the difficulties under which religion laboured, and which were in many respects most injurious to her. But even in these ages we continue to see the fulfilment of our Saviour's promises to his Church. The kingdom of Christ was still expanding itself from the river to the ends of the earth; the tree sprung from a grain of mustard-seed still shewed the vigour of its constitution by putting forth new and flourishing branches; and the fruits of the Holy Spirit's influence, the pledge of our Lord's perpetual presence with his body the Church, were abundantly manifested in the midst of many scandals and sins. It may be said with truth, I believe, that the progress of Christianity in the world during these dark ages was scarcely less than during the first three centuries of its existence.

In the eighth century, the Saracens crossed from Africa into Spain, and having subdued the forces of Roderic, the last king of the Goths, in a pitched battle, made themselves masters of the whole country. They even threatened France, but were defeated with dreadful slaughter by Charles Martel, and compelled to retire within the limits of Spain. They subdued Sardinia, and ravaged Italy and Sicily (of which last they afterwards took possession) so terribly, that in many places the number of towns was reduced by one half. Christianity, however, subsisted under the dominion of the Saracens in the West, as well as in the East, though much oppression was experienced by believers, and some were even delivered to death for the name of Jesus Christ. But the losses of the Church under the Saracen dominion were counterbalanced by numerous conversions in the north of Europe. Christianity was still spreading amongst the Anglo-Saxons; it was carried far and wide amongst the Thuringians, Frieslanders, and Hessians, in Germany, by St. Boniface, or Winfrid, a monk of the order of St. Benedict, and a native of England. Rupert and Corbinian, two French bishops, were invited by Theodo, duke of Bavaria, early in the eighth century, to preach the Gospel in his dominions; and the former baptised that prince, with a large number of his people. Christianity was then established and bishoprics were founded in Bavaria. Firminus preached the Gospel with great zeal in Alsatia, Bavaria, and Switzerland; and Lebuin, a native of England, laboured amongst the Saxons. Carinthia received Christianity from Bavaria, the duke of Carinthia having requested Virgilius, bishop of Saltzburg, to send clergy to instruct his people. St. Virgilius, who was a native of Ireland, and remarkable for his learning and piety, afterwards visited Carinthia, and confirmed the new Christians in the faith. In the latter part of the eighth century, the Emperor Charlemagne having conquered the greater part of Germany and Hungary, established churches throughout his dominions, and obliged his subjects to adopt the Christian religion. In the early part of the ninth century, St. Anschar, a monk of Corby in Westphalia, laid the foundations of the Church in Cimbria, Denmark, and Sweden, in which he was assisted by Anthbert, Ebbo, and many other pious missionaries.

The eastern Church was now also engaging in the same holy work. Methodius and Cyril, two Greek monks, converted to Christianity the Mœsians, Gazarians, Bohemians, and Moravians, about the middle of this century; and the Sclavonians, Aretani, and other nations of Dalmatia, having expressed, in 867, a wish to embrace the Christian religion, they were instructed and baptised by missionaries from the eastern Church. The Bulgarians, a savage nation, who had invaded Thessaly and Epirus some time before, were now converted to the Christian faith by some bishops and clergy from Constantinople, who were called in by the king of Bulgaria. After the people had been thus baptised and instructed in the Christian religion, the king sent to Pope Nicholas I. for further assistance, when that prelate not only sent Italian bishops to Bulgaria, but prevailed on the king to expel the Greek missionaries, and claimed jurisdiction over the Churches which they had founded. A conference was held at Constantinople soon afterwards, to determine whether the see of Constantinople or that of Rome had a right to exercise jurisdiction over these Churches, which concluded in favour of the former; and the bishops of Rome, to their great mortification, failed in their attempt. The vast nations of Russia were also added to the Christian Church in this and the following century; first by the persuasions of the missionaries sent by Ignatius, patriarch of Constantinople, and afterwards by the example of Wlodimir, the sovereign of Russia, who was baptised in 987. The savage Normans, who had invaded and seized a portion of France, now followed the example of their duke Rollo, and embraced the faith; while the conversion of Sweden was completed by Sigfrid; and that of Norway by Guthebald, who went forth on this holy mission from the Church of England. Micislaus, duke of Poland, adopted the Christian religion in 995; and his example so wrought on his subjects, that in a few years they professed the faith, and many episcopal sees were founded in that country. Some of the Hungarians were converted and baptised by Hierotheus, a bishop who was sent to them from Constantinople; but the conversion of that nation is chiefly attributable to the pious zeal of their king Stephen, who having been educated a Christian, resolved to cause his subjects to embrace the true religion; and having subdued a revolt of his pagan subjects, soon after his accession to the throne, in 997, he devoted himself to the propagation of the Gospel with earnest prayer and almsgiving; and sending for Christian teachers from the adjoining countries, he encouraged and assisted them so effectually, that idolatry was entirely banished from his dominions, and ten bishops were ordained for the superintendence of the new Churches.

CHAPTER XII.

ON THE FAITH OF THE CHURCH.

A.D. 680-1054.

DURING this period the faith of Christians did not vary from what it had formerly been: this is proved by the universal adoption of the Nicene creed as the rule of faith, and by the veneration felt by all believers for the decrees of the six holy œcumenical synods. The Trinity, incarnation, atonement, the necessity of Divine grace, original sin, the need of good works, and all the other doctrines taught from the beginning by the Church, were still universally believed. We hear little indeed in these ages, comparatively speaking, of heresies: those which did appear seem not to have had much influence. The errors concerning our Lord's nature, which were taught by Elipandus in Spain in the eighth century, and which were connected with the Nestorian heresy, were condemned by the great council of Frankfort in 794, and they disappeared soon afterwards. The doctrines of the Paulicians in the seventh century, and of Berengarius in the eleventh, seem to have obtained but few adherents; and we can scarcely point to any other errors in faith, which were at this time sustained by bodies of men. The same great truths of religion were universally adopted; the same Scriptures were diligently studied by all who had the means of doing so,—for in those days, before the invention of printing, when all books were transcribed by manual labour, they were both scarce and expensive;—and an universal appeal was made to the sentiments of the ancient fathers and councils in the interpretation of the Bible.

In the seventh century the sect of the Paulicians, or new Manichæans, arose in Asia Minor and Armenia. An Armenian, named Constantine, having received from a captive deacon of the Church the Gospels and the epistles of St. Paul, became the founder of this sect. Observing that the Manichæan heresy was encumbered with a variety of doctrines which rendered it odious to the Church, he threw aside those parts of the system which were most unpopular, and endeavoured to accommodate the language of Scripture to the remainder. The Paulicians believed that there are two gods, one of whom (an evil being) created this world, and was the author of the Old Testament. They accused the prophets of being robbers and impostors, and rejected the sacraments. Their audacity and ingenuity in perverting the plainest passages of Scripture in support of their evil tenets, afford a most instructive example of the danger to which St. Peter alludes (2 Pet. iii. 16), and of the extent of blindness and self-delusion which judicially falls on those who attempt to subject the holy Scriptures to their own inventions, instead of submitting themselves unreservedly, under the guidance of God's Church and the direction of his Holy Spirit, to the instructions of the written Word. The Paulicians were severely, though not undeservedly, punished by the eastern emperors; and after some time they broke into revolt, and uniting with the enemies of the empire, became assailants in their turn; but having been defeated, they were transported into a desert part of Thrace in the tenth century, whence they contrived to propagate their errors in several parts of the western Church, under the name of Cathari, Paterini, and at length Albigenses.

The grand controversy of the eighth century was on a point of Christian morality—the use of images. It is admitted, even by those who approve most highly of their use, that it is no part of Christian duty to possess such memorials; that there is no injunction to that effect in holy Scripture; and that it would be idolatrous to offer them any adoration, as if they were deities, or to attribute to them any peculiar power in themselves. Yet experience informs us that the use of images cannot long continue without the danger of such errors.

We have already seen instances of a tendency to superstition with regard to images: this was carried still further in the East in the course of the seventh and eighth centuries; so that the people, in order to do honour to the saints and martyrs, bowed, lighted candles, and offered incense before their pictures. It is true, that in acting thus, it was intended rather to honour the saints themselves than their pictures; but the tendency of such customs to cause superstition and even idolatry amongst the ignorant, is too obvious to be overlooked. The Greek emperors, Leo, Constantine Caballinus, and several of their successors in the eighth and ninth centuries, seeing these abuses, and desirous to free the Church from them, commenced reformation by breaking down all images, and persecuting those who wished to retain them. To accomplish their object, originally good, the Iconoclasts did not hesitate to condemn the use of any pictures, as absolutely contrary to the word of God, and thus placed themselves in the attitude of arraigning the practice of the universal Church for some centuries as anti-Christian; a line of argument which was as inconsistent with trust in the Divine promises as it was with Christian charity. The western Church at this time generally permitted the use of pictures or images, but forbade any sort of religious honour or worship to be paid to them; and hence, when the bishops of the East, to the number of 338, assembled in synod at Constantinople in 754, and condemned the use of images as idolatrous, the western Churches disapproved of the decree.

After many years, the party in favour of images obtained a temporary triumph in the East, on a change of government. A synod of 350 bishops at Nice, in 787, reversed the decision formerly made at Constantinople, and decreed the lawfulness of images, and the propriety of paying to them a certain honour by bowing, lighting candles, and offering incense before them, which honour was supposed to pass to the person represented, and to be altogether different from the worship which is due to God only. But this synod was soon afterwards rejected by the eastern Church, and so remained till the year 842; while the bishops of the West, to the number of 300, in the great synod of Frankfort, A.D. 794, annulled the decrees of the synod of Nice, which they forbade to be numbered amongst the œcumenical synods, and rejected all worship of images. The western Churches remained for several centuries in the same sentiments. The historians and other writers, from the eighth to the fourteenth century, almost always term the synod of Nice a " pseudo-synod," or " false synod," and condemn its doctrine. It was observed by a Greek writer in the time of the crusades (the twelfth century) that the Germans did not permit the use of images. However, at length superstition in this respect became very common in the West,— an evil which was very much caused by the support always given by the bishops of Rome to the decisions of the Nicene synod.

It appears plainly, from a review of the whole history, that it was always the wish and *intention* of the universal Church to prevent any idolatrous or divine worship of images, and to direct the veneration of Christians to the persons whom they represent. But this intention could not be realised in the case of the ignorant and superstitious, who must always form a great portion of the community; they were placed in most imminent danger of worshipping the images themselves, and with divine honours too; and we know that in later times the abuses in this respect were most lamentable. The removal of images at the Reformation was, in fact, only carrying out the intention of the universal Church in the eighth and following centuries, when experience had amply proved that they could not generally be used without danger of idolatry. It had been held by Agobard, archbishop of Lyons, even in the ninth century, that images ought to be destroyed when they gave rise to idolatrous abuses; as Hezekiah had broken the brazen serpent when it was worshipped by the people.

In the ninth century the doctrine of the holy eucharist became the subject of discussion. It had never been denied by the Catholic Church that this sacrament, when consecrated, continues to be bread and wine, according to the words of the apostle, "The *bread* which we break, is it not the communion of the body of Christ?" and of our Lord, "I will drink no more of this *fruit of the vine*," &c. But Paschasius Radbert, a French monk, in the ninth century, attempted to prove that the sacrament is no longer bread and wine after the consecration, but only the real body and blood of Christ, the same in all respects with that which was born of the Virgin. This doctrine, which has been termed the doctrine of transubstantiation in later ages, gradually obtained many adherents in the western Churches, though it was opposed at first by several of the most eminent

divines; such as Rabanus Maurus, archbishop of
Mayence, and Bertram or Ratramnus, a monk of
Corby. Bertram maintained that the eucharist was
truly the body and blood of Christ, which were present in a spiritual, not a corporeal manner ; and
that there was some difference between the body of
Christ as it is received in the eucharist, and as it
was born of the Virgin and exists in heaven.   This
seems to have been the most prevalent belief for
some ages.   The homily which was then read at
Easter in the Church of England, and which is said
to have been composed by Ælfric, archbishop of
Canterbury in the tenth century, says, that the eucharist " is by nature corruptible bread and corruptible wine, but according to the truth of the
Divine word, is truly the body of Christ and his
blood; yet not corporeally, but spiritually.   There
is much difference between that body in which
Christ suffered, and that body which is consecrated
to the eucharist.   That body in which Christ suffered, was born of the flesh of Mary, with blood
and bones, with skin and sinews, animated with a
reasonable soul in human members ; but his spiritual
body, which we call the eucharist, is composed of
many grains, without blood and bone, without member and soul, and therefore nothing in it is to be
understood corporeally, but all is to be understood
spiritually."   The same doctrine is found in the
writings of the abbot Ælfric, where, having censured the practice of reserving the eucharist consecrated at Easter for the use of the sick during the
remainder of the year, he remarks, that " the eucharist which is consecrated to-day, is as holy as
that which was consecrated on Easter-day.   That
eucharist is the body of Christ not corporeally, but
spiritually ; not the body in which he suffered, but
the body of which he spoke, when he consecrated

bread and wine as the eucharist, and said of the consecrated bread, ‘This is my body,’ and likewise of the consecrated wine, ‘This is my blood, which is shed for many for the remission of sin.’ Understand now, that the Lord, who could spiritually change that bread before his suffering into his body and that wine into his blood, the same Lord daily consecrates, through the priest’s hands, bread and wine to be his spiritual body and his spiritual blood.” Such was the doctrine of the English Church in those ages, which agrees in all material points with what we now receive. For as the Catechism of the Church declares that “the body and blood of Christ” are “verily and indeed taken and received by the faithful in the Lord’s supper,” and as the twenty-seventh homily declares, that “in the supper of the Lord there is no vain ceremony, no bare sign, no untrue figure of a thing absent,” thus acknowledging a real but spiritual presence of the Lord’s body, according to his own words in the Gospel; so, on the other hand, we acknowledge that the spiritual change of the elements into the sacrament of the body and blood of Christ does not cause the nature of bread and wine to be destroyed or cease; but that those elements still remain, and that we may truly and rightly say with St. Paul, “ the *bread* which we break, is it not the communion of the body of Christ?” (1 Cor. x. 16); and again with St. Luke, “ They continued steadfastly in the apostles’ doctrine and fellowship, and in breaking of bread, and in prayers” (Acts ii. 42). Such was the doctrine held by Rabanus and others, in contending against the opinion of Paschasius Radbertus. Scotus, in opposing it, fell into serious errors, as he declared the eucharist to be a bare *sign* of the body and blood of Christ, contrary to the universal belief of the Church ; and in this error he was followed by

Berengarius in the eleventh century, whose doctrine was justly condemned by several councils;
though it is to be regretted, that his opponents
occasionally used expressions with reference to the
eucharist, which were inconsistent with the spiritual
character of that holy mystery. This controversy
only existed in the western Churches; the eastern
Churches continued to retain their ancient doctrines
undisturbed.

During these ages, the practice of private confession to a priest was not held generally to be a
matter of necessity. We have already seen this
custom abolished (as a pre-requisite to the reception of the eucharist) in the East, by Nectarius,
patriarch of Constantinople in the fourth century,
and by the majority of the eastern Church. It was
still practised in many parts of the West, but was
not regarded as an essential of religion. Bede and
Alcuin recommended Christians to confess to the
ministers of God all the grievous sins which they
could remember. But others, as we learn from
Alcuin and Haymo, would not confess their sins to
the priest; but said, " it was sufficient for them to
confess their sins to God alone, provided that they
ceased from those sins for the time to come." The
council of Cavaillon, in the time of the emperor
Charlemagne, acknowledged that it was still a matter
of doubt whether confession to the priests was necessary, in addition to confession before God; and they
attributed the pardon of sins to the latter. " Some
persons say that they ought to confess their sins only
to God, and some think that they are to be confessed
unto the priests; both of which, not without great
fruit, is practised within the holy Church. Namely,
thus; that we both confess our sins unto God, who
is the forgiver of sins, (saying with David, 'I acknow-

ledge my sins unto thee, and mine iniquity have I not hid.' 'I said, I will confess against myself my transgressions unto the Lord; and thou forgavest the iniquity of my sin'), and, according to the institution of the apostle, confess our sins one to another, and pray one for another, that we may be healed. The confession, therefore, which is made unto God, purgeth sins; but that which is made unto the priest, teacheth in what sort those sins should be purged."

It may, perhaps, be advisable to carry our view of this subject beyond the period now under consideration, and to notice the difference of opinions in the western Church previously to the Reformation. Gratian, about 1130, collected the opposite decisions of the ancients as to the necessity of external confession, and concluded thus:—" Upon what authorities, or upon what strength of reasons, both these opinions are grounded, I have briefly laid open. But whether of them we should rather cleave to, is reserved to the judgment of the reader. For both of them have for their favourers both wise and religious men." The council of Lateran, in 1215, directed the faithful to confess their sins to a priest once a-year; but notwithstanding this, the *necessity* of such a confession was not generally admitted. Semeca, the earliest commentator on the canon law; Michael of Bononia, prior-general of the Carmelites; Panormitanus, and a number of eminent writers, asserted that confession to a priest was not instituted by God, but introduced solely by the authority of the Church, and that it was not necessary for the pardon of sin. And this difference of opinion existed in all Churches of the Roman communion, until the council of Trent, when the divine institution and absolute necessity of confession to a priest were declared to be articles of faith, which no one should deny, on pain of anathema.

CHAPTER XIII.

ON THE FRUITS OF FAITH.

A.D. 680-1054.

MENTION has already been made of the great difficulties under which religion now laboured from the disorganisation of temporal governments, and the ravages of barbarians. During these ages, nothing was more frequent than the usurpation of ecclesiastical revenues by kings and feudal lords, or their desecration by the appointment of clergy who were incapacitated by youth or ignorance for the discharge of their duties, and who had nothing to recommend them but nobility of birth. These abuses occurred particularly within the dominions of the emperors in Italy, France, and Germany, where it had been the policy of Charlemagne and his successors to invest the bishops and monasteries with great territories and princely dignities, in the hope that these ecclesiastics would prove more faithful and obedient subjects than the temporal barons, whose turbulence they had found it so difficult to repress. Churches and monasteries were frequently burned or pillaged by the feudal chieftains, or by Saracens, Normans, and Danes. Thus the schools of learning were extinguished, discipline became relaxed amidst the general confusion; and while the clergy were in many places insufficiently educated, the laity fell into extreme ignorance and degradation. We find grievous lamentations over such evils amongst the writers of these ages; yet there is every reason to believe that there was a spirit of repentance at work which could not fail to produce very salutary effects. Those bishops who, when assembled in solemn council, had the courage to proclaim before the world their own remissness, and to confess their sins, with resolution of amendment, could neither have been deficient in a knowledge of their duty, nor in a spirit of Christian humility and repentance.

Hervey, archbishop of Rheims, and eleven other bishops assembled at Troslé in France, A.D. 909, spoke thus: " As the first men lived without law and without fear, given up to their passions, so every one now doeth as he pleases, despising all laws human and divine, and the directions of the bishops. The powerful oppress the weak; violence against the poor, and the plunder of ecclesiastical possessions, are universal. And that it may not be imagined that we spare ourselves—we who ought to correct others—we have indeed the name, but we do not fulfil the duties of bishops. We neglect preaching; we see those who are committed to our care abandon God and fall into sin, without addressing them and stretching forth our hands; and if we wish to reprove them, they say, as in the Gospel, that we bind on them heavy burdens, and will not touch them ourselves with the end of our fingers. Thus the Lord's flock perishes through our silence. Let us think what sinner has ever been converted by our discourses, or who has renounced debauchery, avarice, pride. Yet we shall render an account without ceasing of this business, which has been entrusted to us, in order that we may gain profit by it."—" It has happened through our negligence, our ignorance, and that of our brethren, that there are found in the Church an innumerable multitude of people of every sex and condition, who arrive at old age without ever being instructed in the faith, so that they are ignorant even of the words of the Creed and Lord's Prayer. If there should seem to be any thing good in their lives, yet how can they do good works without the foundation of faith?" These expressions, and the earnest exhortations of the synod, shew that there was still a spirit of real repentance in this part of the Church, notwithstanding the multitude of evils and sins.

That the clergy in those days had, at least, ample opportunities of knowing the obligations which their ministry imposed on them, cannot be doubted. The duties of the priesthood have never been better described, or more earnestly urged, than in the writings of St. John Chrysostom and St. Gregory the Great, whose treatises on this subject were long read and admired in the Church. St. Gregory's book " on the Pastoral Care" was for many centuries after his death, and especially in the ages which we are now considering, the manual of the clergy in all the Western Church, and it was read and inculcated in many councils, as affording the most invaluable lessons. St. Gregory represented to the clergy the great importance and responsibility of their office, and the danger of undertaking it without sufficient preparation. " No one presumes," said he, " to teach an art unless he has previously acquired it by diligent attention. How great, then, is the rashness of those who, without skill, undertake the pastoral office, since the care of souls is the art of all arts! Who does not know that the wounds of the mind are more difficult to be understood than those of the body? And yet those who are unacquainted with the spiritual precepts, are frequently not ashamed to profess themselves physicians of the heart, while those who are ignorant of the effects of drugs would blush to act as physicians to the body. Against such men the Lord complains by his prophet: 'They have reigned, but not by me; they have been princes, and I have not known it.' They are self-appointed rulers, not made by God's will, who, devoid of virtues, uncalled of God, but influenced by their own desire, seize on, rather than obtain, the supreme rule. Those who know not the things of God are unknown of God; for St. Paul says, 'If any man be ignorant, let him be ignorant.' This ignorance of pastors often corresponds with the deserts of their people; for though they are deprived of the light of knowledge through their own sins, yet by a terrible judgment their ignorance is made a stumbling-block to their followers. Hence the Truth itself saith in the Gospel, 'If the blind lead the blind, shall they not both fall into the ditch?'

" Others there are who examine the spiritual precepts with care and ability, but who in their lives trample on that doctrine which their understandings have discerned, who hastily teach what they have not learned by practice but by study, and who by their morals contradict what they themselves preach. Whence it may be, that while the shepherd walks through steep places, the flock also follows him to the precipice. For thus does the Lord complain against the ignorance of pastors, saying, 'When ye drank most clear water, ye have fouled the residue with your feet; and my flock eat that which ye have trodden with your feet, and they drink that which ye have fouled with your feet.' For the pastors ' drink most clear water,' when, with a sound understanding, they drink of the streams of truth; but to ' foul with their feet' the same water, is to pollute the studies of holy meditation by a sinful life. Unworthy persons would fly from the burden of such great guilt, if they would but anxiously dwell on that word of truth which saith, 'Whoso shall offend one of these little ones which believe in me, it were better for him that a mill-stone were hanged about his neck, and that he were drowned in the depth of the sea.' "

St. Gregory afterwards reasons with those pious but timid men, who, through a desire of attending without any disturbance to their own salvation, refuse to undertake the office of the ministry, and declare themselves unworthy of it. To those who thus dissemble the truth, he quotes the words of our Lord: " ' A city set on a hill cannot be hid; and no one lighteth a candle, and putteth it under a bushel, but on a candlestick, and it giveth light unto all that are in the house.' Hence he said to Peter, ' Simon son of Jonas, lovest thou me?' who when he had straightway replied that he did love him, heard, ' If thou lovest me, feed my sheep.' If the care of the sheep is a sign of love, that man who abounds in virtue, and yet refuses to feed the flock of God, is found not to love the chief Shepherd. Hence Paul saith, ' If Christ died for all, then were all dead; and if he died for all, it remains that they which live should not henceforth live unto themselves, but unto him which died for them and rose again.' " The following is his description of one who is fit to be a pastor:—" He then is by all means to be made an example of living, who, dead to all the passions of the flesh, already lives in the Spirit; who has set behind him worldly prosperity; who fears no adversity; who desires only what is within; to whose intentions readily responding, neither the body through weakness, nor the mind through scornfulness, is opposed; who desires not the possessions of others, but bestows his own; who through his mercy and kindness is quickly led to forgiveness, yet never by undue forgiveness descends from the citadel of rectitude; who commits no offence himself, but deplores what is done by others, as if it were his own; who out of an affectionate heart has compassion on another's weakness, and rejoices in the good of another as he does in his own progress; who makes himself an example to all in all his actions, so at least that he has never reason to blush for any of them; who studies so to live that he may with streams of doctrine water the dry hearts of his neighbours; who has learned by the use and experience of prayer, to obtain from the Lord his requests; and to whom by an effectual voice it is specially said, 'Whilst thou art speaking, I will say, Behold, here am I.' "

It must be a subject of gratitude to the Christian to know, that during so many ages, even in times when the light of the Gospel was dimmed by the multitude of abuses, still such high models of Christian sanctity were held up before the ministers of Jesus Christ. Happy indeed would it be, if in these days of knowledge we could in any degree approach to the character of that spiritual and practical religion which St. Gregory has so feelingly and so beautifully described.

Much as we have to lament in the conduct of too many professing Christians in those times, there has, perhaps, never been a period in the history of the Church, when the spirit of religion, where it existed, was more ardent and earnest. The religion of these times was less learned, less accomplished, less free from superstition, than that of earlier ages; but it can scarcely be said to have been less zealous, less productive of good works. Its characteristics were, the deepest humility, renouncement of self, denial of the passions, and even the enjoyments and pleasures of the world; the concentration of all wishes and desires in the glory of God, and the promotion of practical religion; boundless charity to the poor; the foundation of churches, schools, and religious houses; diligent study of the Scripture, singing of psalms, and much prayer. We see not merely one or two, but hundreds of men forsaking all their earthly prospects, the resorts of their youth and the paths of ambition, to devote themselves to the conversion of the heathen. We see them desiring and rejoicing to die for Christ; and by their patience, piety, and wisdom, bringing multitudes of heathen into the way of salvation. We see many of the most powerful monarchs engaged in all the exercises of continual devotion and charity, or descending from the summit of earthly grandeur to spend the remainder of their days in penitence and prayer. However sad may have been the calamities of the Church, and however great the faults of Christians, yet when we see such things as these, we cannot refrain from the conviction that the Spirit of God was still influencing the hearts of many people; nor fail to perceive that the Lord was still, according to his promise, always with his Church.

The monasteries of the East and West, though they gradually degenerated from their original purity, still contained many pious and holy men. In some places discipline was more carefully observed than elsewhere; and it seems that in the East there have been always fewer abuses than in the West, arising perhaps in part from the comparative poverty in which the eastern monasteries remained. The monastery of Studium, at Constantinople, was very celebrated in these ages. The sacred Scripture was diligently studied there; all the offices of the Church were performed with great solemnity; and manual labour was enforced. The monks were chiefly supported by the labour of their

own hands, and they willingly undertook those occupations which seemed mean in the eyes of the
world, in order the more effectually to encourage
humility in their own hearts. All sorts of trades
were carried on by these monks. Some were ma-
sons, others carpenters, smiths, weavers, shoemakers,
ropemakers; and whilst they were at work they
chanted psalms and hymns, so that every one who
beheld them was edified by their industry and their
modesty. The fame of the Studite monks soon became widely spread; and many other monasteries
of the same rule were founded in the East, and assumed the same name. In the West, the occupation
of the monks seems to have generally consisted in till-
ing the ground, and in copying and binding books.

BEDA, the most learned and celebrated writer
of the eighth century, lived and died an humble re-
cluse in the monastery of Yarrow in England. All
his life was devoted to the attainment of various
knowledge, diversified only by the monastic exercises of psalmody, prayer, and manual labour. His
earlier years were applied to the acquisition of Latin,
Greek, versification, astronomy, arithmetic, music,
and other sciences, as well as to the study of holy
Scripture, to which last he gave himself more entirely when he was ordained a presbyter. His
works, which consist of commentaries on Scripture,
homilies, lives of saints, an admirable history of the
Church of England from the earliest period, and
other treatises, fill eight folio volumes. Bede was
eminently distinguished for piety, humility, and all
the graces of the Christian character; he was diligent as a preacher, as an instructor of the ignorant,
and as a spiritual adviser of those who sought his
aid. Amongst his friends was a bishop named Eg-
bert, to whom Bede addressed an excellent letter of
advice. "Before all things," he said, "avoid use-

less conversations, and apply yourself to meditate on the holy Scriptures, especially the Epistles of St. Paul to Timothy and Titus, and also on the Pastoral of St. Gregory, and his homilies on the Gospel. As it is not fitting to employ the sacred vessels in profane uses, it is not less unbecoming that he who is consecrated to minister at the altar should, on leaving the church, discourse or act in a manner unbecoming his station." He urged the bishop to establish presbyters in every village to instruct and administer the sacraments, and that they ought to take especial care that all people knew by heart the Creed and Lord's Prayer; and that those who did not understand Latin ought to repeat them in their own language, whether they were laity, clergy, or monks. Bede had already translated them into English, for the use of many ignorant clergy. He also exhorted the bishop to teach the benefits of frequent communion, as practised in Italy, France, Africa, Greece, and the East; for even the most pious persons in England, as he says, only communicated at Christmas, Epiphany, and Easter; though there were infinite multitudes of people who could easily communicate on all Sundays and feast-days, as was the custom at Rome.

Bede died in 735, aged sixty-three. About a fortnight before Easter, he experienced a difficulty of breathing; but he spent the remainder of his time, till Ascension-day, in joy and thanksgiving, instructing his disciples by day, and spending much of his time, even at night, in singing psalms. He frequently repeated parts of Scripture appropriate to his state, some of which he had translated into English verse. He was still engaged in dictating to Cuthbert a translation of St. John's Gospel into English, and was thus employed on Ascension-day, when feeling his end approach, he sent hastily for the presbyters of the monastery, and having presented to them some small memorials of his regard, he bespoke their religious assistance and prayers for him, and then, extended on the pavement of his cell, full of confidence and joy, and singing Gloria Patri, he departed to his eternal reward.

Such virtues were not confined to the cloister in these ages; they sometimes adorned the throne. Luitpraud, king of the Lombards, in the early part of the eighth century, affords an example of this. He was pious, chaste, good, valiant, and wise, though he was ignorant of letters. He applied himself to prayer and almsgiving; caused an oratory to be built in his palace, and established clergy to chant divine service for him every day: he built churches at every place where he resided. Carloman, prince of the Franks, was celebrated for his victories over the Germans, Bavarians, and Saxons. He for a long time protected and encouraged the missionary labours of St. Boniface, and shewed many indications of a religious mind. At length, finding himself a widower, and being penitent for the severities he had formerly exercised on some of his rebellious subjects, he resolved to retire from the world, and to devote himself to the worship of God. He accordingly resigned his throne, and passed the remainder of his days in the monastery founded by St. Benedict at Mount Casino, where he exercised every sort of self-denial, and, like the other brethren, undertook the humble offices of keeping the sheep, labouring in the garden, and even serving in the kitchen.

Religion was deeply indebted to the Emperor Charlemagne. He devoted himself with the greatest zeal to its propagation amongst the heathen nations subject to his dominion; and endeavoured to correct the disorders into which the Churches of France and

Germany had fallen.   His last days, after the coronation of his son Louis, were occupied in correcting the text of the four Evangelists, in which he was assisted by Greeks and Syrians.   Charlemagne had long shewn a great zeal for religion; he never failed, while his health permitted, to attend divine service daily, morning and evening.   He took great care that the service should be conducted with decorum and propriety; supplied his chapels with abundance of vestments and ornaments; and being perfectly instructed in the best manner of reading and singing, he corrected the mode of performing both; but he himself never read publicly in church, but contented himself with singing in a low tone and with others.   His alms were not only liberally bestowed in his own dominions, but on all the poor and distressed Christians in Syria, Egypt, Africa, Jerusalem, Alexandria, and Carthage; and he cultivated the friendship of unbelieving princes, with a view to assuage the sufferings of the Christians under their dominion.   He died A.D. 814.

The Emperor Louis, his son, who died in 840, usually spent the whole time of Lent in singing psalms, prayer, attendance on divine service, distributing alms, and other works of piety; so that he scarcely mounted his horse and took exercise for more than a day or two during the whole time.

But I must now turn to some of the eminent missionaries who adorned the Church in the eighth and ninth centuries.

St. Boniface, or Winfrid, was a native of England, where he embraced the monastic life at an early age, and was ordained presbyter, by desire of his abbot, in 710; after which he devoted himself to the instruction of the people, and laboured for the salvation of souls.   When he was held in most high esteem in his own country, he resolved to forsake all the worldly prospects which were opening on him, and to devote himself to the conversion of the heathen. Accompanied by some monks, he embarked, and passed over into Friesland and Hesse, where, after some time, he converted and baptised many thousands of the people, and founded a monastery. Whilst he was thus occupied, Boniface and his companions were frequently reduced to great difficulty, from the extreme poverty of the people. They were obliged to live by the labour of their own hands, and were exposed to continual danger from the inroads of the pagan Saxons. At length Boniface went to Rome, by desire of Pope Gregory II., who ordained him bishop for the mission among the heathen east of the Rhine. Returning to the scene of his labours, he confirmed those whom he had baptised, and having boldly cut down a tree of immense size, called the oak of Jupiter, which was held in superstitious veneration by the people, he gained a large increase of converts. Boniface felt himself much impeded in the work of preaching the Gospel by the sinful lives and errors of the neighbouring bishops and clergy; and consulted Gregory and other bishops, whether he ought to hold any communion with such men. He corresponded frequently with Daniel, bishop of Winchester, and received from him very judicious advice, as to the best method of arguing with the heathen. Boniface was a diligent student of the Scriptures. In a letter to his friend Daniel, A.D. 726, he says, "I pray you to send me the book of the prophets, which the abbot Winbert, formerly my master, left me when dying, in which six prophets are comprised in the same volume, written in very distinct letters. You cannot send me a greater consolation in my old age;

for I cannot find a book like it in this country ; and my sight being feeble, I cannot easily distinguish small and contracted letters."

The fame of St. Boniface now attracted a great number of religious men from England, who assisted him in his apostolic labours, and converted multitudes of people in Hesse and Thuringia, so that in 732 he was made archbishop (his see being fixed at Mayence), and empowered to constitute bishops to assist him, which he accordingly did in Bavaria, and other parts of Germany.   In 742 he held a council, under the protection of Carloman, prince of the Franks, for the reformation of the Church in the west of France, where there had been no metropolitan for eighty years, no councils had been held, and the sees had been filled either with laymen, or with bishops altogether unworthy of the name.   In this council it was resolved that the metropolitans should in future request the pall from the bishop of Rome. The views of St. Boniface, with regard to the duties of his station, appear in a letter to Cuthbert, archbishop of Canterbury, written about this time, in which, after complaining of the difficulties which beset him, he says, " Let us combat for the Lord ; for we are in days of affliction and anguish.   Let us die, if it be the will of God, for the holy laws of our fathers, that with them we may arrive at an eternal inheritance.   Let us not be dumb dogs, sentinels asleep, or hirelings who flee at the sight of the wolf ; let us be careful and vigilant shepherds, preaching to great and small, to rich and poor, to every age and every condition, as God shall give us power, in season and out of season."

In 752 he crowned Pepin king of France ; and though now full of years, of honours, and of fame, he continued to act as a missionary to the end of his life. We find him in 754 returning from Friesland, where he had been for a long time preaching to the heathen. In the following year, having ordained Lullus to be his successor, and resigned his see to him, as he was about to depart to Friesland, he said to the new archbishop, " The time of my death draws near: complete, my son, the building of the churches I have begun in Thuringia: apply thee earnestly to the conversion of the people: finish the church of Fulda, and bury me there. Prepare all that is necessary for my journey; and place with my books a winding sheet to bury me." At these words, Lullus wept. St. Boniface then exhorted the abbess Lioba, his old friend, whom he had brought from England, and made abbess of Bischofsheim, to remain still in that foreign country, and to observe her profession, looking for an eternal reward; and he commanded that she should be buried in his tomb. He then departed by the Rhine to Friesland, where he converted and baptised thousands of the heathen, overthrew their temples, and raised churches. He was assisted by the Bishop of Utrecht, and many priests, deacons, and monks. He had fixed a day for the confirmation of his converts, and was encamped with his brethren on the banks of a river; when on the day appointed, they were surrounded by a furious band of heathens. The attendants of St. Boniface went forth to oppose them by force; but he called his clergy together, and said to his attendants, " My children, cease to combat; the Scripture instructs us not to render evil for evil. The day which I have long expected is come; put your hope in God, and he shall save your souls." He then exhorted his clergy and companions to prepare themselves courageously for martyrdom, and soon after fell

beneath the swords of the heathen, in the seventy-
fifth year of his age.

GREGORY, a disciple of Boniface, governed the
church newly founded at Utrecht, where he collected, with great trouble and expense, many volumes of the holy Scriptures; and he also preached
to the heathen in Friesland. Two of his brothers
having been murdered by robbers, the murderers
were arrested, and sent bound to him, to suffer
death in whatever manner he should please; for by
the laws of that barbarous people, the nearest relative of a murdered person was invested with this
power.   Gregory ordered them to be washed,
clothed, and fed; then he said to them, " Go in
peace; never again commit such a deed, lest a
worse thing happen to you; and beware of the
other relations of the deceased." Gregory was
simple in his habits; pretended not to hear what
was unkindly said of him; and treated his calumni-
ators as if they were his best friends. Whenever
he received any money, he immediately distributed
it amongst the poor, keeping no valuables whatsoever, except the sacred vessels of the church.
When this holy man felt his end approaching, he
caused himself to be carried into the church, and
there, having made his prayer, and received the
body and blood of our Saviour, he died—his last
look fixed on the altar.

LEBUIN, an Anglo-Saxon, and a disciple of Gregory, preached among the Saxons in Germany; and
on one occasion, hearing that a great assembly of
the nation was to take place, he presented himself
on the day appointed, arrayed in his vestments,
with the Gospel and the cross in his hands. The
assembly commenced by sacrificing to their false
gods; in the midst of which, Lebuin began with a
loud voice to preach the Gospel, and exhorted the

people to turn from those superstitions to the worship of the true God; for that otherwise, he predicted, they would suffer most grievous calamities, and be reduced to captivity by a neighbouring prince. When the Saxons were about to deprive him of life for this boldness, one of them named Buto, who was generally respected, said, " Listen to me, ye that are wise: the ambassadors of the neighbouring people have often come to us, and we have received them peaceably, listened to their proposals, and sent them away with gifts. Here is an ambassador of the great God, who brings to you salutary promises from Him; and you reject, and wish to slay him: ye ought to fear God's anger." This discourse had such an effect on the Saxons, that Lebuin departed in safety, and continued his missionary labours.

Willehad, an Anglo-Saxon presbyter of Northumberland, being seized with an eager desire of preaching the Gospel to the Saxons and Frieslanders, obtained the permission of his sovereign and his bishop, and in 770 went to Friesland, where he fixed his residence for a time at the very place where St. Boniface had been martyred, and was received with joy by the newly converted Christians. Having strengthened them in the faith, he went amongst the heathen, some of whom wished to put him to death for speaking against their false gods; but others, who were more reasonable, said to them, " We see that this man is not guilty of any crime, and we know not whether the religion which he preaches does not come from God. Let us draw lots to see whether we ought to kill him, or to send him away." Happily, the decision was favourable, and Willehad was permitted to escape. Undeterred by these dangers, he went to another place, where he converted and baptised many of the heathen; but some of his disciples began to destroy the idol-temples, which irritated the pagans so much, that they assailed, beat, and nearly killed this zealous missionary. Soon after, the Emperor Charlemagne, having heard of his learning and piety, sent him to preach the Gospel to the Saxons, whom he had lately subdued; and after labouring with great success amongst them for several years, though on one occasion he was compelled by the revolt of Witikind to fly from that country, he was at last appointed the first bishop of Bremen by the emperor in 788. Here he built a cathedral church, and soon after died.

There were several instances in these ages, of martyrdoms for the name of Christ. A remarkable example of this occurs in the history of the ninth century. The chief of the Saracens having taken the town of Amorium in Asia Minor, in 838, sent the principal men and the military officers to Bagdad, where they underwent a long and rigorous imprisonment; and when it was supposed that their patience was exhausted, every possible effort was made to induce them to change their religion. But in vain did the most learned Mahomedan doctors assail their faith with arguments, promises, and threats: all were alike fruitless. At the end of seven years of imprisonment, they were again offered liberty and life, on condition of joining in the Moslem worship. The renegade who made this offer exhorted them to give an external submission, for that God would surely pardon them, on account of the necessity in which they were placed. This insidious advice was rejected. On the following day the Christians were brought forth from their prison; and the caliph's officer, after inquiring their resolution, said, " You will not then pray with the caliph? I know that there are some of you who desire to do so; when the remainder shall see how these are honoured, they will deplore their own evil fate."   The Christians replied with one voice, " We pray the only true God, that not only the caliph, but the whole nation of the Arabs, may renounce the errors of Mahomet, and adore Jesus Christ, who was announced by the prophets and the apostles. So far are we from renouncing light for darkness." " Beware," replied the officer, " of what ye say, lest ye repent it.   Your disobedience will bring grievous torments upon you."   They answered, " We commend our souls to God, and hope that, even to our last breath, he will give us strength not to renounce this faith."   The officer said, " At the day of judgment ye shall be reproved for leaving your children orphans, and your wives widowed.   The wealth of Egypt might enrich your descendants, even to the tenth generation."   The Christians cried, " Anathema to Mahomet, and to all who acknowledge him as a prophet!"   Then their hands were bound behind them, and they were brought to the banks of the river Tigris, where they were all executed, according to their rank.

We have already seen, that the study of Scripture was frequent in these ages.   Lupus, abbot of Ferrieres, in the ninth century, writing to Godeschalchus, a man of a vain and inquisitive turn of mind, speaks thus: " I exhort you, my venerable brother, not to fatigue your mind with such questions, lest in occupying yourself too much therewith, you may be unable to examine or to teach what is more useful.   Why inquire so much into that which it may be unfit for us to know?   Let us exercise ourselves in the vast field of the holy Scriptures; apply ourselves entirely to study them, and unite prayer with study.   It will be worthy of the goodness of God to manifest himself to us in the manner most suitable to us, when we do not inquire into what is above us." The Council of Pavia in 850, in giving instructions with regard to the life and conduct of a bishop, said, " He shall meditate continually on holy Scripture, in order to instruct his clergy accurately, and to preach to the people according to their understanding." The instruction of the people was carried on chiefly by catechising and sermons, which were delivered in the language of each country. Jonas, bishop of Orleans, A.D. 829, in writing on the duties of the laity, recommends to parents and godfathers the instruction of children, and complains that the ancient penitential discipline was much relaxed, and that most of the laity received the eucharist only three times a-year. Several bishops were very active in the discharge of their sacred duties. Thus it is said that WOLF-GANG, bishop of Ratisbon, who died in 994, preached often to his people, who came to hear him with great eagerness. His discourses were simple and intelligible, but strong and touching. He penetrated to the depths of their hearts, and caused floods of tears to flow. When he visited the clergy of his diocese, he carefully instructed them in their duties, and particularly urged them to purity of life.

ST. FIDUS, bishop of Meissen in Germany, who died in 1015, afforded another example of zeal in the performance of his duties. Brought up in a religious community at Magdeburgh, he only accepted the episcopal office that he might win souls to God. His self-denial was very great: he was continually occupied for the remaining twenty-three years of his life in preaching, baptising, confirming, not only in his own, but in many other dioceses. The continual tears, which expressed his penitence and humility, are said to have weakened his sight. He often went with bare feet on his journeys; and when provision failed him, or he found himself suffering some other difficulty or hardship, he returned thanks to God, and desired his companions to do the same.

England produced many religious princes in these ages, the most conspicuous of whom was King ALFRED, whose undaunted courage in adversity, and wisdom in prosperity, justly gained for him the reputation of being the greatest monarch of his age. The piety of his private life was truly remarkable. He divided his revenue into two equal parts, one of which he applied entirely to works of charity, in the proportions of one quarter to the poor generally; another to two monasteries he had founded; a third to the schools he had established; and a fourth to the monasteries in general, not only in England, but abroad. His time was also divided into two equal parts, one of which was given to religion. He attended the celebration of the eucharist every day; joined in divine service seven other times in the course of the day; and even went to the church secretly at night to pray. He devoted time to reading and meditation, and always carried with him the Psalter and Prayer-book, and a sheet of paper, on which he wrote every day the passages of Scripture which touched him the most; then having collected these sheets, he made a manual, which he used to read with singular pleasure. King Alfred found the education of the clergy and people reduced to the lowest ebb when he ascended the throne: this effect had been produced by the dreadful ravages of the Danes, and the almost total destruction of monasteries, which were at that time the only schools of learning. As soon as public tranquillity was restored, Alfred applied himself to the revival of literature and learning; and for this purpose he sent for the most learned men who could be found in the neighbouring countries, and afforded every possible encouragement to the instruction of the clergy and people. At this period there was a celebrated school at Oxford, which seems to have existed for some time, and which was in after-ages known as the University of Oxford. Alfred brought Grimbald and other doctors to Oxford; but a division arose between these new teachers and the ancient doctors, which the king had much difficulty in terminating.

He was more than twelve years old before he learned to read, and had not leisure, for many years, to apply himself to study. When peace was restored, he devoted himself, with the aid of learned men, to translate such books into English as he judged would be most useful to the people: amongst others, the Psalms of David, St. Gregory's Pastoral and Dialogues, the histories of Orosius and Bede, and the Consolations of Boëtius. In the preface to the Pastoral he says, that in his time but few of the English at this side of the Humber understood their commonest prayers, or could translate any Latin writing into English. He did not recollect to have met any one south of the Thames who could do so when he began to reign, though at the time he was writing there were many persons who were able to teach. " I remember," he says, " before these last ravages (of the Danes), I have seen the churches of England full of ornaments and books; but the clergy did not derive much benefit from them, because they did not understand them; and our ancestors did not translate them into the vernacular tongue, because they did not imagine that we should ever fall into such ignorance." He therefore thought it very advisable to translate the most necessary books into English; and that all the English youth, especially the freeborn, should learn to read.

This excellent prince was grievously afflicted with bodily pains all his life; but his piety never failed. He would pardon a heathen any crime that he might have committed, on condition of his becoming a Christian. All the leisure he had from war and business was devoted to study, and to inquiring how he might do good to others, and improve himself in virtue. He died in peace, A.D. 901.

I now turn to an instance of piety in a very different sphere of life. St. Nilus was born in Calabria, of Greek parentage, in the tenth century. His natural abilities were carefully cultivated by study in his youth. He read holy Scripture continually, and delighted in the lives of the fathers: but when he was in the flower of his youth he fell into sins, from which he was after a time delivered by the grace of God operating on his conscience during his recovery from a violent fever. He then resolved to devote himself wholly to the worship and service of God, and to all the exercises of a religious life; and with this mind he entered a monastery in Calabria, where he was joyfully received; but wishing for more quiet than he found there, he retired to a cavern near at hand, where he spent his days between prayer, copying psalters and other religious books, singing the psalms, and studying holy Scripture and the fathers. In the evening he left his cell to walk abroad and refresh himself, and meditate on some passages of the fathers, without ever forgetting God, whom he contemplated in all the works of creation. After sunset he took his frugal meal, and in the night he slept but for a short time, and then recited the psalms till daylight. His fasts were frequent and long.

One of the brethren having obtained his permission to live along with him, said to him, "My father, I have three pieces of silver; what wilt thou

that I should do with them?"   Nilus replied, "Give
them to the poor, and keep only your psalter."   He
did so; but some time after, being wearied of such
a life, he sought to quarrel with Nilus, and demanded the money which he had given to the poor.
"My brother," said the holy man, "write on a
piece of paper that I shall receive the reward of it
in heaven, and place it on the altar."   Then he departed, borrowed the money, which he gave to the
man, and in twelve days copied three psalters, with
which he paid his debt.   Nilus afterwards refused
to be made abbot of the neighbouring convent.
One of the principal inhabitants of that part of the
country having resolved to live a religious life, and
desiring to place himself under his direction, and
imitate his mode of living, Nilus dissuaded him from
it, saying, "My brother, it is not for our virtue that
we live in this desert, but it is because we cannot
bear the rule of common life, that we have separated
ourselves from men, like lepers.   You do well to
seek your salvation.   Go to some community where
you will find repose of body and mind."

As the Saracens were making many inroads into
that country, Nilus departed to another place, where
several disciples joined him, and a monastery was
formed.   Some brethren in the neighbourhood
spoke evil of him as a hypocrite and imposter, but
he returned it only by giving them blessings and
praise; and one day, when they had extremely mal-
treated him, he came to them as they were eating,
placed himself on his knees, and asked their pardon.
By this conduct he entirely subdued them, and
gained their friendship.   He would not allow any
member of his community to possess any thing but
what was barely necessary, saying that any thing
more was avarice.   When the society increased, he
would never assume the title of abbot or hegumenus.

One day, the metropolitan of Calabria, accompanied by several great men, magistrates, clergy, and a number of people, came to visit him out of curiosity. He caused one of them to read part of a book in which it was written, " that of ten thousand souls, scarcely one at the present time departs into the angel's hands." Many began to say, " God forbid : this is heresy. Where then is the use of baptism, adoring the cross of Christ, receiving the communion, and bearing the name of Christians ?" Nilus replied, " What if I shew you that the fathers, St. Paul, and the Gospel, say the same thing? God is under no obligation to you for what you speak of. You would not dare to profess any heresy : the people would stone you. But know ye, that if ye be not virtuous, yea, exceedingly virtuous, ye shall not escape eternal punishment." Being asked of what tree Adam eat in Paradise, he said, " How should we speak of what Scripture has not revealed to us? Instead of thinking how ye were created; how ye were placed in Paradise; of the commandments ye have received, and have not kept ; of what has driven you from Paradise, and how ye may enter it again; instead of all this, ye inquire the name of a tree !" Many great officers offered him large sums of money for the benefit of his community ; but he said to them, " My brethren will be happy, according to the psalm, if they live of the labour of their hands ; and the poor will cry against you for retaining their goods."

When the Archbishop of Rossano died, the magistrates and principal clergy came to seek for St. Nilus, to offer him the see; but, having heard of their intentions, he retired into the recesses of the mountains, and could not be found; so that they were obliged to elect another person to that see. The incursions of the Saracens at length became so frequent, that Nilus was obliged to take refuge at the monastery of Mount Casino, which St. Benedict had founded. On his way thither, he passed through Capua, and his fame was so great, that he was offered the bishopric of that city. Nilus lived near Mount Casino for fifteen years with his community. In 997, when very aged, he went to Rome to beseech the emperor and the pope to have mercy on the anti-pope Philagathus, whom he had known formerly. The emperor and Pope Gregory having heard of his arrival, went to meet him, and each taking him by a hand, led him to the patriarchal palace, and seated him between them, each kissing his hand. The old man groaned at receiving these honours; yet he endured them, in the hope of obtaining what he desired. He then said to them, " Spare me, for the sake of God. I am the greatest sinner of all men; an old man, half dead, and unworthy of these honours: it is rather my part to prostrate myself before you, and to honour your supreme dignities."

Finding at length that his community at Valdeluce had become seriously relaxed in discipline by the wealth, numbers, and renown, which his sanctity had given to it, he departed and went to a place near Gaëta. " The monks of these times," he said, " do not employ their leisure in prayer, meditation, and reading of Scripture, but in vain discourse, evil thoughts, and useless curiosity. These and many other evils are removed by labour, which distracts the attention from them; and there is nothing equal to eating our bread in the sweat of our countenance."

The princess of Gaëta came to visit him, out of reverence for his piety, and he discoursed to her on purity, almsgiving, and the fear of God. It was always unpleasant to him to meet the great: he

avoided it carefully, as a source of vanity and
danger, and had no intercourse with them even by
letter, except to assist them in their necessities and
their misfortunes. Nilus died soon after, in 1002,
aged ninety-five.

CHAPTER XIV.

ON THE ABUSES AND SUPERSTITIONS OF THIS PERIOD.

A.D. 680-1054.

THE ignorance caused by the disorgan-
ised condition of society during these
ages could not fail to produce many
irregularities, abuses, and superstitions.
I have already alluded to the mischiefs
resulting from the use of images, which were of the
most afflicting character. In many places the superstitious honour which was paid to them approached
the verge of idolatry, and was even sometimes absolutely idolatrous. Such evils chiefly existed in the
East; for the western Churches still rejected the
veneration of images. The honours paid to the remains of the saints also became excessive. What
had arisen from love and a just admiration of their
virtues degenerated into superstition. The relics
of saints were carried with great magnificence from
their original burial-places to churches founded to
their honour. Enthusiasm fancied that their touch
wrought miracles; and as their possession attracted
crowds of pilgrims and great benefactions, it became
the interest of covetous and ambitious monks and
priests to obtain as many relics as possible for their
churches, and to ascribe numerous miracles to those

of which they were possessed. Hence arose a variety
of artifices irreconcilable with honesty and religion;
fictitious relics, the acquisition of relics by strata-
gem and theft, false and exaggerated legends of
saints, which were read on their feast-days. Too
many instances of such unchristian conduct are to be
found in the history of these days; but, at the same
time, it would be unjust to attribute them to all the
Church. Without doubt there were still many who
could not approve of conduct so irreconcilable with
Christian wisdom and morality. The invocation of
saints was also frequent, though we do not find that
direct prayers were, as yet, addressed to them, or
their aid sought, except with a desire for their prayers
to God. The litanies of the western Churches began
to include such invocations; but they did not find
their way into the usual services of the Church.
We have seen, in the last chapter, the lamentable
want of information on religion which existed in
some countries, where the Scriptures and the offices
of religion were unintelligible even to the clergy.
It was a mistaken reverence for antiquity which
led Augustine and Boniface to employ the ancient
Latin liturgies in the Churches which they founded
amongst the heathen. They had not calculated that
the knowledge of that language would be so limited,
or that the people would be so badly instructed.
Succeeding generations wanted ability or courage to
correct a mistake sanctioned by such respectable
authority. Still some means of instruction existed,
though these were not universally found. Such
were, the sermons of the bishops and presbyters;
the exhortations of the monks; the discipline of
penance, which still continued, though much impaired; the system of catechising the young; and
the instruction which was conveyed by parents and
godfathers, who were also reminded of their duties.

And if, as we have reason to believe, a large portion of the community were accustomed to receive the holy eucharist three times a-year, we may trust that the state of religion was in those ages not so bad as it has been sometimes represented; and the present age, with all its advantages of civilisation, peace, and education, would perhaps scarcely be able to prove its greater attention to known duties, or its more conscientious obedience to the impulse of conscience. As time advanced, indeed, we see the words of our Lord verified. The tares began to grow thickly in the field of the Church, and the wheat was oppressed by their multitude. The pure gold of the early times, tried seven times in the fire, was now mingled with the alloy of this earth; and the human heart betrayed daily its tendency to fall away from the service of its Creator. The very chosen resorts of religious zeal and self-denying piety exemplified most lamentably this tendency to decay. The way of life in which an Antony and a Benedict had shewn such eminent virtues was now filled with lukewarm professors. The simple piety, the poverty, and the industry of St. Benedict's rule, gradually gave way before the influence of too ample endowments. Abuses of all kinds arose. The cupidity of barbarians was attracted by the wealth of monasteries and the splendour of their ornaments. Powerful barons usurped their territories or intruded into their precincts, spreading disorder and licentiousness amongst those former seats of religion and learning. When Odo, about 920, was desirous to devote himself to the monastic life, he went himself or sent messengers to all the celebrated monasteries of France; but he could not find a single house in which sufficient regularity and order were observed. He then founded the monastery and order of Clugny, in which the strictness of ancient discipline was re-

vived. Indeed, the observance of St. Benedict's
rule had, even in the preceding century, become so
much relaxed, that Benedict of Anianum was employed to *reform* a number of monasteries in France
and Italy.

The vast possessions which were bestowed on
the Church by the sovereigns of the West, and which
were held by feudal tenure, obliged bishops and abbots to attend the courts of princes, to absent themselves from their dioceses, and to mingle in scenes of
war and civil commotion, which were little consistent
with their sacred characters. Hence too arose that
mutual interference of Church and State, of which
these ages furnished several examples. Princes seized
on the temporalities of churches, kept them vacant
to enjoy their revenues, or insisted on the appointment of bishops who were altogether unworthy. On
the other hand, the bishops began to assume temporal authority. The council of Toledo, in 681,
deposed Wamba, king of the Visigoths, because, as
they pretended, he had taken the monastic habit.
The emperor Louis le Débonnaire was deposed, and
restored again by councils of bishops. When the
patriarchs of Rome had obtained from Pepin, Charlemagne, and their successors, considerable grants
of territory in Italy, those powerful prelates assumed
a still loftier tone of authority, and began to inter-
fere in the disputes and other affairs of princes. Thus
Adrian II. forbade the emperor Charles the Bald to
possess himself of the dominions of king Lothaire
under pain of excommunication, but in this he was
resisted by the bishops of France; and when Gregory IV., about 830, had taken part with Lothaire
against his father the emperor Louis, and threatened
to excommunicate the latter, the bishops of France
informed that prelate, that if he came to excommunicate the emperor, he should return home ex-

communicated himself; and they even threatened to depose him from his see. It is plain that these bishops had no idea of its being necessary to be at all times in the communion of the bishop of Rome.

The extreme abuses which had arisen in the Churches of France during the ages preceding the time of Charlemagne were vigorously assailed by that illustrious prince. The capitularies or codes of ecclesiastical law of Charlemagne and his successors consisted chiefly of selections from the ancient canons, suited to the condition of the Church at that time: and they were collected and enforced in those large councils of the bishops and peers of his kingdom, which in after-ages assumed the name of parliaments. Most of the synods or councils of the western Church, during this period, were of this mixed character, and decided equally on temporal and spiritual affairs. Such a system was not without serious inconveniences, and could not by any means be recommended as the best model for imitation in other times. The presence of a large body of turbulent barons in the synods of the Church could not contribute much to the peace of their proceedings, or to the enforcement of ecclesiastical discipline. This system, however, was gradually put an end to by the usurpations of the see of Rome, which at the close of this period began to arrogate the power of legislating for all the Church.

A great evil in these times was the facility with which excommunications were denounced. A sentence, which ought only to be passed on those who have been guilty of most serious offences against God or their brethren, was used on many trifling and unworthy occasions; and hence we need not wonder at the complaints frequently made in those times, that excommunication was disregarded.

The power of the Roman see in the western

Church was greatly augmented in the ninth century, by the fabrication of a large body of decretal epistles or ecclesiastical laws, which purported to have been written by the popes during the first three centuries, and in which the judgment of all bishops, the holding of all councils, and a right to hear appeals from all ecclesiastical judgments, were claimed for the Roman pontiffs. These epistles, which had been forged in the preceding century, and which are now acknowledged by the most learned Romanists to be mere fabrications, exaggerated to the highest degree the powers and privileges of the popes ; and the ignorance of the ninth century prevented any discovery of their falsehood. The bishops of Rome asserted their genuineness, and carried their principles into practice; though the bishops, especially those of France, offered much opposition. Thus the liberties of Churches were gradually invaded, while their discipline was injured by the obstacles thrown in the way of assembling synods and condemning offenders, and by the facility of appeals to a foreign and too favourable tribunal.

The growing influence of the Roman see in the western Churches is shewn by the gradual adoption of the liturgy of that Church. Originally one liturgy was used in Rome, another at Milan, another in Spain, another in Gaul, and another in Britain and Ireland. It seems that the Spanish, Gallican, and British liturgies were all derived from the same parent-stock; and there are reasons for supposing that they owed their origin to the apostle John, or the Asiatic Churches. The African Churches had also peculiar rites of their own. Thus it appears that for six centuries at least the Roman liturgy was not used out of Italy. But Augustine and Boniface carried that liturgy into England and Germany in the seventh and eighth centuries; and in the ninth, Pepin and Charlemagne, to gratify the bishops of Rome, obliged the clergy of France to adopt it; while in Spain, the ancient Mosarabic liturgy was abolished at the end of the eleventh century by the princes of that country, assisted by the papal legates, and the Roman was received in its stead. Milan alone, in all the West, was able to maintain its ancient rites against those of the dominant Church of Rome. It thus appears that the unity of worship and liturgy which Romanists so often boast of, was altogether unknown in the earlier and purer ages of the Church.

The bishops of Rome gradually acquired power over the metropolitans of the West by conferring on them the pall, which was an ornament originally given to the patriarchs by the Roman emperors, and which from the sixth century the patriarchs of Rome bestowed on those bishops whom they constituted their vicars. This honour became an object of extreme desire to the western metropolitans and bishops; and from the middle of the eighth century, the metropolitans generally began to receive it. But they were obliged to solicit it earnestly, and at length to go to Rome for the purpose; and, in fine, about the end of the eleventh century, it was represented by the popes as essential to the discharge of the duties of metropolitans; and this point being gained, the metropolitans were at last compelled to take oaths of obedience to the pope, before they could obtain their palls.

CHAPTER XV.

ON THE DIVISIONS OF THE EASTERN AND WESTERN CHURCHES.

A.D. 680-1054.

URING the period now before us the rival Churches of Rome and Constantinople had several disputes.   When the controversy about images broke out in the eighth century, Gregory II. and Gregory III. of Rome excommunicated the emperors of the East, and forbade the payment of tribute to them, in consequence of their opposition to images.   The emperors in return confiscated the possessions of the Roman see in their dominions, and withdrawing the various Churches of Illyricum, Macedonia, Greece, as well as those of Sicily, Apulia, and Calabria, from the jurisdiction of Rome, subjected them to the see of Constantinople.   The three former provinces had been under the see of Rome for about 350 years; the latter for a much longer time: however, the eastern Church offered no objection to this arrangement, nor was communion interrupted between the East and West on this account, though the bishops of Rome made frequent efforts to obtain a restoration of their authority. Their requests were fruitless, as long as they were addressed to the eastern emperors or Churches; but when the Normans subdued Sicily and Naples, in the eleventh century, those provinces, after an interval of three centuries, again became subject to the Roman jurisdiction.   During the disputes on image-worship, the Roman see was for some time separated from the communion of the Church of

Constantinople; but it does not appear that the western Church generally regarded either party as heretical, or refused communion with them.

In the ninth century a dispute arose between the bishops of Rome and Constantinople about the province of Bulgaria, which each claimed. This was heightened by the controversy in the case of Photius, who had been made patriarch of Constantinople when Ignatius, the last patriarch, was expelled from his see by the emperor, and deposed by a synod of 318 bishops, by whom Photius was acknowledged patriarch. The Roman see took part with Ignatius, and deposed Photius, who retaliated by deposing the bishop of Rome : but after a time he was expelled, and Ignatius restored by another emperor. The majority of the eastern Church, however, adhered to Photius; and on the death of his rival Ignatius, he was again placed in his see by a synod of 383 bishops, in 879, with the approbation of pope John VIII. The latter consented to his restoration, on condition that Bulgaria should be transferred to the Roman jurisdiction; but this transfer was opposed by Photius and his successors; and though he became, in consequence, very obnoxious to the popes, who withdrew their communion from him, the communion of the universal Church was not seriously affected, and the two rival Churches afterwards remained in communion till 1054.

In this year, however, a division began between the eastern and western Churches, which has never yet been entirely healed. For when Cerularius, bishop of Constantinople, wrote to the bishop of Trani, in Italy, condemning several of the rites and ceremonies of the Roman Church, and shut up the Latin churches and monasteries of Constantinople, the legate of the Roman see, Cardinal Humbert, insisted on his implicit submission to the pope; and, on his refusal, left an excommunication on the altar of his patriarchal church of St. Sophia at Constantinople. And as the eastern Churches adhered to Cerularius, and the western to the Roman see, they gradually became estranged from each other, though for many ages some communion still existed between them.

I have thus endeavoured to trace briefly the principal features in ecclesiastical history from the beginning to the division of the eastern and western Churches, and to shew that in every age the Church of God still existed, notwithstanding all the temptations of the devil, the world, and the flesh. It will next be my endeavour to carry on the same plan from the division of the East and West to the Reformation.

CHAPTER XVI.

ON THE PROGRESS OF CHRISTIANITY.

A.D. 1054-1517.

THE period under consideration is chiefly remarkable as exhibiting the progress of the division between the eastern and western Churches, and the rise and increase of the prodigious spiritual and temporal power of the popes. It was the unreasonable claims of this power which separated the eastern from the western Church, and which still continues to be the great obstacle to their re-union. The spirit of worldliness, of craft, cruelty, and avarice, which so often disgraced professing Christians, and even ministers of Christ, in these ages, was but too faithfully copied from the example of the pretended heads of the universal Church; while the ancient laws and liberties of churches, the rights of kings, and the sound discipline of the Church, were without scruple invaded and subverted by these imperious pontiffs. But we should remember that the visible Church was now becoming co-extensive with the world, and therefore that "it was impossible but that offences should come." The good seed was now mingled thickly with tares, and the love of many waxed faint: but still there was a remnant left; still the Church, however afflicted, might point to new evangelists and saints, and behold the verification of our Saviour's promises.

The great work of evangelising the heathen was continually proceeding, and the zeal and piety of the early missionaries were occasionally revived. In 1124, Boleslaus, duke of Poland, having subjugated the duchy of Pomerania, and wishing to introduce Christianity into that country, invited St. Otto, bishop of Bamberg, to preach the Gospel there, informing him that the people had consented to be baptised, and that he should be aided and assisted in every way by the sovereign power. St. Otto having learnt that the Pomeranians were wealthy and despised poverty, went into that country with a considerable train, and with every thing that could convince the natives that he came not to derive any pecuniary advantage, but solely to win their souls. At the town of Pirits, where they first proceeded, about four thousand men were assembled from all parts to keep the feast of one of their idols. The principal inhabitants of the place were informed by one of the duke's officers of the approach of the bishop, and of the commands of their sovereign that he should be received and heard with respect. The officer added, "that this prelate was a great and wealthy man in his own country; that he sought none of their goods, but only their salvation; that they ought to remember their promise to become Christians, and the sufferings they had experienced in war, and not to provoke again the anger of God." After some demur, the pagans, finding that St. Otto was close at hand, agreed to hear him; and the bishop then came with all his company and encamped outside the town, where the barbarians ran in great numbers to behold and assist them. St. Otto then ascended an elevated place, adorned with all his episcopal vestments, and by means of an interpreter addressed the people, who were very eager to hear him.

"May ye be blessed of God," he said, " for the good reception you have given to us. You already know, perhaps, the cause which has brought us so far. It is your salvation and your happiness; for you will be happy for ever, if you will acknowledge your Creator and serve him." While he thus simply exhorted the people, they all declared that they would receive his instructions. He spent seven days in instructing them carefully, with the assistance of his priests and clergy. Then he ordered them to fast three days, to bathe themselves, and clothe themselves with white garments, to be ready for baptism. He then prepared three baptisteries, for the men, women, and children, respectively. These baptisteries were great wooden vessels sunk in the earth and filled with water. They were surrounded by curtains, and at the part of each where the priest stood, was another curtain. When any one was to be baptised, he came accompanied by his godfather, to whom, on entering the baptistery, he gave his garment, and who held it before his face until the ceremony was concluded. The priest, as soon as he observed any one in the water, drew aside the curtain a little, and baptised him, immersing his head three times in the water. He then anointed him with chrism, gave him a white garment, and dismissed him. The godfather received him, covered him with his garment, and led him away. In winter, baptism was administered with warm water, in places well heated.

Otto and his companions remained three weeks at Pirits, instructing the converts in the duties of religion, the observance of Sundays and holydays; exhorting them to attend the celebration of the eucharist, and to communicate at least three or four times in the year. He explained to them the sacraments, desired that their children should be brought for baptism at Easter and Whitsuntide, exhorted them to give some of their children to be educated as clergy, and left them a priest to administer the sacraments, whom the people, to the number of seven thousand, received with the greatest joy and devotion.

In the next town he remained six weeks, and baptised so great a multitude, that his alb was often wet with perspiration even to the waist. At another town he was less fortunate. The Pagans fell with fury on him and his attendants. St. Otto was with difficulty saved, after having received many blows and fallen in the mud. At Stettin, the people declared at first that they were satisfied with their old religion, and refused to become Christians; but they afterwards gave hopes that if the duke would remit certain taxes, they might be induced to adopt Christianity. While the negotiation was going on, the bishop and priests, arrayed in their vestments and bearing a cross, preached twice a-week in the market-place, that is, on market-days. The novelty attracted many hearers, and several were converted. On the return of their messengers with a favourable answer from the duke, the inhabitants resolved to receive the Gospel. Otto exhorted them to destroy their idols; but as they feared to do so, he himself led the way with his clergy, and struck the idols down, when the people, seeing that their gods could not avenge themselves, completed the work of destruction. Thus he went throughout Pomerania, converting multitudes of the people, and at length returned to Bamberg, after a year's absence. In a few years he again visited Pomerania, many of the people having relapsed into paganism; but as he approached Stettin, the clergy who accompanied him, dreading the barbarity of the people, remonstrated with him, and endeavoured to dissuade him from his journey. He said to them, "I would fain exhort you to martyrdom, but I shall not constrain any one. If you will not aid me, at least do not hinder me; but leave to me the same liberty which I do to you." Thus saying, he shut himself up in his chamber, and remained in prayer till the evening. But in the night he placed on his shoulders a bag containing his vestments and the vessels of the altar, and privately left the place, taking the road to Stettin, and chanting the nocturnal service as he went. Early in the morning, the clergy found him, after an anxious search, as he was entering a boat; and casting themselves at his feet, with many tears, promised that they would follow him even to death. St. Otto succeeded in recovering the people from their apostacy, and after many labours and dangers returned at last to Bamberg.

In 1168, the natives of the isle of Rugen, in the Baltic, were converted to Christianity; the capital of that island having been surrendered to Waldemar, king of Denmark, on condition that the idol Suantovit, and all his treasure, should be delivered to the king, and that the people should embrace the Christian religion. Suantovit, whom these barbarians regarded as their principal deity, was originally the martyr St. Vitus. The monks of Corby, in Saxony, had formerly introduced Christianity into this island, and they had dwelt so much on the merits and miracles of this saint (whose relics were preserved at Corby), that the people, after their departure, fell into most dreadful idolatry, forgot the true God, and placed the martyr St. Vitus, whom they called Suantovit, in his stead, and made an idol of the saint with four heads, to which the people offered human sacrifices; and the idol-priest had greater wealth and authority than the king. Such are the dangers which arise from the excessive honours paid to saints and images. The idol was dragged into the Danish camp, where it was split to pieces, and the wood was employed in the camp-kitchens. The idol-temple was burnt, churches were built, and the people converted and baptised by the bishops of Roschild and Mecklenberg, who accompanied the king of Denmark.

The Sclavonians who inhabited the borders of the Baltic sea were, in a great measure, converted by the pious and judicious zeal of Vicelinus, bishop of Oldenberg. He devoted thirty years of his life to the glorious work of an evangelist among the northern nations, and few names in these ages deserve more reverence.

About the same time, the Armenians, who had been for a long time involved in the Eutychian heresy, condemned by the fourth œcumenical synod, were reunited for a time to the communion of the patriarch of Constantinople. In the following century they also received for a short time the dominion of the bishop of Rome.

The conversion of the Maronites, a small nation of Mount Lebanon, in Syria, took place about 1182. They had been involved in the Monothelite heresy since the seventh century; but now, finding themselves surrounded by the various principalities established by the Latins in the time of the crusades, they embraced the faith, discipline, and obedience of the pope. About this time, the Gospel was introduced into Livonia, a country on the Baltic, by Meinard, canon of Sigeburg, who made several voyages there with the merchants, and gained many converts. Finding his work prosperous, he applied to the archbishop of Bremen for additional authority, and was ordained bishop, when he fixed his see at Riga, and converted great numbers of the heathen. Berno, bishop of Suerin, who died in 1195, had also baptised many of the Sclavonians, abolished their idols, and cut down their groves.

In 1210, some Cistertian monks preached the Gospel in Prussia; and some years afterwards, the pagans of that country having most dreadfully persecuted the Christian converts, they were subdued by Crusaders, and by the powerful order of Teutonic knights, and gradually converted to Christianity. In this century also, the Mohammedans were deprived of their dominion in the greater part of Spain, and Christianity was re-established in that country. They had already been despoiled of Sicily by the Normans. In 1230, the king and people of Courland, on the Baltic sea, made a treaty with the Roman legate in Germany, by which they undertook to receive the Gospel. The Franciscan and Dominican friars, in the latter part of this century, preached in Tartary with considerable success. They were sent by Nicholas IV. with letters to the emperor of Tartary, and to the Nestorians; and they succeeded in erecting several Christian churches in China, which was then under the dominion of the Tartars. One of these pious missionaries, named John à Monte Corvino, translated the Psalms and the New Testament into the Tartar language. In 1307, 1311, and 1338, Clement V. and Benedict XII. sent several bishops into Tartary and China; but after that period, their missions seem to have fallen into decay. The last country in Europe which received the Christian religion was Lithuania. Jagello, duke of Lithuania, was still a pagan, when on the death of Louis, king of Poland, he was named amongst the candidates for the vacant throne; but his infidelity was an invincible obstacle to the attainment of his wishes. It is to be hoped that his conversion was sincere, as he persuaded all his subjects to embrace Christianity, at the same time that he himself did, in 1386.

The conquests of the Portuguese in Africa and India led to the spread of Christianity in those countries. The sovereigns of that nation felt themselves bound to use all their influence for the propagation of the Gospel in their dominions; and the first result was the conversion of the king and people of Congo in Africa, in 1491. The subsequent settlement of the Portuguese in India was distinguished by similar blessings. The conquest of South America and of the West Indies, by the Spaniards, was also made the means of disseminating the Christian faith through those wide regions, though we cannot but deplore the cruelties which were practised in the subjugation of the unfortunate inhabitants of those countries.

CHAPTER XVII.

ON THE FAITH OF THE CHURCH.

A.D. 1054-1517.

THE belief of the eastern and western branches of the universal Church remained the same in all articles of faith, during the period now before us, as it had been before the division. The Nicene creed was universally received as the rule of faith. The six holy œcumenical synods were still regarded with the greatest veneration; but the decrees of the Nicene synod in favour of images, which pretended to be the seventh œcumenical synod, were only approved by the eastern and by a portion of the western Churches. The principal point of doctrinal difference between the East and West, was the procession of the Holy Spirit; for the former asserted, that the Holy Spirit proceeds from the Father only, while the latter believed that He also proceeds from the Son. However, as the former allowed that the Holy Ghost proceeds from the Father *by* the Son, the difference did not seem irreconcilable. The doctrine of purgatory, which was held by the popes, and a large party in the West, as an article of faith, was another point of dissension between them and the Greek Church, by which this doctrine was constantly denied. With the exception of these points, there was no difference in matters of faith between the East and West. The doctrines of the Trinity, incarnation, divinity of our Lord, the atonement, original sin, and the need of divine grace; the obligation of good works, of repentance, prayer, fasting, alms-giving, charity, and all other Christian acts and habits, were universally maintained. The faith of the western Church is shewn by its condemnation of various heretics, such as Peter de Bruis and Arnold of Brescia, who, in the twelfth century, denied infant baptism, and destroyed churches. The Albigenses, who held Manichæan heresies, and were a branch of the Paulicians already mentioned, were condemned in several councils, especially the great Lateran synod, in 1216, which, in opposition to their errors, made a definition of faith in the Triune God, the only Principle and Author of all things; the authority of the Old Testament; our Lord's incarnation, suffering, bodily ascension into heaven; the resurrection of the body at the last day; the importance of the eucharist, and the real presence of Christ's body and blood; the necessity of baptism, and lawfulness of marriage. The Manichæans denied all this: and the decree furnishes a clear proof that the western Church always maintained its ancient faith.

This celebrated decree was as follows: " We firmly believe and sincerely confess that there is but one true God, Eternal, Infinite, Almighty, Unchangeable, Incomprehensible, and Ineffable, the Father, the Son, and the Holy Ghost, three persons, but one essence, substance, or nature, altogether uncompounded. The Father is derived from none, the Son is of the Father only, the Holy Ghost is from both alike, without beginning and without end. The Father begetting, the Son being born, the Holy Ghost proceeding, of the same substance, co-equal, alike Almighty and Eternal, one principle of all things, Creator of all things visible and invisible, spiritual and bodily; Who, by his own almighty power, created from the beginning of time, out of nothing, both the spiritual and the corporeal, the angelic and the earthly creatures, and then the human creature as composed both of spirit and body. But Satan and the other devils were created naturally good by God, but became evil of themselves; and man sinned by the instigation of the devil.

"This holy Trinity, which is undivided as regards its common essence, but distinguished as regards its personal qualities, bestowed saving doctrine on the human race through Moses and the holy prophets and others, according to a most settled order of time; and at length the only-begotten Son of God, Jesus Christ, being made flesh by the whole Trinity in common, conceived of Mary, ever-virgin, by the co-operation of the Holy Spirit, and made true man, composed of a reasonable soul and human flesh, one person in two natures, shewed to us more plainly the way of life; Who, though he was immortal and incapable of suffering according to his divine nature, yet according to his human nature was mortal and liable to suffering; and having suffered and died on the wood of the cross for the salvation of the human race, he descended into hell, rose from the dead, and ascended into heaven. He descended in soul, rose again in body, and ascended with both alike, and shall come again at the end of the world to judge the living and the dead, and to render to every one according to his works, as well the reprobate as the elect; who shall all rise with their bodies which they now bear, to receive every one according to what he deserves, whether it be good or evil, the one perpetual punishment with the devil, the other eternal glory with Christ.

"And there is one universal Church of the believing, out of which no one is saved, in which the same Jesus Christ himself is both priest and sacrifice; whose body and blood are really contained in the sacrament of the altar, under the form of bread and wine, the bread being changed* into his body, and the wine into his blood by divine power, that, in order to perfect the mystery of union, we may receive of his what he received of ours. And no one can consecrate this sacrament, except a priest who has been lawfully ordained according to the keys of the Church, which Jesus Christ himself gave to the apostles and to their successors.

"The sacrament of baptism, which, in the name of the undivided Trinity, that is, the Father, the Son, and the Holy Ghost, is consecrated in water, when conferred on infants and adults by any one rightly and according to the form of the Church, avails to their salvation. And if any one, after having received baptism, fall into sin, he may always be restored by true repentance. And not only virgins and the unmarried, but those who are married, pleasing God through right faith and good works, deserve to attain everlasting happiness."

If we compare this confession with that which S. Irenæus made in the name of the whole Church in the second century, we shall find that the same great truths had substantially continued to prevail

---

* The word here translated "changed" is in the original *transubstantiatis*, whence arose the common use of the word "transubstantiation;" and as many persons supposed that by this was meant such a change of the elements as made them cease to be bread and wine, that doctrine was by them considered to be an article of faith approved by the Church; whereas there is every probability that the decree did not mean to determine any such doctrine, but merely to condemn the Albigenses, who denied that the body of Christ was received in the holy eucharist.

during the course of more than a thousand years in the Christian Church.

During the period now under consideration, all the most eminent and learned theologians of the western Church continued to believe that man cannot merit salvation by his own works, but that he must place his whole trust and confidence in the mercy of God, and the atonement, merits, and intercession of our Lord Jesus Christ. It has been shewn by a learned writer (Archbishop Usher*), that this truly Christian doctrine was included amongst the instructions and consolations which were prescribed for the use of persons ready to depart from this life. Amongst other questions which were to be put to the sick man, were the following: " Dost thou believe to come to glory, not by thine own merits, but by the virtue and merit of the passion of our Lord Jesus Christ?" and, " Dost thou believe that our Lord Jesus Christ did die for our salvation, and that none can be saved by his own merits, or by any other means but by the merit of his passion?"   In other copies of the same office for visiting the sick, the last question is this: " Dost thou believe that thou canst not be saved but by the death of Christ?"   And when the sick person has replied in the affirmative, he is exhorted in these words: " Come, therefore, while thy soul remaineth in thee, place thy whole confidence in this death alone; have confidence in no other thing; commit thyself wholly to this death; with this alone cover thyself wholly; mingle thyself entirely in it, fasten thyself in it, wrap thyself wholly in it.   And if the Lord will judge thee, say, Lord, I oppose the death of our Lord Jesus Christ betwixt me and thy judgment; no otherwise do I contend with thee.   And

* Answer to a Jesuit, ch. xii.

if he say unto thee, that thou art a sinner, say, Lord, I put the death of the Lord Jesus Christ betwixt thee and my sins. If he say unto thee, that thou hast deserved damnation, say, Lord, I set the death of our Lord Jesus Christ betwixt me and my bad merits, and I offer his merit instead of the merit which I ought to have, but yet have not. If he say, that he is angry with thee, say, Lord, I interpose the death of our Lord Jesus Christ betwixt me and thine anger."

Such was the belief and such the practice of the Latin Churches, in ages when great corruptions had undoubtedly become prevalent; and surely it is impossible to trace such sentiments, without a feeling of gratitude to that GOD, who, in spite of so many scandals, so much ignorance, and such heavy sins, still continued to fulfil his gracious promises, and to preserve always in his Church those vital truths, which constitute the only solid foundation for a Christian's hope of salvation. It would be easy to trace the same doctrine in the writings of St. Bernard, St. Anselm, Petrus Blesensis, and many of the most eminent scholastic writers of the middle ages. But at length some ignorant and wicked men maintained that our " good works are properly *meritorious*, and the very *cause* of salvation; so far that God would be *unjust*, if he rendered not heaven for the same." These arrogant sentiments were held by some of the Romish controversialists in the sixteenth century; but they had been for some time before slowly working their way in the Church.

The following extract from the writings of the celebrated Gerson, chancellor of the university of Paris in the fifteenth century, and a zealous defender of the liberties of the Church of France, will afford a specimen of the moral and spiritual system of instruction in those ages:—

"'Come unto me, all ye that labour and are heavy-laden, and I will give you rest.' It is well for us, most beloved brethren, to proclaim this with all reverence, although we can by no means comprehend this 'great mystery of godliness' which 'was manifested in the flesh' and appeared in the world, namely, that Jesus Christ came into this world 'to save sinners,' and to 'seek what was lost.' He came not as he was 'in the beginning,' the Creator and Judge of all worlds, but as was suitable to us, 'fairer than the children of men,' abundant 'and rich in mercy' to all who call upon him. He came, a saviour for the lost, a redeemer for the captives, a king for his soldiers, a lord for his servants, a rich man for the poor, a physician for the sick:—as he found no one free from infirmity, so he came for the salvation of all. He came, the fairest of flowers, the guide of life, the channel of pardon, the fountain of goodness and grace, which is open to the house of Jacob, to pardon the sinner and the polluted. He came as a kind instructor, a gracious master, a preacher of truth and of mercy, 'meek and humble in heart.' He came from the throne of Majesty, from the bosom of God the Father; and the draughts which he had there received from the fountain of goodness, he poured forth to us.

" And what but love was sufficient for this? It was love alone which moved the compassion of our God to send to us a deliverer and defender, to free us from the slavery of the devil, by which we were oppressed. The apostle testifies this, saying, 'For his great love wherewith he loved us,' God the Father sent his Son; and again, 'God spared not his own Son.' Urged by this love, the Son of God came from heaven; urged by this, he suffered himself to be hanged upon the cross; urged by

this, he descended to deliver his own, who were
held captive in hell. This he taught by words,
confirmed by example, sealed by the shedding of
his blood.   He taught it when he said, ' Love your
enemies ;' he exemplified it when, hanging on the
cross, he prayed the Father for those that crucified
him—' Forgive them, for they know not what they
do ;' he confirmed it by shedding his blood, because
he ' laid down his life for his sheep,' and, as ' a good
shepherd,' condescended to die for his flock.   And
he marked it too in this place, ' Come unto *me*,
all ye that labour and are heavy-laden.'   He himself, then, is the very centre of charity or love.
But examine whether this be in respect of his own
divine nature, or of us.   If we say that it is in
respect of himself, no one can doubt it, for ' in
him dwelleth all the fulness of the Godhead bodily,'
and if the fulness of the Godhead, then the fulness
of love also, for ' God is love.'   If we say that he
is so in respect of us, it is clear that he is the centre
of our love, for who resembles *us* more nearly than
that wounded man, or who deserves more of his
love than that good Samaritan who took care of
him with wine and oil?   In the same centre, then,
from every side, human and divine love meet together, insomuch that he is truly ' the mediator
between God and man, the man Christ Jesus.'

   " To this centre of love, then, that is to itself,
love itself invites us, that being rooted and grounded
in love, we may hold it fast and delight therein.
He saith, therefore, ' Come unto me.'   It is the
voice of one that calleth, inviteth, persuadeth, en-
courageth, and beseecheth, and all for our salvation.   He wants not our goods, yet he wishes to
shew forth his love, and communicate his blessedness to us.   For this, he calls us to his kingdom,
and invites us to that feast which hath been pre-

pared for all his elect from the foundation of the
world.   He calls those that are afar off, invites the
hungry, persuades the willing, commands the unwilling, encourages the weary, compels the reluctant, yea, to all in common he saith, ' Come unto
me.'

"O, what amazing goodness, what wondrous
condescension of God—of Him whom we ought to
entreat that he would deign to receive us;—we are
entreated by HIMSELF to come to him!   What
else doth he set forth in this, but that primary
grace which no man can deserve; I mean that
grace which bringeth the faithless and unbelieving
to faith, which converts the wicked and sinful to
religion, and excites the weary and negligent to
devotion.   This grace is the free gift of God, flowing from the unspeakable mercy of the Lord Jesus,
and from the inmost recesses of his love.   No
crimes are too grievous, no sins too great, no
bonds of habit too hard, no difficulties too impass-
able for it.   This grace leads us to desire what is
good, it afterwards enables us to perform it; it
strengthens those who stand, lest they fall; makes
those who run, to run with more alacrity; compels
those who are fallen to rise from the lake of misery
and the mire of filthiness.   No will, no merit, no
devotion of ours precedes it; but it cometh to us
voluntarily, it cometh to us undue, and therefore
rightly claims as its own the whole man.   For it is
only fitting, that when so free and so great a blessing of God has been received as to renew and
change the whole man, that man should entirely
change from what he was to what he was not, from
unjust to just, from unholy to holy, from sin to
innocence, and devoting himself to thanksgiving,
should not remain ungrateful for the mercy of
God.   But true gratitude is shewn by unceasing

labours to do good works; for that man who still resists the commandments of him who bestoweth grace is plainly ungrateful. . . .

" Wherefore, my beloved, if ye hear his voice, harden not your hearts, despise not his advice, neglect not the time of grace which is now at hand. Think, brethren, think what severity of judgment will hereafter be exercised by Him who hath first offered the multitude of his mercies. He who now opens the bosom of his mercy to the penitent, then shuts the door of heaven for ever against the despisers; he who now healingly cries, ' Come unto me, all ye that labour and are heavy laden, and I will give you rest,' shall then terribly thunder, ' Go, ye cursed, into everlasting fire, prepared for the devil and his angels.' .. While we have time, then, beloved brethren, let us go before his face with confession, that we may escape so horrible a malediction; let us go to meet our Saviour, let us ascend upward in our hearts, let us ascend to the mountain of the Lord, that we may come to the glory of his kingdom. That ascent, indeed, is hard, but inestimable is the fruit when we have attained to it.

" Five steps are before us by which we are to come unto him, but in four we shall approach to him, in the fifth we shall obtain him. The first step of our approach to him is faith; the second, love; the third, obedience; the fourth, perseverance; the fifth, incorruption. Of the first, the Lord himself speaks in the Gospel, ' He who cometh to me shall never hunger, and he that believeth in me shall never thirst;' of the second, ' Every one who hath heard and learned of the Father cometh to me,' that is, whoever hath heard what is inspired of God, cometh to me, that is, follows me through love; of the third, again, ' If any man will come after me, let him deny himself,' that is, obey the commandments of another; of the fourth, 'All that the Father giveth me shall come to me, and him that cometh to me (that is, who perseveres), I will in no wise cast out;' of the fifth, it is said to the bride in the Canticles, 'Come with me from Lebanon,'—come to be crowned. The first three steps are comprehended in a brief but admirable sentence by the apostle, saying, 'Faith worketh by love.' The other two are expressed by the Truth itself in these words, 'He that shall persevere to the end, the same shall be saved,' that is, shall possess incorruption. . .

"As it is impossible to erect a building without a foundation, so without faith it is impossible to please God; which faith is rightly called 'the desire of discipline' (Wisd. vi. 17); because true faith always desires to know the law of life and discipline, lest perchance it may overflow, or 'run in vain,' or follow the spirit of error instead of the Spirit of truth. After the 'desire of discipline' follows love, that you may know how to study and love that discipline which you desire, that it be not troublesome and grievous to you, though sometimes it may seem to have more of grief than joy. After love follows 'keeping the law,' that is, obedience; for, as St. Gregory testifies, 'The proof of love is the exhibition of good works.' But obedience itself must be constant, real, joyful, affectionate. Their obedience is not constant, whose only object is to obey their own will. Their obedience is not real, who obey for the sake of worldly gain or convenience. Their obedience is not joyful, who with murmuring or reluctance do what they are commanded. Their obedience is not affectionate, who, if they dare not refuse, revolve rancour and ill-will in their hearts . . .
And to obedience we must join perseverance; for

what profit is there in the beginning of a good work, if perseverance faileth? This may be well called the completion of incorruption, which having begun on earth, it causeth to be finished and crowned in heaven. We may rightly infer that uncorruptedness bringeth us near to God, and that the sight of God is promised to it alone; for the Lord saith, ' Blessed are the pure in heart, for they shall see God.' ... Yet know that this uncorruptedness of life can never be perfectly attained by us in this world; for however great be the splendour of purity in this life, however great may be its power through faith, still man ever beareth within himself that which compels him to endure corruption. He may have preserved his body in integrity, and mortified not only its works, but its senses. But who shall boast, that his heart is in all respects clean? For from the moment when the human mind, in our first parents, forsook the Author of purity, it cannot fail to be defiled by evil thoughts, even if it desired not to be so. Yet, through God's grace, there shall be a time when it may both wish and accomplish without difficulty; when our nature shall change into glory; when corruption shall put on incorruption; when ' the woman' (that is, human weakness) shall be ' clothed with the sun' of brightness, and ' shall have the moon' (of changeableness) ' beneath her feet' (that is, cast down and trodden under foot)."

The Roman pontiffs regarded their own supremacy over the whole Church, by divine right, as a prime article of faith; and their adherents, the monks, friars, and schoolmen, maintained it so vigorously, that in this period it came to be regarded generally in the western Church as a matter of faith, or at least as a settled and indisputable point. On this basis the fabric of the papal power was raised to a gigantic height. As for the eastern

Churches, they rejected and denied this novel doctrine, which was never declared to be an article of faith by any general synod; for the synod of Lyons in 1274, in which this doctrine was advanced by the ambassadors of the Greek emperor, to gratify the pope, and by some Greek bishops who acted under intimidation; and the synod of Florence, in which it was forced on those Greek bishops who were present, were rejected by the eastern Church. The latter synod, indeed, was of doubtful authority even in the West, as it consisted only of Italian bishops, while the rival synod of Basle was sitting at the same time. The doctrine, however, became deeply rooted throughout the western or Latin Churches.

The synod of Florence, just referred to, was the first synod which taught the doctrine of purgatory as an article of faith. It had, indeed, been held by the popes and by many writers, and it became the popular doctrine during the period under review; but it was not decreed by any authority of the universal, or even of the whole Latin Church. In the eastern Church it was always rejected.

Nearly the same may be said of transubstantiation; for though the persuasion of the majority of the schoolmen was, that after consecration the bread of the eucharist no longer exists, there were several learned men during these ages who held different notions; such as Durand, and many others mentioned by Cardinal D'Ailly. The council of Lateran, indeed, in 1215, as I have said, had made use of the *word* "transubstantiation," to express the change by which the bread and wine become the sacrament of Christ's body and blood; but this word might be, and in fact was, used in many senses inconsistent with the Romish interpretation of it; and the object of the synod itself seems to have been merely to establish the old doctrine of the presence and reception of Christ's body and blood in the sacrament, in opposition to the Manichæan errors. There is also much reason to believe, that the great mass of the people in these ages did not understand or believe the doctrines of scholastics on this subject; and that they held simply the doctrine of the real presence, without denying the existence of the bread after consecration. The eastern Church in these ages knew nothing of transubstantiation. Such in general was the condition of the Christian faith up to the beginning of the Reformation. No article of faith was denied by the Church generally; the erroneous doctrines which existed were held by a greater or less number of individuals, but without any solemn decree or determination of the universal Church. Now it is certain that errors not directly contrary to the articles of faith may occasionally exist in the Church, because they do not destroy its faith. Even the Roman Catholic theologian Bossuet says, that the majority of writers in any age may suppose some doctrine to be a matter of faith which is not really so; and other Roman theologians allow that the opinion most commonly held at any particular time in the Church may not be true. Hence, although many persons in the western Church during the period now under consideration, believed that the doctrines of transubstantiation, purgatory, and the papal supremacy, were matters of faith; and though many also believed equally in the infallibility of the pope, the immaculate conception of the Virgin, and other points which are now disputed by Romanists themselves; yet still the real faith of the Church was not essentially changed. These doctrines were received under a mistaken notion, that they had been established by the unerring authority of Revelation, and inquiry into the *fact* was always liable to remove these additions to religion. Independently of which, the doctrines themselves, though mistaken and erroneous, were not directly contrary to any of the articles of faith; and the promises of our Saviour to his Church only extend to the preservation of the articles of the faith, all of which were revealed by himself and the apostles, and are written in holy Scripture.

CHAPTER XVIII.

ON THE FRUITS OF FAITH.

A.D. 1054-1517.

HAVE already adverted to the pious labours of evangelists and missionaries during these ages: it now remains to speak of some of the most eminent saints who adorned the Church; and I shall commence with some account of St. Anselm. He was born in Piedmont, of noble parents, about A. D. 1033, and was brought up by his pious mother in the ways of godliness. When he was about fifteen years of age he wished to enter the monastic state, but was refused by the abbot to whom he applied, for fear of his parents' displeasure. During the course of his studies after this time, he neglected to cultivate the spirit of religion in his heart; and having lost his zeal for piety, and becoming insensible to the fatal tendency of vanity and worldly pleasures, he began to walk in the broad way of worldliness. Anselm in his writings expresses the deepest sorrow and contrition for these disorders of his early life, which he never ceased most bitterly to deplore to the end of his days.

After several years of diligent study in France and Burgundy, he was attracted by the great celebrity of Lanfranc, prior of Bec in Normandy, and afterwards archbishop of Canterbury, to place himself under his tuition. After some years, Anselm reverted to his early design, embraced the monastic state, and became successor to Lanfranc's office and celebrity. He applied himself most earnestly to every part of theology by the clear light of Scripture and tradition, and acquired great fame by his theological writings, his skill in metaphysics, and his ability in teaching, which attracted multitudes of disciples from all the adjoining kingdoms to the monastery of Bec. In 1078 he was elected abbot of Bec ; and as that house possessed lands in England, he was occasionally obliged to visit this country, where he was held in the highest esteem by William the Conqueror, by Lanfranc, then archbishop of Canterbury, and by many great nobles in the kingdom.

On the death of Lanfranc in 1089, the possessions of his see, like those of several others, were seized by king William Rufus, who kept many of the English bishoprics vacant for years, and applied their revenues to his own use. At length, in 1093, having fallen into a dangerous illness, and apprehending that his end was near, he was touched with compunction for his ill-spent life, and endeavoured to make amends for his sins, by issuing proclamations for the release of prisoners, the discharge of debts due to him, and a general pardon ; and at the same time he nominated Anselm, who happened to be at the court, to the metropolitan see of Canterbury, which, notwithstanding the strongest opposition on his part, Anselm was obliged at last to accept, and he was soon after consecrated with great solemnity.

It may be here observed, that the pope had not yet acquired the power of appointing to bishoprics in England. Anselm was elected and consecrated archbishop of Canterbury without any papal bulls. It was after this that the pope sent him the pall, which constituted him vicar of the Roman see.

Anselm was soon exposed to the enmity of the wicked prince who had, in a moment of transitory remorse, advanced him to the highest office in the Church of England. His refusal to pay the king an immense sum, which was demanded for his nomination to the archbishopric, and his persevering solicitations for the removal of gross corruptions in ecclesiastical patronage, and for permission to hold synods with a view to enforce the discipline of the Church, excited the wrath of the tyrant, who resorted to every possible expedient in the hopes of depriving him of his bishopric. At length, unwilling to witness grievous oppressions of religion which he was unable to prevent, Anselm retired to France, and thence to Rome, where he earnestly wished to resign his see, but was prevented by pope Urban II., who enjoined him to retain his office, and to maintain the cause of the Church. He was received with great honours in all parts of Italy, and assisted at the council of Bari, where a conference took place between the oriental and the Latin Churches, and where Anselm was commissioned to argue against the doctrine of the Greeks on the procession of the Holy Spirit. After the death of William Rufus, he returned to England, and was received with much friendship by king Henry I.; but this harmony was ere long interrupted by demands of homage and investiture on the part of the king, which Anselm, in accordance with certain principles lately laid down by a synod at Rome, thought it his duty to refuse. Notwithstanding this he opposed himself with all his power to an attempt made by Robert duke of Normandy to obtain the crown of England; and Henry I. was much indebted to him for retaining possession of his throne. After many other troubles, this venerable man died peaceably at Canterbury in 1109.

St. Anselm had a most lively faith in all the great truths of the Christian religion. His hope of heavenly things gave him a great contempt for the vanities of the world; and he might truly say, that he was dead to the world and to all its desires. By the habitual restraints he imposed on his appetite, he seemed to have attained perfect indifference to the nourishment which he took. His fortitude was such that neither fear nor favour could ever induce him to swerve from the way of justice and of truth. He seemed to live not for himself, but for others. Amidst all his troubles and public distractions, prayer was his great and continual resource. He often retired in the day to his devotions, and not unfrequently continued the whole night in prayer. An anecdote has been preserved, which shews how continually his mind was engaged on the great and awful realities of religion. One day as he was riding, at one of his manors, a hare, pursued by the hounds, ran under his horse for refuge; on which he stopped, and the hounds stood at bay. The hunters began to laugh at the circumstance; but Anselm said, weeping, " This hare reminds me of a poor sinner just upon the point of departing this life, surrounded by devils waiting to carry away their prey." The hare going off, he forbade her to be pursued, and was obeyed. In this manner, every circumstance served to raise his mind to God; and, in the midst of noise and tumult, he enjoyed all that tranquillity and peace which naturally arose from the continual contemplation of his God and Saviour, and which elevated him above the cares and anxieties of this life.

The following prayers and meditations may afford us some notion of the spirituality and piety of this holy man.

"I call on thee, my God, I call on thee, because thou art nigh unto them that call on thee, that call on thee in truth; for thou art Truth. Enable me, O holy Truth, to call on thy mercy, for I know not how it should be done, but I humbly entreat to be taught of thee, O blessed Truth. Wisdom without thee is folly; to know thee is the perfection of knowledge. Instruct me, O divine Wisdom, and teach me thy law. The guilty are delivered from their prison, the emancipated from their chains, the condemned receive not only life, but unexpected favour, when they intimate to angry fathers the love of their children; and disobedient servants escape punishment, when their master's children kindly intercede for them. Thus do I entreat thee, Almighty Father, by the love of thine Almighty Son, bring forth my soul from its prison to confess to thy name; deliver me from the bondage of my sins, through thine only Son, coeternal with thee; and through the intercession of thy precious Child, who sitteth at thy right hand, restore me, whose sins threaten condemnation, to life.

"For I know not what other I shall choose for my intercessor with thee, but he who is 'the propitiation for our sins,' who 'sits at thy right hand,' who, in the glory which he hath with thee, 'maketh intercession for us' with thy mercy. Behold my Advocate with thee, my God and Father; behold that High Priest, who needeth not to be cleansed by another's blood, because he is resplendent, washed in his own blood; behold the holy Sacrifice, well-pleasing and perfect, offered and accepted as a sweet-smelling savour; behold the spotless Lamb which was dumb before the shearers; who, when beaten with stripes, spat on, and insulted, opened not his mouth; behold him 'who did no sin,' but 'bore our sins,' and by his bruises healed our sickness; consider, O loving Father, thy meek Son suffering so grievously for me a sinner; look, most merciful Father, on him that suffers, and graciously remember for what he suffers.

"Behold those innocent hands dropping with blood, and forgive the sins which mine have committed; regard that unarmed side pierced with the cruel spear, and renew me by that holy fountain which I believe to have flowed from thence; see those stainless feet, which never stood in the way of sinners but ever walked in thy law, transfixed with the terrible nails, and perfect my goings in thy paths, make me to hate every way of iniquity, remove the way of iniquity from me, and enable me to choose the way of truth.

"What hast thou done, most dear Son, to be thus condemned? What hast thou committed, most loving Child, to be thus treated? What is thy crime, what thy guilt, what the cause of thy death, what the reason of thy condemnation? It is I who am the wound of thy pain, the cause of thy slaying, the severity of thy suffering, the pain of thy torture. I am the sin for which thou diest, the crime for which thou art punished. O, wondrous way of judgment, appointment of ineffable mystery! The unjust sins, and the righteous is punished—the good suffers what the evil deserves, the master pays for the servant's crime, and what man has committed, God endures. How, O Son of God, hath thy humility descended! how hath thy love burned, thy mercy advanced, thy benevolence increased! whither have thy love and compassion attained to!

" What, my God and my King, 'what reward shall I give thee for all thy benefits unto me ?' Nothing in the heart of man can be found which may worthily be likened to such blessings. Can human wisdom devise ought to which Divine mercy can be compared ? Nor is it the place of a creature even to attempt to recompense his Creator's aid. But in this thy admirable appointment, O Son of God, there is somewhat which my frailty may in a degree supply, if my mind, touched by thy visitation, crucifies the flesh with its affections and lusts. If this be granted, it begins to suffer and to live unto thee, because thou hast died for sinners; and thus guided and inwardly victorious, it will be prepared for the outward palm; subdued by inward persecution, it will not fear for thy love to be subject to the material sword. Thus, if it please thy mercy, shall the frailty of the creature be able to respond, according to its strength, to the greatness of its Creator....

" Forgive, Creator of light, forgive my sins, for the immeasurable sufferings of thy beloved Son; let my impiety be pardoned for his piety, my perverseness for his moderation, my fierceness for his meekness. Let his humility buy my pride, his patience my impatience, his mercy my hard-heartedness, his obedience my disobedience, his tranquillity my disquietude, his sweetness my bitterness, his gentleness my wrath, his love my cruel obstinacy; and, O holy comforting Spirit, the consolation of mourning hearts, descend, with thy mighty power, into my heart, enlighten its dark recesses, and mercifully dwelling there, make fruitful with thine abundant dews all that hath been long withering in dryness."

St. Bernard was born in France in 1091, the third of six brothers, and was remarkable in his childhood for diligence in his studies, and for the purity of his morals. When he had attained his

twenty-second year, finding himself surrounded by
the temptations of the world, he resolved to follow
the example of Antony, and to seek a retreat in the
newly-founded monastery of Citeaux; and he persuaded his five brothers, his uncle, and many other
persons of wealth and merit, to unite with him.
Accompanied by thirty disciples, he was admitted at
Citeaux, where he sought to hide himself from the
world; and so entirely was he absorbed in the contemplation of heavenly things, that all the ordinary
affairs and objects of life ceased to excite his attention or curiosity. His watchings and fastings brought
on an infirmity of body, which never left him. In
accordance with the rule of St. Benedict, which was
here strictly observed, he laboured diligently with
his hands, while at the same time he was inwardly
occupied in the worship of God. He prayed and
meditated on Scripture, and afterwards said that it
was chiefly in the woods and fields that he had learnt
the spiritual meaning of holy writ. In the intervals
of labour, he was always engaged in prayer, reading,
or meditation. He studied Scripture by simply reading it regularly through many times; and said that
there was nothing which enabled him to understand
it better than its own words, and that all its truths
had more force in the text than in the discourses
of commentators. He, however, read with humility
the expositions of the fathers, and followed in their
footsteps.

After St. Bernard had been a year at Citeaux,
he was sent by the abbot to take charge of the new
monastery at Clairvaux. The society began in extreme poverty. They were often obliged to make
their pottage of leaves, and mingle their bread with
millet and vetches. Assistance, however, came to
them often when it was least expected. St. Bernard
proposed to his disciples in this place a piety so pure

and elevated, that it seemed beyond them ; but his
exalted sentiments, and the strictness of his discipline, gradually produced a revival of the ascetic life
in all its purity.   On approaching Clairvaux, a different scene presented itself from that afforded by
other monasteries, which were magnificently built
and adorned, and exhibited every sign of opulence.
The buildings here were plain and poor.   The valley
was filled with men, each silently engaged in his
appointed task ; and nothing interrupted the silence
but the sound of labour, or the praise of God when
the monks chanted their offices.   They lived on the
poorest fare, and denied themselves all earthly pleasures and enjoyments.

The fame of St. Bernard soon spread far and
wide, and men began to resort to him; but wherever
he was, or with whomsoever conversing, he could not
refrain from preaching and speaking of the blessed
truths of religion, and of his God and Saviour.   His
zeal, the extent of his learning, the acuteness of his
intellect, his dauntless courage, and a piety which
shed the splendour of sanctity over all his great
endowments, soon distinguished him as a man who
was calculated for a wider sphere than the limits of
his cloister afforded ; and for the last thirty years of
his life (he died in 1153), St. Bernard was consulted
by popes, emperors, kings, and bishops.   He was
engaged in most affairs of importance; was called to
many councils ; subdued several heretics in controversy ; was commissioned to preach the crusade to
the assembled sovereign and nobles of France; influenced the Christian world in favour of pope Innocent, whose election he supported against a rival ;
lived to see one of his own monks placed on the
papal throne ; and at his death left a hundred and
sixty monasteries, who regarded him as their founder or their governor.

I cannot pass on from this brief account of St. Bernard without presenting to the reader the following specimen of his spiritual and moral instructions and exhortations.

" Man," he said, " is ever changing amidst prosperity and adversity, and knows not when he is to die. For as a glimmering star shoots swiftly from the heavens and is suddenly extinct, and as a spark of fire is extinguished in a moment and reduced to ashes, so suddenly may we behold the close of life. For man in this world is ever ready and willing to stay God, and thinks that he hath long to live, and he is arranging many things to be done for a long time, when he is suddenly hurried away to death, and his soul is unexpectedly separated from the body. But yet that separation is accompanied by grievous terrors and sore pains; for the angels come to receive the soul and to carry it before the tribunal of the awful Judge; and then, remembering its evil deeds which it hath wrought by day and night, it trembles, and desires to flee from them, and begs for a truce, saying, 'Give me but the space of one hour.' And then shall all its works say together, 'Thou hast made us, we are thy works, we will not leave thee, but be with thee for ever. We will go with thee to judgment.' Then the soul, finding the eyes and the mouth shut, and the other senses of the body by which it used to 'go forth' and delight itself in outward things, returns into itself; and finding itself alone, and struck with great horror, shall faint despairingly and sink within itself. And because, through the love of the world and the lust of the flesh, it had forsaken God, it shall be forsaken of Him in its misery, in the hour of extremest necessity, and shall be delivered to the devils to be tormented in hell. Thus the soul of the sinner, in a day when he knows not, and an

hour which he looketh not for, is seized by death
and separated from the body, and departs full of
miseries, trembling and sorrowing ; and having no
excuse for its sins, faints and exceedingly fears to
appear before God.

"O soul ! dignified with the image, adorned
with the likeness of God, espoused to Him by faith,
endowed with the Spirit, redeemed by blood, accounted with angels, capable of happiness, heir of
goodness, partaker of the inheritance,—what hast
thou to do with the flesh, from whence thou suf-
ferest all this ?...Why dost thou so lightly esteem thy
soul, and prefer the body to it ? That the mistress
(*i. e.* the soul) should be servant, and the servant
(*i. e.* the body) should be mistress, is an exceeding
abuse. All this world is not as valuable as one soul ;
for God, who gave his life for the soul of man,
would not have given it for the whole world. The
value of the soul, therefore, which could not be redeemed save by the blood of Christ, is most sublime.
What then shalt thou give in exchange for thy soul
—thou who givest it away for nothing? Did not
the Son of God, who was in the bosom of the Father,
descend from his kingly throne for it, that he might
deliver it from the power of the devil? which when
He beheld, ensnared as it was in the cords of sin,
and about to be forthwith delivered to the devils to
be punished with eternal death, He wept over it,—
wept over that which knew not how to weep for
itself ; and not only wept, but permitted himself to
be slain, that by the precious price of his blood he
might redeem it.

"Behold, O mortal, what a sacrifice is given for
thee ! Confess, O man, how noble is thy soul, and
how deadly are its wounds, for which it was necessary that Christ the Lord should be wounded ! If
these thy wounds were not unto death—eternal

death, never would the Son of God have died for their remedy.

"Then think not lightly of thy soul's suffering, to which thou seest so great compassion shewn by such great Majesty. He shed tears for thee—do thou also wash thy bed each night with a contrite heart and continual weeping. He poured forth his blood —do thou also shed thine by continual mortification of the body, which if thou canst not lay down at once for Christ, yet do so by a gentle though longer martyrdom. Attend not to what the flesh desires, but to what the Spirit demands. Now then let us choose one of these two, either to be tormented for ever with the wicked, or to rejoice perpetually with the saints; for good and evil, life and death, are set before us, that we may stretch forth our hands to whichever we prefer.

"If torments do not terrify us, at least let rewards invite us. It is a reward to behold God, to live with God, to live by God, to be with him and in him, who shall be all in all, to possess God who is the chiefest good; and where the chiefest good is, there is supremest happiness and joy, true liberty, perfect love, eternal security, and secure eternity. There is true enjoyment, perfect knowledge, all beauty, and all blessedness. There are peace, piety, goodness, light, virtue, honesty, joy, pleasure, sweetness, eternal life, glory, praise, rest, love, and sweet concord. Thus blessed shall that man be with God, in whose conscience sin shall not be found ... and this is the whole good of man, to know and to love his Creator.

"The time of man is but as a shadow on the earth, and it delays not; when it seems to stand still, it is gone! Why then will men lay up treasures on earth, when the gatherer and the gathered pass away without lingering? And thou, man—what fruit dost thou expect in the world, whose fruit is ruin, whose end is death?   O, that thou wouldst be wise and understand, and wisely provide against the end!   I kuow one who hath lived familiarly with thee for many years, who hath sat at thy table, taken food from thine hand, slept in thy bosom, held converse with thee.   He is by hereditary right thy slave, but because in youth thou hast nourished him delicately, and spared the rod, he hath become disobedient—hath lifted his heel against thy head, reduced thee to slavery, and cruelly ruled over thee. Perhaps thou askest 'who is this?'   Thy 'old man,' which trampleth down thy spirit, which valueth not that desireable land, but savours only of fleshly things.   Already he hath cast thee into the ditch which he hath made; thou art enfeebled, oppressed beneath the yoke of most miserable slavery, wretch-edly and vilely trampled beneath his feet.   O, un-happy, miserable man! who shall deliver thee from the bondage of this reproach?   Let God arise, and let that armed one fall; let him fall and be broken into powder, that hostile man, that despiser of God, that worshipper of self, that lover of the world, that servant of the devil!   How thinkest thou?   If thou judgest aright, thou wilt say with me, 'He is guilty of death; let him be crucified.'   Then do not dis-semble, do not defer, do not spare; but speedily, boldly, instantly, crucify that man—but with the cross of Christ, in which is salvation and life, to which if thou criest from thine heart, the Crucified will hear thee, and will benignantly reply, 'To-day shalt thou be with me in paradise.'

"O compassion of Christ!   O unexpected sal-vation to the wretched!   O, how great is the mercy of God, how unspeakable the change wrought by the right hand of the Most Highest!   Yesterday thou wast in darkness, to-day in the splendour of light; yesterday in the mouth of the lion, to-day in the hand of the Mediator; yesterday at the gates of hell, to-day in the delights of paradise! But what avail these letters of warning, except thou shalt blot from thy conscience the letters of death? What avails it to read and understand these words, unless thou shalt read and understand *thyself?* Give thyself then to read what is *within,* to read, examine, and know thyself. Read, that thou mayest love God, resist and subdue every enemy; that thy labour may change to rest, thy lamentation to joy, and after the darkness of this world, thou mayest see the dawn of the rising morn, behold the meridian Sun of righteousness, in which thou shalt behold the Bridegroom and his bride, even that one and the same Lord of glory, who liveth and reigneth for ever and ever."

These are, indeed, words of eloquence, of the highest and noblest eloquence. They are the words of truth, filled with that burning zeal and affection, which the influence of Divine grace, operating on minds of peculiar energy, has occasionally produced. Who can fail to recognise in these words of Bernard, the same vehemence of charity, the same fervour of faith, the same devotedness of spirit, which shone so conspicuously in the Apostle of the Gentiles?

At Cremona, in Italy, about this time, lived a man named HOMOBONUS, who was a merchant, and remarkable for honesty in all his dealings. He was married; but finding himself more free to follow his wishes after the death of his father, he resolved to labour no more for the wealth of this world, but to give himself up to prayer, watchfulness, fasting, and other religious duties. He distributed to the poor what he had gained in traffic, and performed every office of charity both to their souls and bodies. His wife reproached him with his want of care for the things of this life; but he calmly reminded her, that what is given to God is never lost. He often went at night to pray in the church; and one morning early, while the service was proceeding, he prostrated himself on the ground, his hands extended in the form of a cross, and after a time he was found to be dead. He died in 1197.

Some of the most learned and pious of the schoolmen flourished in the twelfth and thirteenth centuries. Amongst these may be named PETER LOMBARD, ALEXANDER DE HALES, BONAVENTURA, AQUINAS, and SCOTUS. These were men of very ardent piety; but some of them were deeply tinged with superstition. The founder of the order of Franciscan friars was also endowed with a zealous spirit of religion. ST. FRANCIS, amidst much enthusiasm, displayed a spirit of devotion and piety, a contempt for all earthly things, and a simplicity of purpose in the endeavour to win souls to God, which reflect honour on his memory. But it is to be lamented, that the spirit of credulity, if not of imposture, has been so largely at work in attributing to him a mass of fabulous miracles, some of which have excited derision in later times, as they did even in the thirteenth century.

RICHARD, ordained bishop of Chichester in 1245, affords an example of piety and charity. After his consecration, king Henry III. withheld the revenues of his see; so that he was obliged to depend on the charity of those of the people of his diocese who were willing to minister to his necessities; but he, nevertheless, made visitations, and administered the sacraments, as he saw need. At length, after enduring the deprivation of his lands with patience, they were restored to him by the king, but in a miserable state, and plundered of every thing.

He, however, began to distribute abundant alms; and when his brother, who managed his affairs, represented that his revenue was insufficient, he replied: "Is it right that we should eat off gold and silver, while Jesus Christ suffers hunger in the persons of his poor? I know how to content myself with earthen vessels, as my father did. Let every thing be sold, even to my horse, if there be need." He was fervent in prayer, in fasting, and all good works.

He never gave benefices to his relatives; he resisted, with invincible firmness, the king and the archbishop of Canterbury, who wanted him to prefer an unworthy curate in his diocese. He preached assiduously, even out of his diocese; consoled and encouraged those penitents who came to consult him as their spiritual adviser; and died, in 1253, as he was engaged in the active and diligent discharge of his sacred duties.

Robert Grosteste, bishop of Lincoln, who flourished at the same time, was remarkable for sanctity of life, and purity and severity of discipline. He opposed himself, with remarkable firmness, to the exactions and pretensions of the popes. On one occasion, when he had received a mandate from the pope to appoint an improper person to a benefice in his diocese, he wrote in reply, that the mandate he had received could not be genuine, as it pretended to the power of subverting all the canons, and as it prescribed a positive sin, in requiring the introduction of a false pastor into the Church. The pope was very much irritated, and threatened to have him punished by the king of England; but the cardinals represented that this prelate's reputation stood so high in France and England, that no remedy could be hoped for. Grosteste complained of the pretension of the popes

to dispense with all the canons and constitutions of
the Church at pleasure; of their ordering the Dominican and Franciscan friars to persuade the dying
to leave their goods to the crusade, and to take the
cross themselves, in order to defraud their heirs of
their goods, and to enrich the papal coffers; of
their measuring indulgences in proportion to the
money given for the crusade; of their ordering
bishops to institute to benefices persons who were
foreigners, ignorant, or absent; of their permitting
persons to be bishops without ordination, in order
that they might enjoy the revenues of the Church;
and of the general avarice, extortion, and impurity,
which reigned in the court of Rome.   Grosteste is
said to have performed miracles; but, though adorned
with many virtues, his resistance to the Church of
Rome prevented his ever being numbered amongst
the saints of that calendar.

The most eminent theologians in the following
centuries were OCKHAM, an English ecclesiastic,
who refuted the doctrine of the infallibility of the
pope; NICHOLAS DE LYRA, who wrote a commentary on Scripture, which was much valued by the
Reformers; GERSON; and PETER D'AILLY, who,
in the fifteenth century, argued against the papal
pretensions, and ably defended the rights of the
Church. GERSON was a man of eminent piety,
and wrote many devotional treatises.   The celebrated book " Of the Imitation of Christ," which
was written in the fifteenth century by THOMAS A
KEMPIS, a canon in Germany, is a sufficient proof
that Christian faith and devotion of the highest
order were still existing in the Church.

There cannot be a stronger exemplification of
this consolatory truth than in the life of LAURENCE
JUSTINANI, bishop and patriarch of Venice.

This venerable man, whose excellent piety and

abundant good works were worthy of the brightest ages of the Church, was born in Venice in 1389, of a noble and ancient family; and at nineteen years of age devoted himself to the monastic life in his native place, where he was remarkable for prayer, fasting, and vigils, and for the fervour and zeal of his piety. He was endued with a remarkable spirit of Christian fortitude; and being afflicted with an illness which rendered a surgical operation indispensable, he said to his surgeons, who trembled at the danger to which his life was exposed, "What do you fear? Let the razors and the burning irons be brought in. Cannot He grant me constancy, who not only supported but even preserved from the flames the three children?" On another similar occasion he said to a surgeon, "Your razor cannot exceed the burning irons of the martyrs."

While he resided in the monastery, he was remarkable for his humility: he willingly undertook the lowest and most menial offices in his community, and evinced a spirit of poverty and self-denial which the most eminent ascetics might have applauded. After some time, he was ordained priest, and became general or superior of his order, which he reformed and regulated with so much strictness, that he was afterwards regarded as its second founder. The saying of our Lord, that "out of the abundance of the heart the mouth speaketh," was verified in this holy man. All his conversation was replete with a spirit of piety, which melted the hearts of those with whom he discoursed. His confidence in the infinite power and goodness of God kept pace with a perfect humility and distrust of himself; and assiduous prayer was his continual support.

In 1433 he was made bishop of Venice, which was afterwards, in honour to his transcendent merits, made a patriarchal see by the pope. He endeavoured ineffectually to decline this appointment; and being exceedingly averse to pomp and ostentation, he took possession of his church so privately that his friends knew nothing of the matter till the ceremony was over.

When he was placed at the head of so great a church, his manners and habits of life underwent no alteration. His household was placed on the most moderate scale; it consisted only of five persons. He had no plate in his house, but used only earthenware, lay on a straw bed, and wore no rich clothing. His example, his severity towards himself, and his affability and kindness to others, won the hearts of all, and enabled him to introduce most important reforms in discipline. Great multitudes of people resorted every day to his palace for advice, comfort, or alms. His gate, provisions, and purse, were always open to the poor. His alms were carefully and judiciously distributed; provisions and clothing were more frequently given to applicants than money. With a feeling of the most considerate sympathy, he employed pious matrons to find out and relieve those poor whose modesty prevented them from soliciting alms, and to assist persons of family in decayed circumstances. These abundant charities were but the result of a spirit of divine love, which influenced all his conduct. Nothing could exceed his zeal for the glory of God; and he was rewarded by the gift of wisdom, which enabled him to pacify most violent dissensions in the state, and to govern his diocese in most difficult times with perfect ease.

In his last illness, his servants were preparing a bed for him, at which this self-denying man was troubled, and said to them, "Are you laying a feather-bed for me? No, that shall not be; my Lord was stretched on a hard and painful tree. Do not you remember what St. Martin said in his agony, that a Christian ought to die on sack-cloth and ashes?" He forbade his friends to weep for him; and as his strength failed, often exclaimed, with rapture, "Behold the Bridegroom; let us go forth and meet him." He added, with his eyes raised towards heaven, "Good Jesus, behold, I come." When it was remarked to him, that he might go joyfully to his crown, he was much disturbed, and said, "The crown is for valiant soldiers, not for base cowards such as I am." During the two last days of his life, all the city came in turn, according to their ranks, to receive his blessing. He commanded even the beggars to be admitted, and addressed to every class some short pathetic instructions; after which he departed in peace, in the year 1455. Such examples suffice to shew, that even when the Church was most in need of reformation, the grace of God still continued to produce saving faith, and to sanctify his people.

That serious corruptions in practice, and even in doctrine, had now become common among Christians, is indeed but too evident. Learned and godly men were longing for a reformation of the many evils by which religion was afflicted: but amidst much of human infirmity and sin, we still cannot avoid recognising the continued fulfilment of the promises of God to his Church. The following expressions of Luther on this subject are well worthy of attention. "In this Church," he says, "God miraculously and powerfully preserved baptism; moreover, in the public pulpits, and the Lord's-day sermons, he preserved the text of the Gospel in the language of every nation, besides remission of sins, and absolution as well in confession as in public. Again, the sacrament of the altar, which at Easter, and twice or three times in the year, they offered to Christians, although they administered only one kind (*i. e.* the bread). Again, calling and ordination to parishes, and the ministry of the word, the keys to bind and loose, and to comfort in the agony of death. For amongst many it was customary to shew the image of Christ crucified to those who were dying, and admonish them of his death and blood. Then, by a Divine miracle, there remained in the Church the Psalter, the Lord's Prayer, the Creed, the Ten Commandments. Likewise many pious and excellent hymns, which were left to posterity by truly Christian and spiritual men, though oppressed with tyranny. Wherever were these truly sacred relics —the relics of holy men—there was and is the true holy Church of Christ; for all these are ordinances and fruits of Christ, except the forcible removal of one part of the sacrament from Christians. In this Church of Christ, therefore, the spirit of Christ was certainly present, and preserved true knowledge and true faith in his elect."

CHAPTER XIX.

ON THE EASTERN CHURCH.

A.D. 1054-1517.

THE eastern or Greek Church existed under the Greek emperors, in the country now called Turkey in Europe and Asia Minor, and also in Russia, Poland, Bulgaria, Moravia, Sclavonia, Georgia, Mingrelia, Circassia, Syria, Palestine, and Egypt. It was governed by the patriarchs of Con-

stantinople, Alexandria, Antioch, and Jerusalem.
After the division between the Churches of Rome
and Constantinople in 1054, the eastern and western Churches did not immediately withdraw from
mutual communion. In 1155, Basil, archbishop of
Thessalonica, in an epistle to Adrian IV., allowed
that the Latin Churches held the orthodox faith,
and formed part of the universal Church, while he
denied that the Greek Church was guilty of schism :
and in 1203, Demetrius, archbishop of Bulgaria,
denied that the Latins were heretics. On the other
hand, Peter, abbot of Clugny, and William of Tyre,
in the twelfth century, admitted the Greeks to form
part of the Catholic Church; and several modes of
intercourse existed between the Churches. The
popes, however, being full of the notion of their
own supremacy over the whole Church, always
treated the Greeks as schismatics; and though
they entered into many negotiations with the Greek
emperors, for the re-union of East and West, the
first article always insisted on was, that the Greek
Church should *obey* the pope. Had the popes
merely desired to restore the communion of the
Churches, leaving the Greeks their ancient independence and equality, there would have been no
difficulty; but they refused, and rightly refused, to
place their religion, their discipline, their property
and persons, at the feet of pontiffs who pretended
to infallibility, and who refused to be bound by
any laws or canons.

The views of the eastern Church on this subject are exemplified by the words of Nechites,
archbishop of Nicomedia, in his conference with a
Latin bishop, in 1137: "We do not refuse the
Roman Church," he said, "the first rank among
her sisters the patriarchal Churches, and we acknowledge that she presides in a general council;

but she separated from us by her pride, when, exceeding her power, she divided the empire and the Churches of the East and West. When she holds a council of western bishops without us, it is well that they should observe their own decrees; but how can we be expected to obey decrees made without our knowledge? If the pope pretends to send us his orders, fulminating from his lofty throne, and to dispose of us and our churches at his own discretion, without advising with us, what paternity or what fraternity is there in that? We should be only slaves, not children of the Church. The Roman Church alone would enjoy liberty, and give laws to all others, without being subject to any herself. We do not find in any creed, that we are bound to confess the ROMAN Church in particular, but one holy, catholic, and apostolic Church. This is what I say of the Roman Church, which I revere with you; but I do not with you believe it a duty to follow her necessarily in all things, nor that we ought to relinquish our rites, and adopt her mode of performing the sacraments, without examining it by reason and the Scriptures."

The crusades, which the popes set on foot for the recovery of the Holy Land, but which led to the subjugation of Constantinople, Cyprus, and a great part of the Greek empire by Latin chieftains, tended much to promote unfriendly feelings between the Churches. Latin bishops were instituted in Jerusalem, Antioch, Constantinople, Greece, and Cyprus, although there were already Greek bishops in those sees; and the crusaders in many places profaned the Greek churches, expelled their clergy, or forced them, on pain of death, to become obedient to Rome. The Greeks retaliated when they were able; and the Churches became much more estranged from each other.

In the year 1261, the Greek emperor Michael Paleologus recovered Constantinople from the Latins; and fearing that the pope would proclaim a crusade against him, he entered into negotiations for the union of the Churches, and compelled some of the Greek bishops to write to the pope and the council of Lyons in 1274, admitting the primacy of the Roman see, and expressing their wish for union. A letter from the emperor was also read in the council, in which he professed his belief in the Roman primacy, in purgatory, transubstantiation, and seven sacraments, as the pope had commanded. The council then permitted the re-union of the Greek Church to the Latin, and did not require any alteration in their form of worship. But in 1280 the pope again excommunicated the Greeks for not obeying his commands, and the temporary union came to an end. When Constantinople was threatened by the Turks, in the fifteenth century, the Greek emperor John Paleologus, desirous of obtaining the pope's assistance for his falling empire, came with several Greek bishops to the synod of Florence in 1438, where, after much disputation, those prelates were compelled to subscribe to the doctrine of purgatory, the papal primacy, and the procession of the Holy Spirit, as held by the Roman Church: but on their return to Greece, they were condemned by the eastern Church, and the proposed union fell to the ground. Constantinople was taken by the Turks in 1453; and the Christians of those countries have been ever since much oppressed by these infidels: but the popes discovered that the attempt to reduce the Greek Church beneath their sway was a hopeless one.

CHAPTER XX.

ABUSES AND CORRUPTIONS.

A.D. 1054-1517.

THE grand and crying evil of these ages was the position of the Roman pontiffs, who were now exalted in the western Church to such a height of power, and invested by themselves and their adherents with such extravagant privileges, that the temporal as well as spiritual governments throughout Europe were every where agitated and enslaved, and the rights of sovereigns, the liberties of Churches, the holiest discipline of antiquity, were ruthlessly invaded and subverted. The spirit of the world discovered itself in the proceedings of the court of Rome; and ambition, cupidity, and pride, were but too frequently the characteristics of the Roman pontiffs. These evils were the result of false maxims. The flatterers of the popes had, for several ages before those now under consideration, attributed too extensive powers to them. It had become a settled notion in the western Churches, that the bishops of Rome were the successors of St. Peter in the primacy of the Church by *divine appointment*. The spurious decretals, already alluded to, represented them as, even from the time of the apostles, claiming and exercising an extended jurisdiction over all Churches. Hence it followed necessarily that it was the duty of every Church and every Christian to be in communion with, and to be subject to, the pope; and therefore that those who were out of his communion, or disobedient to him, were not Christian. This was, in fact, to invest the Roman pontiff with absolute power in temporal as well as spiritual matters; for if, as it was maintained, it was absolutely necessary for every Christian to be in his communion, the only thing requisite to obtain obedience, whether from kings or bishops, was to threaten or inflict excommunication upon them. Sooner or later this formidable sentence was pretty sure to weigh upon the consciences of those who were disobedient to the papal commands, or on those of their adherents; so that these prelates had little to do except to wait for the issue of events, and always, in fine, to receive the most humble apologies and entreaties for pardon, together with the whole, or at least some part, of their demands, however unreasonable or extravagant.

The papal power was first developed in all its extent by the celebrated Hildebrand, or Gregory VII., who ascended the throne in 1073. He was a man of undaunted courage and energy, and deeply imbued with notions of the extent of the papal supremacy. He accordingly excommunicated and deposed the Emperor Henry IV. of Germany, for disobedience to his mandates, and compelled him at last to sue for absolution with the greatest humility. On further symptoms of disobedience, he again deposed and excommunicated him, gave his dominions to another prince, and excited a rebellion against him. He claimed, and in many instances succeeded in obtaining, the acknowledgment of his feudal superiority, or temporal jurisdiction, over France, England, Hungary, Denmark, Poland, Russia, Norway, Dalmatia, Italy, Sicily, Sardinia, Corsica, &c. France and England for the present resisted these claims successfully; but in the reign of Pope Innocent III., John, king of England, was obliged to declare himself a subject of the Roman

see, and to pay tribute to it.   As for the affairs of
the *Church* in every country, Gregory disposed of
them as if the whole world were his diocese, and the
bishops were merely his assistants or deputies. This,
indeed, was a notion which in the following centuries was boldly avowed and acted on by the popes.
Legates, or papal viceroys, were continually going
from Rome into all countries, and enforcing the
new mandates or exactions of their masters, to the
infinite trouble, expense, and annoyance of kings,
prelates, and people; but it was in vain that they
protested, petitioned, complained, and threatened,
or offered resistance. Their own notions of the
papal authority were a chain round their necks,
which never failed to bring them ultimately into
subjection.

The history of Europe from this period, for two
or three centuries, is little more than a history of
the popes; of their contests with emperors and
kings; their deposal of some monarchs, their creation of others; of armies which they commanded
to be fitted out for the recovery of the Holy Land,
for the extermination of heretics, for the subjugation of heathen, or for the dethronement of their
own enemies; of the taxes which they levied from
all churches and states, either for the crusades, for
their own wars with princes, or for their pleasure;
of the controversies and wars which their disputed
elections excited. All this was done on principle.
There were good men among the popes and among
their adherents; but the false maxims, to which I
have before adverted, were so deeply engrained in
their minds, that it was a matter of conscience with
them to act as they did. The history of these ages
is alone sufficient to shew that there were some great
mistakes abroad with regard to the papal authority;
it occupies far too large a space in the transactions

of the period before us. Even St. Bernard was obliged to expend a great portion of his energy, zeal, and piety, for many years, in maintaining the disputed election of a pope. The world and the Church were disturbed with controversies of this kind, to the neglect of the practical duties and elevated contemplations of true religion.

No part of the Church smarted more severely under the papal tyranny (for such it became) than the Church of England. Let us dwell a moment on some particulars of its history in the thirteenth century. In 1240, Cardinal Otho, one of those legates with whom the popes were continually troubling the Churches, published at London a mandate, in which permission was given to all persons who had taken the cross (*i. e.* vowed to fight for the recovery of the Holy Land,) to obtain absolution from their vow, on condition of paying to the pope the sum which they would have expended in their journey. This was a frequent practice of the popes, by which they much injured these expeditions. The money went into their coffers, with the understanding that it was to be applied to the use of the crusaders actually engaged in Palestine; but it was frequently diverted to other purposes. The clergy of England shortly after assembled at Reading, when Cardinal Otho represented that the pope was sorely pressed for money, in his dispute with the Emperor Frederick, and demanded instantly a *fifth* part of their revenues. The bishops objected, but at length paid the exaction. Some time after, a mandate came from the pope to the archbishop of Canterbury, the bishops of Lincoln and Salisbury, to appoint *three hundred* Roman subjects to the next vacant benefices, on pain of being suspended from conferring all benefices!

In 1244 the pope sent an emissary into Eng-

land with a letter to the abbots of the diocese of
Canterbury, stating that the sums drawn by the
late pope from England and other states had been
insufficient to discharge his debts contracted for the
defence of his patrimony and the liberties of the
Church. He therefore ordered them to aid him
with the sums of money which his agent should
mention within a given time. The nuncio was supplied with many bulls, in order to bestow the best
benefices, or their revenues, on the pope's relatives.
The pope soon after wrote to the clergy of England,
commanding them to give liberally to the king. In
1245 the ambassadors of the king of England, in
the council of Lyons, read a letter addressed by the
kingdom of England to the pope, complaining that
his predecessors, wishing to enrich the Italians, who
had become excessively numerous, had given them
such a multitude of benefices in England, that their
income amounted to 60,000 marks of silver, a
greater revenue than the king possessed; that these
Italians, indifferent to the souls entrusted to them,
and only desirous of the revenues of their benefices,
lived abroad; that the nuncio had recently conferred all vacant benefices worth thirty marks on
Italians, and provided that on their death others
should succeed, to the destruction of the rights of
patrons. Many other abuses were mentioned; but
the pope, having heard the letter, would make no
reply further, than that an affair of so much consequence deserved full consideration. In the following year another vigorous attempt was made. It
was resolved by the parliament of England that an
embassy should carry to the pope *five* letters, from
the bishops, the abbots, the lords and commons, and
the king, respectfully demanding redress, and threat-
ening, in case of not obtaining it, no longer to obey
the Church of Rome. While these letters were on

their way, the pope, having learnt that many rich English ecclesiastics died intestate, decreed that the possessions of all who should hereafter die intestate should revert to himself; and commissioned the Franciscan and Dominican friars to see to the execution of this mandate. The pope was enraged when he heard of the opposition offered to his exactions, and resolved to place England under an interdict; but he was appeased by the ambassadors, who assured him that the king would speedily yield what he desired. The next year he sent over a mandate that all the resident clergy of England should pay *one-third* of their revenue, and the non-resident *one-half*, to the see of Rome. The clergy, however, were prevented from paying this exaction by the king. In 1252 we find that the king had obtained from the pope *a tenth* of the incomes of the clergy and people of England for three years, under pretence of a crusade. In 1255 a papal nuncio came to levy a tenth in England, Scotland, and Ireland, for the pope or the king. The nuncio then preached a crusade against Mainfroy, king of Sicily, an enemy of the pope, and demanded immense sums from the English bishops for this object.

The proceedings of these few years will afford a sufficient specimen of the servitude to which the prevalence of false maxims had reduced the Church. Some princes resisted such claims more effectually than others; but they were continually liable to recur, and the papal power was always encroaching and usurping the rights of the Church and State.

During the period now under consideration, the evil of appeals to the popes came to its height. No cause could occur in spiritual matters which might not be carried by appeal directly before the tribunal at Rome, to the delay of justice, the impoverishment of suitors, and the subversion of the authority of bishops and metropolitans. Vast sums of money were in this way continually draining out of England; and it should be remembered too, that by custom, or the concession of princes, the jurisdiction of the Church extended in those ages to a great number of temporal causes, besides those of wills, matrimony, tithes, and ecclesiastical property, the right of patronage, and the correction of morals, to which it is now chiefly limited. It is admitted, even by the most learned Romanists, that appeals to the papal see are of mere human institution.

About the twelfth century it became customary with the popes to give dispensations or exemptions from the laws of the Church. They would, either for money or favour, permit one person to hold several benefices or even bishoprics. They would dispense with a bishop elect remaining without ordination for years, or would permit children or other improper persons to be nominated to benefices. They would give dispensations for non-residence, for irregularities of all sorts. In short, there was scarcely any law or rule of the Church which they did not continually dispense with. The consequence was, that ecclesiastical discipline became most grievously relaxed. The bishops and clergy were too frequently infected by such evil examples; and a spirit of worldliness, self-indulgence, and habitual neglect of duties, began largely to prevail.

About this time the popes successfully claimed the appointment to archbishoprics, bishoprics, and all other benefices. The appointment to the former was first seized on. The ancient custom of sending a pallium to the bishop of the principal see in each country, was made the pretext for first exacting an oath of obedience to the pope, then prohibiting the discharge of any metropolitical powers without it. At length the popes began to issue bulls, appointing the metropolitan to his see; and afterwards, especially during the great western schism, from 1378 to 1414, when rival popes divided the whole of Europe into two or three different communions, the appointment to bishoprics, and to all other benefices, was usurped.

The plenary indulgences which the popes issued first to the crusaders, but afterwards to many other persons, completed the ruin of the penitential discipline of the Church. These indulgences or pardons were the remission of the lengthened works of penitence imposed by the ancient canons. All that was necessary to obtain them, was to confess to a priest all past sins, to go to the crusade in Palestine or in some other country, or to perform some other work assigned by the pope.

Such were some of the principal evils under which the western Churches suffered from the papal supremacy. In connexion with this subject, it may here be well to notice more particularly the history of those celebrated expeditions for the recovery of the Holy Land from the dominion of the infidels, which are commonly called THE CRUSADES. The Christians of the Holy Land, who were subject to the patriarchs of Jerusalem, had been under the Mahommedan dominion from the seventh century; and though they were exposed to many trials and temptations, yet were in general treated with tolerable forbearance by the infidels until about the eleventh century, when the Turks having succeeded to the power of the Mahommedan caliphs of Bagdad, the Christians found themselves subject to great difficulties and persecutions. Jerusalem continued to be the resort of innumerable pilgrims from the western Churches, who went to visit the scenes of their Saviour's life and death; and on their return to Europe, they carried into every country accounts of the oppression which the Christians of Palestine were enduring, the insults which their religion suffered, and the danger which the pilgrims encountered from the unbelievers. Amongst others, Peter, a hermit of the diocese of Amiens in France, was filled with grief and indignation at what he beheld during a visit to Jerusalem; and he inquired of the patriarch Simeon, "whether no remedy could be found for such great evils?" The patriarch said, "Our sins are so great, that God heareth not our prayers. We are not yet sufficiently punished. But we should have some hope, if your people, who serve God truly, and whose strength yet remains unbroken and terrible to our enemies, would come to our help, or at least pray to Jesus Christ for us. For we expect nothing more from the Greeks, though they are near at hand and connected with us, and abound in wealth. They can scarcely defend themselves, and within a few years they have lost half their empire."

Peter immediately requested the patriarch to address letters to the pope and the sovereigns of the West, describing the persecution which the Christians were suffering, and offered to carry them into all parts of Europe. His request was readily conceded; and setting forth on his mission, he came to Bari in Apulia, and thence to Rome, where he delivered the patriarch's letter to Pope Urban II., who received him favourably, and promised to take measures in furtherance of the design, when a proper opportunity should arrive. Peter the hermit then proceeded on his mission, traversed the whole of Italy, crossed the Alps, and penetrated into the various countries of Europe, addressing himself to the sovereigns, and exhorting the people every where to engage in liberating the Holy Land.

Shortly after, Urban II. assembled a great council of bishops at Clermont in France, A.D. 1095, where, after several canons of discipline had been enacted, and amongst the rest, that the sacrament of the eucharist should be received in both kinds by all the people, the pope made a discourse to the assembly in the following terms: "You know, brethren, that the Saviour of the world honoured by his presence the land which he had promised to the ancient fathers; that he has called it his inheritance, and especially loved it; and though he has delivered it for a time into the hands of unbelievers, on account of the sins of its inhabitants, we should not think that he has rejected it. For many years the impious nation of the Saracens have tyrannised cruelly in the holy places. They have enslaved the believers, and overwhelmed them with taxes and injuries. They seize their children, compel them to apostatise, and if they refuse to do so, put them to death. The temple of God has become the seat of devils; the Church of the Holy Sepulchre is defiled by their impurities; the other holy places have become stables. No one is secure; priests and deacons are slain, and women grossly insulted in the very sanctuary. Arm yourselves, then, my dear children, with zeal for God; march to the succour of your brethren; and the Lord be with you. Turn against the enemies of Christianity the arms which you unjustly employ against each other. Redeem by this service, well-pleasing to God, those acts of pillage and burning, those homicides and other crimes, which exclude from His kingdom, that you may quickly obtain their pardon. We exhort and enjoin you, for the remission of your sins, to have compassion on the affliction of our brethren who are in and around Jerusalem, and to repress the insolence of the unbelievers, who wish to subdue all kingdoms and empires, and design to extinguish the name of Christianity.   Otherwise it is to be feared that the faith will soon perish in those lands.   Many of you have witnessed personally the persecution which prevails there, and we have learnt it by this letter, which the venerable Peter here present has brought to us.

"For our part, confiding in the mercy of God, and the authority of St. Peter, we forgive to those who shall take arms against the infidels, those immense penances which are due to their sins.   And those who die in true penitence ought not to doubt that they receive pardon of their sins and an eternal reward.   We take under the protection of the Church, and of the apostles St. Peter and St. Paul, those who engage in this enterprise, and command that their persons and their goods be in perfect security."

This discourse of the pope, in which the reader will observe the erroneous notion, that good works can atone for past sins, and the assumption of authority to dispense with the acts of penance imposed by the canons of all Churches, had so great an effect on the assembled multitude, that it was unanimously agreed to commence the crusade; and Adhemar bishop of Puy, and Raymond count of Toulouse, were appointed leaders of the expedition.   But the flame of religious enthusiasm soon spread far and wide through Europe; and in the following year, eight hundred thousand armed men, under different leaders, marched for Constantinople on their way to the Holy Land.   Peter the hermit led a vast but undisciplined body through Hungary and Thrace; but their disorders caused the inhabitants of those countries to take up arms against them.   Vast multitudes, however, crossed over into Asia Minor.   Nice, the capital of Bithynia, was besieged and taken by the crusaders, who penetrated through Asia Minor, and subdued Antioch and Edessa, which were formed into principalities, and assigned to some of the chiefs of the crusade. In fine, the Christian army, led by Godfrey of Bouillon, duke of Lorrain, laid siege to Jerusalem in 1099, and after five weeks gained possession of that holy city, where they immediately established their general as king. The kingdom of Jerusalem continued to exist for about eighty years. It only included the city of Jerusalem and a few towns in the neighbourhood, and the subjects of the new monarch consisted chiefly of the small body of crusading troops which remained to support his dominion. The country in general was under the dominion of the Mahommedans; and the Christian principalities, established at such enormous sacrifices, maintained only a feeble existence.

In 1147, a second crusade was proclaimed by Pope Eugenius III., in consequence of the alarming accounts which had reached Europe of the progress of the infidels in the East, their capture of Edessa, and the dangers of the other Christian principalities. St. Bernard, abbot of Clairvaux, at the desire of Louis VII., king of France, and the pope, preached the crusade at Vezelai, where the king, the queen, and many of the nobles and prelates of France, took the cross (the emblem of the crusaders); and soon afterwards the king of France and the emperor of Germany led immense armies towards the Holy Land, but failed in affording any effectual aid to the Christians, and returned in 1149 with the miserable remains of their hosts. The kingdom of Jerusalem continued to exist for about forty years longer; but in 1187, Saladin, sultan of Egypt and Syria, availed himself of the divisions and corruptions of the Latins of the East to wage war on them with vigour; and having captured Guy of Lusignan, king of Jerusalem, soon after took that city, and extinguished the dominion of the Latins.   In consequence of these events, a third crusade was undertaken by the emperor Frederic Barbarossa of Germany in 1189; but this prince was drowned in a river of Cilicia on his way to the Holy Land, and his army was swept off by a most terrible pestilence.   In the following year another expedition was headed by Philip Augustus, king of France, and Richard Cœur de Lion, king of England.   The former of these monarchs soon became weary of the wars in Palestine, and returned home again : king Richard gained great advantages over Saladin ; but finding himself unsupported, was obliged at length to retire, leaving the Mahommedan power established in Palestine.

In 1203 a fourth crusade was engaged in by the French and the Venetians.   At the desire of the latter, the whole expedition was directed to Constantinople, to procure the restoration of a young prince, who had been unjustly deprived of the empire; but these crusaders soon forgot the end of their expedition, took possession of Constantinople, where they established a Latin emperor, and a patriarch subject to the pope, and subdued the European possessions of the Greek emperors, in which they appointed schismatical bishops subject to the see of Rome, and most cruelly persecuted the Greek bishops and clergy.   The Greek emperors and patriarchs maintained their succession at Nice in Bithynia ; and in 1261 recovered the city of Constantinople, and expelled the Latin usurpers from their countries.

Several other expeditions for the recovery of the Holy Land took place in 1217, 1228, 1239, 1240, 1249, and 1270, which produced no permanent effects.   Jerusalem was for a short time recovered, but it soon fell again under the dominion of the

Mahommedans; and in 1291, the city of Acre, where the feeble relics of the crusaders, and the titular king and patriarch of Jerusalem, had long resided, was captured, and the Christian power in Palestine came to an end.

The influence of the crusades in extending and consolidating the power of the see of Rome was very great. The plenary indulgence, or remission of the canonical penance of all persons who should engage in these expeditions, was in itself based on the notion that the bishop of Rome had jurisdiction in every part of the Church, and that he might relieve the laity and clergy of other bishops from those canonical penances and external marks of contrition for their sins which had been imposed by their own pastors. This was an usurpation on the part of the popes; and yet on the admission of this usurpation the whole fabric of the crusades rested. For two centuries the popes had the power of directing all the armies of Europe against the infidels, or against those whom they chose to term heretics and schismatics; and they exacted enormous sums of money from every country, on pretence of sending assistance to the crusaders. We cannot wonder that, under such circumstances, they should have conceived themselves entitled to create kings, to deprive sovereigns of their thrones, and to claim temporal dominion over all kingdoms of the world. However absurd such claims may now appear, and however plainly inconsistent such assumption of temporal power was with the gospel of Christ, in those ages they were very commonly received; and along with them came the notion of the pope's infallibility and superiority to a general council.

The most vehement supporters of the papal authority were the monks and begging friars. The reason of this was, that the popes, amongst other usurpations, took on them to exempt monasteries in general from the jurisdiction of their respective bishops, to whom they had always been subject from the most ancient times, and made them immediately subject to the papal see. The monks and friars, who were glad to be relieved from the inspection of their bishops, and to be left almost entirely without control, became, of course, advocates for the papal power in every diocese, and over every bishop. It also led them to set the power of the popes above all the laws of the Church; for the whole body of ancient canons had placed the monasteries under the jurisdiction of their bishops. And the next step was to infer that a power which was above all laws was infallible and almost divine.

The monks, who were distinguished from the friars by possessing property and endowments, gradually became extremely relaxed in discipline, and fell into contempt. In the thirteenth century they received incomes from their monasteries, and their situations became so many good benefices. They went out without permission, accepted invitations from laymen, and remained out of their cloister. They had property of their own, borrowed money, became security for others, and partook of all the indulgences of ordinary life. Labour was now commonly discontinued; the time of fasting very much abbreviated, on the pretence that human nature had less strength than in ancient times. The monks were now no longer in deserts apart from society, and devoted to meditation and silence: they studied at the universities, mingled in the affairs of Church and State, undertook the care of parishes, and indulged in recreations.

All this was widely different from the manners of the ancient monks, who were religious in deed, as a learned writer has said, and not merely in name. There was little thought at that time of following the example of the venerable St. Columbanus. When Sigebert, king of France, had offered him large possessions in that country, in the hope of retaining him there, the holy man replied: "We who have forsaken our own, that, according to the commandment of the gospel, we might follow the Lord, ought not to embrace other men's riches, lest peradventure we should prove transgressors of the divine commandment." The rule universally adopted by the primitive ascetics was, that " they which live in monasteries should *work in silence, and eat their own bread.*"

The begging friars, who were instituted in the thirteenth century, and consisted of the four orders of Dominicans, Franciscans, Augustinians, and Carmelites, exhibited for a time a very ardent zeal, and a spirit of poverty and self-denial, which in some degree resembled that of the ancient ascetics. Superstition, however, prevailed amongst them to a greater extent than in any other part of the Church. Their great boast was, to possess no property whatever, either personally or as a community. Still, this did not prevent them from having large funds at their disposal; for while they would have esteemed it an unpardonable offence to receive any thing for themselves directly, they had no scruple in receiving donations and benefactions to any amount " for the pope and the Roman Church," to be applied, however, to their own particular uses. This ingenious distinction enabled them to profess their own utter poverty, to beg with the utmost importunity, and to be at once theoretically the poorest, and practically the wealthiest orders in Europe.

Richard Fitz-Ralph, archbishop of Armagh, in the fourteenth century, who was a strong opponent of the begging friars, objected against them, in the presence of the pope and cardinals, that in his time "scarce could any great or mean man of the clergy or the laity eat his meat, but such kind of beggars would be at his elbow; not like other poor folks, humbly craving alms at the gate or the door, (as St. Francis did command and teach them in his testament,) by begging, but without shame intruding themselves into courts or houses, and lodging there, where, without any invitation at all, they eat and drink what they find among them; and not content with that, carry away with them either wheat, or meal, or bread, or flesh, or cheeses, although there were but two in a house, in a kind of extorting manner, there being none that can deny them, unless he should cast away natural modesty." Religion was degraded by this mean and sordid system, which clothed itself with the character of superior piety and perfection, while it disgusted every pious mind by its habits of grasping extortion. The spirit of secularity and of luxury soon found an entrance amongst these begging friars; they became still more engaged in the affairs of the world than the monks, and fixed their residences in the midst of populous cities and of the world.

What might naturally be expected followed. The monasteries, which had been originally intended to afford examples of perfect purity, devotion towards God, and deadness to the world, were polluted by the spirit of worldliness, and other gross sins; and having ceased to be advantageous to Christianity,—though even in the worst times they were useful to a certain extent in preserving ancient books and monuments, and in affording education, —they had become an incumbrance to the Church, which it was necessary to remove.

The bishops and clergy themselves shared but

too often in the evils of the times. We read of archbishops and bishops engaged in wars, crusades, and other temporal avocations. They were chancellors, chief-justiciaries, ministers, regents, embassadors. Hunting and hawking were their not unfrequent amusements. They were engaged more in temporal than spiritual affairs. The clergy of cathedrals became idle and luxurious. They neglected their canonical duties, and heaped up preferments and wealth in a manner altogether alien to the spirit of Christianity. The parochial clergy were still ignorant, though less so than in former ages. They too much neglected preaching; and the mendicant friars, by permission of the popes, half superseded them in their offices,—preached, administered the sacraments, and became spiritual directors of their parishioners. The bishops and clergy were often exceedingly unpopular amongst the laity, and bitter complaints were made of their ambition and exactions. The evil practice of pluralities, *i.e.* of clergy holding several parishes and offices in the Church, arose in these ages, and was encouraged by the popes, who set the example of most scandalous abuses, by accumulating quantities of preferments on their own relatives, and on the cardinals or principal clergy of the city of Rome. This practice was in direct contradiction to the laws of the Church; nevertheless it became so customary, that, although the abuse is much diminished, the Church has never yet been able to extinguish it entirely.

Let me now notice a few other corruptions introduced in these ages. In the eleventh century it was supposed that for every particular sin it was necessary to fulfil the time of penitence prescribed by the ancient canons; so that if ten years had been appointed for homicide, a man who had committed that sin twenty times was bound to discharge two hundred years of penance. This led ingenious men to discover ways of paying the debt. Peter Damian, in the twelfth century, affirmed that the repetition of the Psalter twenty times, accompanied by discipline (that is, scourging), was equal to a hundred years of penitence. A friend of his requested him, at the beginning of Lent, to impose on him a thousand years of penitence, and he nearly finished his satisfaction before the end of Lent! Another invention was the discharge of penitence by one person for another. These strange doctrines obtained much popularity, though many persons disapproved of them.

A singular illustration of the superstitions current in these ages is afforded by the history of the Flagellants, or Scourgers, in the thirteenth century. We have seen that Peter Damian in the preceding century had recommended the newly invented discipline of scourging as a means of speedily discharging the great debt of penance due to the Church. This notion was soon adopted and disseminated by the pious but ignorant and superstitious monks of Monte Cassino, and gradually made way amongst the common people in Italy till the middle of the thirteenth century, when a strange scene of mingled devotion and superstition was witnessed. . The movement began at Perugia in Italy, thence passed to Rome, throughout Italy, Germany, Poland, and other countries. All classes of the people, nobles and serfs, old and young, even to children five years of age, filled with apprehension of the wrath of God on account of the sins of their nations, were seen walking in procession with bare feet, and almost in a state of nudity, through the streets, each holding in his hand a scourge of leather, with which, amidst many tears and lamentations, they lashed themselves until the blood flowed, while they besought the mercy of God, and the assistance of the Virgin Mary. These processions frequently continued during the night by torch-light, and in the midst of a severe winter. They consisted of many thousands of people, and became common even in the remotest and obscurest districts. The effects of this enthusiasm on the morals of the people were truly extraordinary. The customary amusements and occupations of life were forgotten in the universal excitement. Instead of instruments of music and songs, nothing was heard but the cries and wailings of these processions. Even the women of all ranks took a part in this enthusiastic movement; but as modesty forbade their appearance in public, they practised all the severities of the Flagellants in their private chambers. Enemies became reconciled to each other; usurers and robbers hastened to restore the possessions of others, of which they had unjustly deprived them; sinners of every kind confessed their sins, and amended their lives. Prisons were opened, and captives set at liberty. Exiles were recalled, and all sorts of good works abundantly performed.

In Germany and Poland, the Flagellants who went in procession concealed their heads and faces, that they might not be known. They scourged themselves twice a day for thirty-three days, in remembrance of the thirty-three years of our Saviour's life on earth, and chanted hymns on his death and passion. After a time they asserted that no one could be pardoned of all his sins, unless he had first undergone this discipline. They confessed their sins to each other, and gave absolution, though they were only laymen, and pretended that their penance or discipline could benefit even the dead. This strange superstition or enthusiasm was soon suppressed. The temporal sovereigns of Italy and Germany became apprehensive of the assemblage of such great bodies of men in their dominions; and many of the bishops, having discovered the excesses and errors which began to flow from this system, forbade and condemned it, so that it was soon abandoned and forgotten; but the history affords an interesting example of the tendency of the popular mind in those ages, of zeal unregulated by knowledge, of piety mingled with superstition. It may be added, that the practice of flagellation, which was first introduced in the twelfth century, continued long after the suppression of this enthusiastic popular movement, though it was no longer publicly or commonly used. It has been occasionally practised by devotees in the Roman Church even to the present day.

A distinct office in honour of the Virgin was used by some persons in the tenth century; it became common in the eleventh; and the monks, about the same time, added the office of the dead to their daily devotions. In these ages, persons not unfrequently, on the approach of death, caused themselves to be arrayed in the garments of monks, imagining that these holy vestments would protect them against the devil. In the thirteenth century, a new devotion for the laity was invented by Dominic. Men were taught to repeat the angel's salutation to the Virgin 150 times, and the Lord's Prayer fifteen times, that is, once after each decade of Aves. The prayers were reckoned by beads; and the whole ceremony obtained the name of Rosary. Dominic invented some other devotions to the Virgin Mary. The scapulary, a portion of the monks' dress, was now worn by some persons as a sort of charm: the Carmelites were loud in their assurances of the blessings which might be expected by its possessors. Several persons wore sackcloth or haircloth next their skin, by way of voluntary mortification. The mendicant friars introduced a custom which was extremely prejudicial in its effects. They granted absolution immediately to those who confessed their sins, without waiting for the accomplishment of the penitence which they assigned them. This led men to think that they might sin without danger; as a simple confession, with a promise of amendment, was sufficient to procure the priests' remission of their sins. In the thirteenth century also, the eucharist began to be elevated after consecration, and the people were taught to bow or prostrate themselves at the same time. Hence many persons were in danger of offering worship to the bread and wine. It became customary in this age to administer the sacrament to the laity only in one kind, that is, the bread. This custom was inconsistent with the institution of our Lord, and the practice of the whole Church for more than a thousand years: it was in direct opposition to the decree of the synod of Clermont, A.D. 1095, where more than two hundred bishops were present with Pope Urban II.: but it was nevertheless sanctioned by the councils of Constance in 1414, and Basil in 1438. I have not spoken of the invocation of saints, the veneration for relics and images, which in these ages continued to be excessive, nor of many other minor superstitions and errors. These will sufficiently shew the great necessity for reformation in the Church. It is true, indeed, that many persons were more or less free from superstitions; but a great change was imperatively called for. Few things needed reformation more than the system of theological instruction in universities, commonly called the scholastic theology.

Schools for the instruction of the clergy and

laity had existed generally in cathedral churches and monasteries from the remotest antiquity; but, about the twelfth century, the schools in some cities became very celebrated and extensive, and were known under the name of *Universities*. The principal universities, during the middle ages, were those of Paris, Oxford, Bologna, and Salamanca. They were endowed with revenues, and granted many privileges, by princes and popes. Instruction was given to students in the four faculties of theology, law, medicine, and the arts, by the doctors in those faculties. Peter Lombard, bishop of Paris, a celebrated doctor of theology, published, in 1172, a treatise entitled *The Book of Sentences*, in which the various doctrines of revelation were collected and explained from the writings of the fathers. This work formed the basis of the scholastic theology; it became the text-book on which all the subsequent theologians commented, and to which they added all the subtilties of the Aristotelic philosophy. The Christian faith and morality were not, in the writings of these theologians, proved so much by Scripture, and the scriptural doctrine of the ancient fathers and œcumenical synods, as by mere reasoning and philosophy. Every thing was questioned and disputed, and the most insignificant as well as the most essential points were settled, and frequently on erroneous grounds. The ablest of the scholastic writers were Thomas Aquinas and Scotus.

The text-book of the canonists, or students of canon law, was the work of Gratian, a Benedictine monk, entitled *Decretum*, and written about A.D. 1130, in which the ancient canons of councils were collected, and reconciled with each other and with the decretals of the popes. In this collection all the spurious decretals of the early popes, fabricated

in the eighth and ninth centuries, were introduced;
and as Gratian entertained very exaggerated notions
of the papal authority, this book, which was immediately received as of the highest authority in all
the schools of Europe, tended greatly to increase
the influence of the popes. The study of canon
law became so popular, and led so certainly to
advancement in the Church, that theology and the
arts were much neglected; and more than one pope
felt himself bound to discourage this exclusive application.

From the twelfth century, the writings of the
early fathers and the decrees of councils were little
known in the schools, except through the medium
of *The Book of Sentences* or the *Decretum.* This
is allowed by a learned Roman Catholic historian,
the Abbé Fleury, who says, that " it was the misfor-
tune of the doctors of the thirteenth and fourteenth
centuries to know but little of the writings of the
fathers, especially the more ancient, and to be deficient in the aids requisite for well understanding
them. It is not that their books were lost; they
existed, for we have them still; but the copies were
scarce, and hidden in the libraries of the ancient
monasteries, where little use was made of them."
He adds, that King Louis IX. of France, in the
thirteenth century, caused many of them to be
transcribed; and that Vincent of Beauvais made
extracts from them, and John of Salisbury cited
them frequently: " but," he continues, " this was
merely the curiosity of some individuals. The ge-
nerality of students, and even of doctors, limited
themselves to a few books, chiefly those of modern
authors, which they understood better than the
ancients." " I do not cease to wonder," he continues, " that in such calamitous times, and with
such small aid, the doctors so faithfully preserved

to us the deposit of tradition with regard to doctrine." The Abbé Goujet, another Roman Catholic divine, confirms this; and observes also, that the study of *Scripture* "had been extremely neglected" in these ages. "They did not study it even in the schools of theology but with lukewarmness; and often contented themselves with such extracts from it as were found in the writings of some superficial theologian. Hence arose the ignorance of the clergy, and the few defenders which the Church found against heresies....... At length the study of holy Scripture caused men to escape from this lethargy; men then perceived the crowd of errors and false opinions which had inundated the whole Church, and had nearly choked the good seed." The fallen state of theological study at the time of the Reformation may be collected from the complaints of the faculty of arts in the university of Paris in 1530. "The study of sacred Scripture," they said, "is neglected. The holy Gospels are no longer cited. The authority of St. Chrysostom, St. Cyprian, St. Augustine, and the other fathers, is not employed. Theology has become nothing but a sophistical science." Under such circumstances it was to be expected that erroneous opinions would become more or less prevalent in the Church. The holy Scriptures had been undoubtedly given by God, that "the man of God might be perfect, thoroughly furnished unto all good works;" and when this divine means of grace and wisdom was neglected, as it certainly was to a considerable degree in these times, it could not be supposed that the same purity of doctrine or of practice should exist as in the primitive ages of the Church.

CHAPTER XXI.

THE FOREIGN REFORMATION.

A.D. 1517-1839.

THE enormous power usurped by the popes, and the abuses in its exercise, at length paved the way for its own subversion, and for the Reformation. Never were its exactions and abuses so excessive as in the time of what is called the great schism, from 1378 to 1414, when Europe was divided under the domination of rival popes, one of whom resided at Avignon in France, and was acknowledged pope by France and Spain; while the other, who resided at Rome, was obeyed by the rest of Europe. The papacy was greatly lowered in public estimation by this division; and France, on more than one occasion, withdrew itself from the obedience of both popes. The contests which arose between the councils of Pisa, Constance, and Basil, in the early part of the fifteenth century, and the popes, in which each party asserted its own infallibility, and its superiority to the other, excited a spirit of inquiry.

The council of Pisa was called together in 1409 by many of the cardinals of the two contending popes, in order to put an end to the schism. In this council both popes were deposed, and a third was elected; but this measure only increased the division; for there were now *three* rival popes, each of whom excommunicated and deposed his opponents and all their adherents. This division was terminated by the council of Constance in 1414, when one of the rival popes was degraded, another

resigned, and a third sunk into obscurity and insig-
nificance, after the election of a new pope, who was
acknowledged by all Europe.   The council of Basil
in 1437 having made reforms which were disliked
by pope Eugenius IV., the latter called a rival
council at Florence; on which he was deposed by
the council of Basil in 1439, and a rival pope was
elected; but this division did not last long. "The
REFORMATION OF THE CHURCH, in its head and
members," was now one of the objects avowed by
every considerable council that assembled.   Wickliffe had, in the preceding century, declaimed against
the popes and against several abuses; and he was
closely followed by Huss, and Jerome of Prague:
but their opinions were mingled with much that
was exceptionable; and they seem to have been
unfitted rightly to conduct the mighty work of reformation.   The revival of learning in the fifteenth
century was the great forerunner of improvement.
Men now began to study the writings of the fathers,
which had only been known at second-hand, from
the books of Lombard and Gratian.   The introduction of the Greek and Hebrew languages (entirely
unknown during the middle ages) rendered the study
of Scripture in the originals possible; and the scholastic writers began to lose their credit with men of
education.

At length the Reformation began; but not as it
could have been desired; not promoted by the heads
of the Church, not regulated by the decrees of councils.   An individual monk in Saxony was made the
involuntary instrument by which this great work was
set on foot.   Martin Luther, an Augustinian friar,
when he declaimed against the scandalous sale of
indulgences by the papal agent Tetzel, in 1517,
had little notion of opposing the papal supremacy,
or reforming the Church.   He simply rejected with

indignation the notion, that by purchasing certain indulgences, the soul was to be freed from torments after death ; and reminded men that indulgences were originally nothing more than the remission of canonical penance in this life. When assailed by Eckius and many others with the most furious violence, he was led to further investigation ; and he shewed, in his conference with Eckius, in 1519, that the Roman Church had not originally any supremacy over the universal Church. He, however, testified to the pope his earnest desire for peace, and submitted himself entirely to him : but when Luther declined to retract, without any discussion, whatever Cardinal Cajetan might censure in his doctrine, the pope, notwithstanding his submissive tone, and his protestations that he did not intend any separation from the Church, excommunicated him and his favourers, in 1521.

Luther, and his friends Melancthon, Carlostadt, and all who were of the same sentiments, were thus separated from the communion of the pope, and of his adherents in Germany, not voluntarily, or by their own act. They were now, however, able to examine and to speak more freely; and a strong controversy immediately arose, in which the prevalent errors and superstitions were assailed unsparingly; while every effort was made by the Romish party to procure the extirpation and destruction of their opponents. The Lutheran party were protected by the electors of Saxony and Brandenburg, and many other princes and states in Germany; and they continually called for the assembling of a free and general council, to whose decision they offered to submit themselves. In the meantime, various abuses were corrected in the churches of those states, and a temporary system of Church-government was established by the Lutherans, which they intended to be replaced by the ordinary episcopal government, when the council had arranged their disputes, and they should be united again to the Church. But Providence forbade the accomplishment of their wishes: an arrangement which the contending parties had come to in the diet or parliament of Spires in 1526, and which left the Lutheran states free to regulate their own ecclesiastical affairs until the general council could be called together, was set aside by a new diet at the same place, in 1529, in which all alterations were prohibited by a majority of votes. The Lutheran princes and states entered A PROTEST against this edict, and from this they were termed PROTESTANTS. The term Protestant, therefore, does not properly signify a protest against the errors of the Church of Rome, but against the edict of Spires. It belongs properly to the Lutherans, by whom in fact it is claimed, as being peculiarly their own; while the Church of England has never applied the term to herself, nor ever used it in any of her formularies. It came gradually, however, to be applied to all who were in favour of the Reformation. In the following year (1530) a diet was convened at Augsburg, by the Emperor Charles V., with the intent of terminating these differences. The Lutheran party here presented their confession of faith, which has since been called the Confession of Augsburg, and which contains a brief summary of the Christian doctrine, together with their objections to the chief errors and superstitions then prevalent. It professes a belief in the doctrine of the Holy Trinity, the Godhead of the Son and the Holy Spirit, according to the decree of the synod of Nice, and rejects the Manichæan, Arian, Sabellian, and other heresies; acknowledges that man is naturally sinful; that we cannot be justified by our own merits, but only through Christ; that there is need of the sacred ministry in the Church; that good works and obedience to God are necessary ; that baptism is requisite to salvation, and that children ought to be baptised; that the body and blood of Christ are truly present and received by those who partake of the Lord's supper; that private absolution should be retained, but that it is not necessary to confess every particular sin to a priest; that the Church may absolve those who truly repent; that faith is necessary to receive the sacrament rightly ; that man cannot do good works without the aid of the Holy Ghost; and that the memory of the saints should be honoured, but that they ought not to be invoked or assistance sought from them, because the Scripture declares that Christ is our only mediator, propitiation, priest, and intercessor.

The Confession of Augsburg, having thus stated the belief and doctrine of the Lutheran party, next proceeds to remark on the abuses to which they objected as " novel, and contrary to the intention of the canons" or laws of the Church. They objected to the recent abuse of giving the bread only in the eucharist; to the celibacy of the clergy, which had produced such great abuses, and which was enforced by capital punishments ; to the use of an unknown language in public service ; to the system of paying for masses, and to those private or solitary masses where the priest alone communicated, and which were unknown to Christian antiquity. They blamed the opinion of those who imagined that partaking of particular sorts of food, or the practice of certain ceremonies invented by men, entitled them to remission of their sins, or to an increase of divine grace. They objected to the system of exacting vows from those who gave themselves to a monastic life, which had been unknown to Christian antiquity; and censured the doctrine of those who supposed that sins were remitted by adopting the monastic profession, and that this state of life was much holier and deserved far higher rewards than any other. These are the principal points which, in the opinion of Luther and his friends, needed reformation.

The Confession of Augsburg professes that there is nothing in it "which differs from the Scriptures or the *Roman Church*." It declares that they "differ concerning no article of faith from the Catholic Church, but only omit some abuses." "There is no design," they said, "to deprive the bishops of their authority; but this only is sought, that the gospel be permitted to be purely taught, and a few observances be relaxed."

Notwithstanding this moderation, the diet, by order of the emperor, condemned the Protestants, and ordered them to submit themselves to the pope. They were then obliged to confederate in their own defence, in the league of Smalcald; and by this means they obtained toleration from the emperor. Various controversies and conferences afterwards took place between the opposed parties, especially in 1541, at Ratisbon, when many of the points of difference were removed, and both parties, including the papal nuncio, were in great hopes of an entire agreement.

The Protestants had continued their appeal to a free general council from the year 1520; but the pope, who had usurped for some centuries past the privilege of assembling such councils, refused to do so in the present instance, except in places where there was no security for the safety of the Protestants. The pope at length fixed on Trent as the place of meeting; and when the Protestants objected to it on various grounds, the emperor and pope conspired to crush them by force. Accordingly, Charles V. declared war against them, and overthrew them in the battle of Muhlberg, in 1547. In the meantime the council of Trent had met in 1545; and having decided several points in controversy in the absence of the Protestants, had been prorogued in 1547. The emperor, therefore, being unable to compel the Protestants to send deputies, was obliged to be satisfied with issuing a formulary of faith and discipline, called *The Interim;* in which the chief points permitted to the Lutherans were, the marriage of the clergy, and the use of the cup in the sacrament. When the council again assembled, in 1551, the Protestants were compelled to send deputies there; but when they required that the articles already decided by forty or fifty bishops at Trent should be re-examined, they were not listened to. They were consequently obliged to withdraw from the council, and to retain their own observances, without any hope of reconciliation with the Church. They were enabled to maintain their religious liberty by the advantages gained over the emperor by the Elector Maurice of Saxony, in 1552, which led to the pacification of Passau, by which the religion and liberties of the Protestants were secured from further molestation.

In the meantime, the Reformation, as established by Luther and Melancthon, spread itself widely. Denmark, Norway, and Sweden, together with a great part of Germany, embraced it. Monasteries were suppressed; purgatory, indulgences, invocation of saints, worship of pictures and relics, flagellations, communion in one kind only, rosaries, scapularies, and a number of other errors and superstitions, disappeared. The Scriptures were translated afresh, and read by all the people. Divine service was celebrated in a known language, and sermons were frequently delivered. Episcopacy was never condemned by the Lutherans; they even retain the form of that ecclesiastical government in several countries, and it is said that their bishops in Sweden are validly ordained.

It is to be lamented, however, that the Lutherans after a time forgot that their system was merely provisional, and designed only to last till a general council could be lawfully assembled. They then began to pretend that their ancestors had separated *voluntarily* from the western Church, and justified this act by reasons which sanctioned schism and separation generally. In the seventeenth century there were many learned men amongst them; but they were much troubled by religious parties, and were threatened with destruction in the war which was waged against them for thirty years by the emperors and the Romish party, and which was at length terminated by the peace of Westphalia, in 1648. In the middle of the following century, a spirit of false liberality and scepticism began to infect the Lutheran communities. The Confession of Augsburg, and other formularies of the sixteenth century, to which their ministers had subscribed, lost their authority, and an unbounded freedom of op - nion on all points was encouraged. The result was, the rise of a party headed by the notorious Semler, who, under the mask of Christianity, explained away all the doctrines of revelation, denied the miracles and other facts of sacred history, and subverted the genuineness and authenticity of the Bible. This infidelity became dreadfully prevalent among the Protestants of Germany and Denmark in the course of the last and present centuries; the universities were full of it, the ministers of religion tainted with it; and the Lutheran faith seems under an eclipse, from whence we fervently pray that it may be delivered.

It is now time to consider the Reformation in

Switzerland, France, and the United Provinces. Zuinglius, a clergyman in Switzerland, from the year 1519 preached in the church of Zurich against the corruptions of that period; but after some time he was treated as a heretic by the adherents of the pope, and had he not been protected by the magistrates, would have fallen a sacrifice to their rage. A reformation then took place in Switzerland, which was carried too far in some respects; and on the subject of the sacraments especially, Zuinglius was severely condemned by Luther for considering the eucharist a mere sign of our Lord's body. His views on baptism were also very defective. Some years after his death, Calvin, a man of abilities and learning, obtained a vast influence among the reformed in Switzerland, France, Holland, Germany, &c. He was called to Geneva by the inhabitants of that city, and became their pastor. His well-known doctrinal system of irrespective election and irresistible grace obtained a wide currency. His views on the eucharist were apparently very much more sound than those of Zuinglius. He was the founder of the Presbyterian system of Church-government.

In France, the doctrines of Luther obtained adherents very early; but their professors were most bitterly persecuted for a long series of years. They were favoured by many of the nobility, and headed by the Queen of Navarre, and afterwards by her son Henry IV. of France. A league was formed for their extirpation by the powerful family of the Guises; and, in 1572, the massacre of St. Bartholomew, commanded by Charles IX., destroyed many of their leaders, and a vast multitude of the people. At length, after much cruel persecution, they obtained toleration by the edict of Nantes, in 1598. The reformed party in France at that time followed the doctrines of Calvin, and Beza his coadjutor. They continued to exist during the seventeenth century; but in the year 1685, Louis XIV. revoked the edict of Nantes, and they were then either compelled to emigrate, to conform to the Church of France, or to conceal themselves. They have latterly become a small and feeble party, and have too generally ceased to believe the articles of our faith.

The persecution of the Spanish government for the sake of religion obliged the seven United Provinces of Holland to arm in their own defence in the latter part of the sixteenth century ; and after a desperate struggle, they succeeded in obtaining civil and religious freedom. They also adopted the doctrines of Calvin ; but in the following century they were torn by controversies between his followers and those of Arminius. The latter seem to have held errors in some degree resembling those of Pelagius. They were condemned in the Calvinistic synod of Dort in 1618, the decrees of which are not of any authority in the Church.

It may be observed in general of the reformed communities in Switzerland, France, and the United Provinces, that they have too generally fallen away from the doctrines originally believed by them into the Socinian or Arian heresies.

It remains now to notice briefly a few of the principal leaders of the Reformation on the continent.

Martin Luther was born in Saxony in 1483; and having been early instructed in letters, he went to the university of Erfurt, where he studied the classics, the Aristotelic philosophy, and the civil law, with the intent of advancing himself at the bar; but he was diverted from this intention by the following accident. As he was walking with a friend one day in the fields, he was struck by lightning, which threw him to the ground, and which killed his companion at his side. This circumstance so profoundly affected him, that, without communicating his design to his friends, he immediately entered the order of Augustinian friars. Here he applied himself closely to the study of the scholastic writers, and afterwards to that of the Bible; and was ordained priest in 1507, after which he was chosen by the elector of Saxony to a professorship in his new university of Wittemburg. In 1510 he was appointed by his order to go to Rome to plead their cause, on occasion of a dispute with their general; and this afforded him an opportunity to see and condemn the gross corruptions and scandals of all sorts in that city: but it was not till Tetzel began the scandalous sale of indulgences in Germany, and promised remission of all past and future sins for money, that Luther was led to examine deeply into the existing abuses. He had, however, no intention of separating from the communion of the Church; he repeatedly, in the course of four years, between 1517 and 1521, declared that he was ready to be silent and to submit himself to the judgment of bishops, or of the Roman see, provided that his adversaries were also commanded to be silent. Even when he found that the pope was under the influence of his personal enemies, he did not reject the jurisdiction of the Church, but appealed to the next general council; and, in fine, he and his friends were expelled from the communion of the Roman Church in a very unjustifiable manner, and did not voluntarily forsake it.

In 1521 Luther was called to the diet of Worms by the emperor, to ascertain whether he really held the errors imputed to him. His friends were very reluctant that he should attend the diet, fearing lest, in spite of the emperor's safe-conduct, he might be seized and put to death by his enemies: but Luther said, "I am lawfully called to appear in that city, and thither will I go, in the name of the Lord, though as many devils as there are tiles on the houses were there combined against me."   In this diet Luther firmly refused to retract his doctrines, unless they were proved contrary to the word of God; and being dismissed unhurt, he was presently seized and hid in the castle of Wartburg by his friend the elector of Saxony ; for a severe edict had been issued against him by the diet immediately after he had departed. In this solitude Luther began the translation of the Bible into the vernacular language, and composed several books in defence of his doctrines.   In 1522 he returned to Wittemburg to check the excesses of Carlostadt, who had broken the images of saints, and was proceeding with reforms indiscreetly and irregularly.   Soon after, great part of the Bible was published, and had much effect in promoting the progress of the Reformation throughout Germany. From this time Luther continued to reside at Wittemburg, and was the head of the Reformation in Germany.   He composed commentaries on the Bible; was always vehemently opposed to the papal authority, which he regarded as an anti-Christian usurpation; and died in 1546, in the sixty-second year of his age.

PHILIP MELANCTHON, a friend of Luther, and who succeeded at his death to the chief influence amongst the Protestant party in Germany, was born in 1495, and was distinguished at an early age by his attainments in every sort of literature ; so that, in 1518, when only twenty-three years of age, he was appointed professor of Greek at Wittemburg, where he contracted a close intimacy with Luther, and was converted to his opinions by the disputation which took place between Luther and Eckius. Melancthon, in 1520, read lectures on St. Paul's epistles, which were highly approved by Luther, and printed. He afterwards drew up the Confession of Augsburg, and the Apology or defence of that confession, which became the standards of doctrine among the Lutheran party. He was remarkable for his moderation; was always most desirous that the Church should be re-united; and was ready to make considerable sacrifices in order to attain so desirable an object. He wished the authority of bishops to be preserved, and would even have been contented to allow some authority to the see of Rome; but his views were far too moderate to satisfy the papal party; and the Lutherans had been too severely persecuted to regard them with much favour. Melancthon wrote largely in defence of Luther, and against the Romish errors; and died in 1560.

JOHN CALVIN was born in France in 1509, and studied at the university of Paris. The discipline of the Church at that time was so relaxed, that although he was not in sacred orders, he had been presented successively to three benefices when he was but twenty years old. Having studied the Scriptures, and becoming alive to the errors and superstitions then prevalent, he resolved to relinquish the design of taking holy orders, and to apply himself to the law; on which he resigned his benefices. His studies led him to embrace the doctrines of the Reformation; and a violent persecution arising against all who "were of that way" in France, he was compelled to fly for his life into Switzerland, where, in 1535, he published his *Institution*, as an apology for those who were burnt for their religion in France. The next year, as he passed through Geneva, the citizens of that town compelled him to be their pastor and professor of divinity; but, in consequence of his resolution to put a stop to the immoralities and factions of that place, by enforcing a rigorous discipline, he was banished from Geneva.   He was again recalled in 1541, when he established a form of Church-discipline, and a consistory, invested with power to inflict canonical censures and excommunications; to which the magistrates and people of Geneva promised obedience.   Calvin was a vigorous opponent of the common errors and superstitions; and caused Servetus, who blasphemed against the Holy Trinity, to be put to death.   He wrote many commentaries on Scripture.   His influence was widely extended throughout the reformed communities by his correspondence.   Calvin was a man of great genius, considerable learning, and irreproachable private character; but of a zeal which was too little under the guidance of charity.   His position, as the minister of the people at Geneva, was certainly an irregularity and anomaly, as he had never received holy orders.   It was only excusable under the difficulties of the times, when the bishops of the Continent were too generally under the influence of the pope, and the adherents of the Reformation were unjustly cast out of the Church, and treated as heretics.   It seems to have been held by many persons, and not without some grounds of probability, that in such an extreme case, a Christian community might constitute pastors; although we cannot feel *certain* that divine grace accompanies such ministrations.   It was, perhaps, a reliance on the uncovenanted mercies of God, which consoled many pious men in the unavoidable absence of that lawful ordinary ministry, which was instituted by Jesus Christ, and which has continued by successive ordinations in all ages.   Calvin died in 1564.

ULRICH ZUINGLE was born in Switzerland in 1484, and studied at Basil and Vienna; after which he received holy orders, and became successively

pastor of Glaris, and preacher at the abbey of Ein-
seldeln. Having diligently studied Scripture, the
fathers and schoolmen, he began to see the corruptions so generally prevalent; and he addressed himself, in the first instance, to the bishop of Constance
and the cardinal bishop of Sion, urging them to reform the Swiss churches. Being appointed in 1519
to the principal church in Zurich, he declaimed
against the sale of indulgences, and against other
common errors. Controversies ensued between
Zuingle and the vicar-general of the bishop of Constance, who accused him of heresy and sedition to
the magistrates of Zurich. Zuingle and his friends
declared "that they did not, either in act or intention, separate from the Church." Zuingle was again
accused, in 1522 and 1523, by the Romish party,
as a heretic; but he overcame his adversaries in
controversy; and the magistrates of Zurich decreed that he should not be molested, and that the
clergy should preach nothing except what could be
proved from holy Scripture. After this, Zuingle
and his friends being entirely separated from communion by the Romish party, they effected various
reforms and changes in rites; and they became involved in controversy with Luther on the subject of
the holy eucharist. Zuingle seems to have fallen
into the error of Berengarius on this point; but it
was hoped for a long time that he and his adherents
might be brought to a sounder mind. Conferences
with this object continued long after his death,
which took place in 1531.

CHAPTER XXII.

ON THE BRITISH CHURCHES.

A.D. 1530-1839.

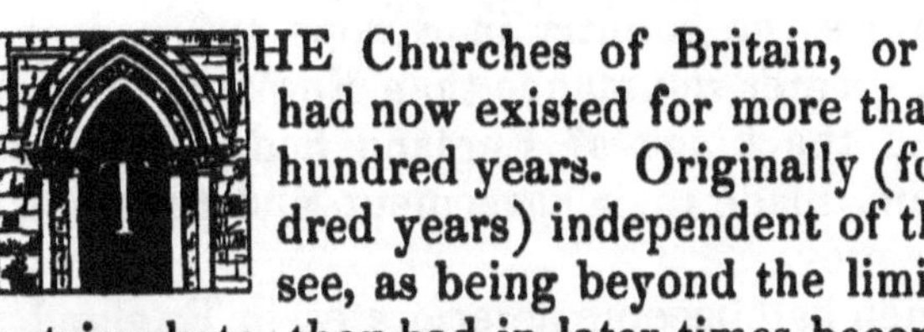THE Churches of Britain, or England, had now existed for more than thirteen hundred years. Originally (for six hundred years) independent of the Roman see, as being beyond the limits of that patriarchate, they had in later times become subject to its jurisdiction. The invasion of Britain by the Saxons, and the subsequent mission of St. Augustine, by Pope Gregory, afforded the opportunity for extending the Roman power; and Augustine was sent the pall, the emblem of honour and authority, as vicar of the holy see. For many ages, however, we hear little or nothing of any exercise of jurisdiction by the popes in England: the English bishops and kings did not permit appeals to Rome. When Wilfrid, bishop of York, appealed against an English synod which had deposed him from his diocese, and obtained a decree in his favour from the pope, that decree was disregarded in England. Pope Gregory I. had made a regulation in accordance with the canons, that the bishops and metropolitans of England should be always appointed and consecrated in their own country, and had no sort of intention to claim the right of confirming or ordaining them. And accordingly the metropolitans and bishops of our churches were always consecrated without reference to the see of Rome, till the twelfth or thirteenth century. Nor were our bishops summoned to attend synods held by the popes, until about the same period.

At length, from the time of Gregory VII., the papal jurisdiction was pushed into England, as it was into other countries; legates made frequent visits, held councils, exacted subsidies. Appeals, dispensations, mandates, reserves, annates, bulls, and all the other inconveniences of papal usurpation, followed each other in rapid succession; and for four centuries no country in Europe suffered more and with greater reluctance than England. But the popes and the kings of England had, after much disputation, made their agreement, and the Church was their prey.

Religion had become deteriorated in England, as well as in the remainder of the western Church. A spirit of opposition to prevailing errors had been excited by Wickliffe; but he, and his followers the Lollards, advocated several erroneous and seditious opinions: they were condemned by the clergy, and persecuted by the state. The Scriptures, however, were translated by Wickliffe; and thus the way was prepared for religious improvement.

The scruples of Henry VIII. as to the lawfulness of his marriage with Catharine, the widow of his elder brother, led ultimately to the removal of the papal power in England, and to the Reformation. Henry in 1526 commenced negotiations with the pope for the dissolution of his marriage, requesting that the papal dispensation by which it had been contracted might be examined, or declared invalid. But the pope, under the influence of the Emperor Charles V., the nephew of Catharine, protracted the affair, by various expedients, for six years. At length Henry, wearied by the arts and chicanery of the court of Rome, had recourse to an expedient, first suggested by Cranmer, a learned doctor of Cambridge, who was soon after made archbishop of Canterbury,—namely, to consult all the universities of

Europe on the question, "whether the papal dispensation for such a marriage was valid;" and to act on their decision, without further appeal to the pope. The question was accordingly put, and decided in the negative by the universities of Oxford, Cambridge, Paris, Bologna, Padua, Orleans, Angiers, Bourges, Toulouse, &c., and by a multitude of theologians and canonists. Henry now being satisfied that his marriage with Catharine had been null and void from the beginning, privately married Anna Boleyn, in 1532; and the convocation of the Church of England immediately afterwards declared his former marriage null, and approved that recently contracted.

In 1532 and 1533 the king and parliament of England suppressed by law various usurped or superfluous privileges of the pope. First-fruits, tenths, pensions, annuities, payments for bulls, palls, &c., censes, portions, Peter's-pence, and all the other pecuniary exactions of the court of Rome, were abolished. Bulls of institution to bishoprics or archbishoprics, and palls, were no longer to be sought from Rome. The prelates were (as they had been for twelve centuries) to be elected and ordained in England. All appeals to Rome in ecclesiastical causes were suppressed; and every cause was to be determined finally in England, according to ancient custom. All that great multiplicity of licenses, dispensations, compositions, faculties, grants, rescripts, delegacies, &c., by which the pontiffs had so grievously enervated the discipline of the Church and enriched themselves, was put an end to. Dispensations were in future only to be issued by the primate of England. Thus the various branches of the papal jurisdiction, most of which had been usurped within the four preceding centuries, were removed. The Church of England acquiesced in these proceedings, well knowing that no principle of justice or of right was infringed by them; and in fine, as the pope and his adherents exclaimed loudly against these reforms, and pretended that the papal jurisdiction thus suppressed was founded on "the word of God," and that it was most impious and wicked to deprive the papal see of any powers which it had possessed; the question was proposed to the bishops and clergy, assembled in the provincial synods of Canterbury and York in 1534, "whether the bishop of Rome has, in the word of God, any greater jurisdiction in the realm of England than any other foreign bishop?" It was determined in the negative. The universities, chapters, monks, friars, &c., throughout the kingdom, declared their assent; one bishop only (Fisher) refused to unite in this general decision of the Church of England; and thus the ordinary jurisdiction of the pope over England was regularly and lawfully suppressed.

The door was now open for gradual improvement; and though the king remained attached to some errors and abuses, several valuable reforms were made during the remainder of his reign. In 1537 and 1543, the convocation published two formularies of doctrine, entitled the *Institution of a Christian Man*, and the *Necessary Doctrine and Erudition;* in which various abuses connected with purgatory were disclaimed. Indulgences were rejected by the same authority, together with all kneeling, bowing, and offering to images; and all worship before them was to be directed to God only, not to the image of the saint represented. Images abused by pilgrimages, and other special honours, were removed; prayer to saints was prohibited, and their invocation only permitted under certain limitations intended to prevent idolatry and superstition. The superstitious use of relics was discouraged; and various other superstitions, such as using gospels for charms, drinking holy water for the cure of diseases, &c., were prohibited. These were great advances and improvements ; but the king opposed a full reformation, and in the parliament of 1539 made penal laws against any who rejected the doctrine of transubstantiation, the celibacy of the clergy, and some other points. The convocation of the clergy in 1531 had acknowledged the king to be " head of the Church of England, as far as it is allowable by the law of Christ," a limitation by which they intended to save all the spiritual rights and jurisdiction of the Church. In virtue of this office, which Henry seems to have understood in a somewhat different sense from that of the convocation, he appointed Lord Cromwell his vicar-general, and visitor of monasteries ; and a visitation of these institutions having been set on foot, they were found to be so generally corrupt and fallen from their rule, that they were all suppressed, and their enormous revenues were given to the king, with a portion of which he founded six new bishoprics in England.

On the death of Henry VIII. in 1547, and the accession of Edward VI., the work of reformation proceeded freely. The communion was now given in both kinds to the laity, according to our Lord's institution and the practice of the Catholic Church ; images and relics, so long abused to superstition and even to idolatry, were removed ; the clergy were permitted to marry ; and the public prayers were translated from the old Latin offices of the English Church, with various improvements from the Greek and Oriental liturgies. These reforms were made by the united authority of the bishops, or convocation, and the parliament.

The popes had thought proper to consider England in a state of schism and separation from the

Church, as soon as their own usurped jurisdiction was abolished. The Church and realm of England repeatedly disclaimed any intention of separating from the communion of the Roman, French, Spanish, and other western Churches, subject to the pope; they never thought of refusing communion to the members of those Churches; but the popes and their party in the West still adhered obstinately to the mistaken notion, that the bishop of Rome was, by divine right, head of the universal Church; and therefore they looked on the conduct of the English Church, in removing his power, as sinful; and when the pope deposed and excommunicated Henry VIII. and his adherents, they considered England as out of the pale of the Church. There was a party in England which secretly held the same views, and were attached to the old superstitions, though they did not venture to separate from the Church.

On the death of Edward in 1553, and the accession of Mary, who was a devoted adherent of the pope, the popish party obtained the ascendant for a time, and involved the Church in confusion and misery. No fewer than *fourteen* of the bishops, who were favourable to the Reformation, were expelled from their sees, by intimidation, by packed commissions irregularly appointed by the crown, or by mere intrusion of persons who had been schismatically ordained. They were replaced by others, who were constituted by the pope, in opposition to the laws and regulations approved by the Church of England during the two preceding reigns, and in violation of its liberties. Independently of which the pope acted without any right of jurisdiction whatever; for his jurisdiction had been many years before regularly and validly suppressed by the Church of England, by whose permission alone it was at any time lawful; and the Church had never, by any decree of its convocations, revived or created again that jurisdiction: but the popish party merely implored the papal absolution for their schism. Consequently, all acts performed by the pope or his authority at this time were unauthorised and null. At the same time, an obsequious parliament repealed all the laws in favour of the Reformation; and at their humble request the pope granted his *absolution* to the English nation for the *schism* of which it had been guilty. A most savage persecution assailed all who were in favour of reformation, and who rejected the papal supremacy. The venerable Cranmer, archbishop of Canterbury, Bishops Ridley, Latimer, Hooper, and hundreds of others, bishops, presbyters, and pious men and women, fell victims to the ferocity of the papists, and attested with their last breath their adherence to the cause of pure religion. Three thousand of the clergy were expelled from their churches; multitudes of confessors were driven into exile, where they lived till the death of this persecuting queen in 1558.

The accession of the illustrious Queen Elizabeth was followed by the restoration of the Church to its former state. The laws which had been formerly made with the full concurrence of the Church, in the reign of Henry and Edward, and which always remained in their spiritual obligation, having never been condemned by the Church of England, were now restored. The popish intruders into English bishoprics, who had been appointed to those sees by virtue of the papal authority, which was null and void in England, and also without the consent of the legitimate metropolitans, Cranmer and Holgate, (which was absolutely requisite to their canonical appointment,) were expelled by the civil power, and their places were filled by orthodox prelates, who were ordained by some of the bishops who had been persecuted by Mary and driven into exile. The clergy generally approved of the return to pure religion, and retained their benefices, administering the sacraments and rites according to the English ritual. In 1562, the synod or convocation of England published a formulary of doctrine, divided into thirty-nine articles, in which the doctrines of the Catholic faith were briefly stated, and various errors and superstitions of the Romanists and others were rejected. This formulary was again approved by the convocation in 1571, and ordered to be subscribed by all the clergy. There was no schism for many years in England: all the people worshipped in the same churches, and acknowledged the same pastors. It is true that persons were to be found, who secretly cherished a love for the old superstitions and abuses, and for the Roman sway. This was not to be wondered at. Men's minds will differ on almost every subject; but more information would have probably removed in the end any such tendency.

The pope was much annoyed at these proceedings in England; he took no decided steps, however, for some time. At last, in 1569, Pius V. issued a bull, in which he excommunicated Queen Elizabeth and her supporters, absolved her subjects from their oaths of allegiance, and bestowed her dominions on the king of Spain. This bull caused the schism in England; for the popish party, which had continued in communion with the Church of England up to that time, during the eleven past years of Elizabeth's reign, now began to separate themselves. Bedingfield, Cornwallis, and Silyarde, were the first popish recusants; and the date of the Romanists in England, as a distinct sect or community, may be fixed in the year 1570. This separation was also fomented by priests and Jesuits, who were sent from abroad to pervert the people: but they did not succeed to any great extent. It may be here added, that with the exception of about six years, when a titular bishop sent by the pope resided in England, the Romanists had no bishops till 1685.

The same year which witnessed the separation of the Romanists, was also the commencement of the puritan separation. The origin of this sect, which at last acquired such power, may be traced to some of the exiles in the reign of Mary, who in foreign lands imbibed a taste for the doctrines and discipline of Calvin and Zuinglius, and who, on their return, endeavoured vainly to reform the Church of England according to those models. When they beheld the Reformation re-established according to the forms adopted in the reign of King Edward, they became dissatisfied; and after much fruitless agitation to alter the Church, they at length began to declaim against her as infected with popish errors and superstitions; and affirming episcopacy to be anti-Christian, they separated from the Church, and formed conventicles, about 1570. From this time the Puritans, and those who followed their principles and practices without separating from the Church, became exceedingly troublesome. They were opposed and punished by Queen Elizabeth, and by Archbishops Whitgift and Bancroft. Archbishop Abbot, in the early part of the seventeenth century, relaxed all vigilance, and permitted them to increase. Archbishop Laud, who succeeded in 1633, used his utmost efforts to repress this sect, and to restore order and uniformity in the Church, which had been much troubled by puritan innovations. His exertions were very successful for some time; but the puritan party were filled with enmity against this great man, and vowed his destruction.

The Church of England continued to be defended by the state till the great rebellion in 1640, when the king and parliament being at variance, the Puritans, and a number of other sects, were permitted to increase. Of these sects, the principal were the Brownists or Independents, and the Anabaptists, which had been set on foot in England a few years before. The parliament, under the influence of the Puritans, beheaded Archbishop Laud, abolished episcopacy as anti-Christian, rejected the Liturgy, and expelled several thousands of the clergy who adhered to the regulations of the Church of England, intruding in their place Puritans and other sectarians.

In 1660, on the restoration of King Charles II. to the throne of his ancestors, the Puritans were expelled in their turn, and the Church was delivered from persecution, and prospered exceedingly for many years. Many learned and great men were now appointed to preside over the Church, and the various sects of separatists or dissenters diminished. James II. attempted, by many arbitrary and illegal proceedings, to establish popery, which excited the indignation of his subjects so strongly, that he was compelled to abdicate his throne in 1689, and William III. of Orange, and Mary, were declared king and queen. On the refusal of Sancroft, archbishop of Canterbury, and some other bishops and clergy, from conscientious scruples, to take the oaths of allegiance to the new government, they were deprived of their sees and benefices by the civil power, and they, with their adherents, obtained the name of Non-jurors. Bishops were ordained in their places, and accepted by the great body of the Church of England; but a warm controversy ensued, which, however, terminated in the gradual return of the Non-jurors to the Church.

In 1717 a controversy arose on occasion of the

writings of Hoadly, bishop of Bangor, in which he maintained that it was needless to believe any particular creed, or to be united to any particular Church; and that sincerity, or our own persuasion of the correctness of our opinions (whether well or ill founded), is sufficient. These doctrines were evidently calculated to subvert the necessity of believing the articles of the Christian faith, and to justify all classes of schismatics or separatists from the Church. The convocation deemed these opinions so mischievous, that a committee was appointed to select propositions from Hoadly's books, and to procure their censure; but before his trial could take place, the convocation was prorogued by an arbitrary exercise of the royal authority, and has not been permitted to deliberate since. The temporal government, influenced by the schismatics, protected and advanced Hoadly and several persons of similar principles. In 1766, Archdeacon Blackburn, who was supposed to be an Arian, anonymously assailed the practice of subscribing the Articles; and in 1772 a body of clergy and laymen petitioned parliament to put an end to it; but their request was refused. Many of these petitioners were secret disbelievers in some of the Christian doctrines.

The sect of Methodists had now become numerous. It was founded by Wesley and Whitfield, in the early part of this century. Originally they designed only to assist the clergy in preaching to the poor in populous places; but they were gradually urged on to establish a sect. It was not, however, till after the death of Wesley that they pretended to administer the sacraments in their communities, and became absolutely separated from the Church.

The Church had been suffering much for a long time from appointments to its offices made from unworthy motives. The bishoprics, and other dignities, were bestowed by the ministers of the crown on men distinguished only by birth or connexions. Patronage in general was distributed on low and worldly considerations. Theological learning received no encouragement ; and active zeal was viewed with jealousy, as an approximation to Methodism. Prosperity had begun to inspire confidence, security, and sloth. The danger to religion arising from the French Revolution in 1789, which let loose an atheistic spirit throughout the world, stimulated the Church to renewed exertions. At the beginning of the present century, a great revival of religious zeal took place ; numerous societies for various purposes connected with religion were instituted and vigorously supported, though not always on principles accordant with those of the Church, as several of them evinced too great an intimacy with Dissenters.

The aspect of the times has since contributed to stimulate the activity of the Church. The weakness of the temporal government, and the influence which parties hostile to the Church have for the last twenty years exercised over it, have taught the Church to depend less on the protection of the state than on the Divine blessing on a zealous discharge of pastoral duties, and have led her to perceive more clearly the necessity of inculcating her own sound and Christian principles on all classes of the community. The violent hostility which Dissenters and Romanists have for some time exhibited towards the Church of England, and their avowed, though fruitless intention and endeavours to destroy her, have likewise produced most salutary effects in promoting union, zeal, and attachment to her doctrines.

The Churches of IRELAND have been suffering severely from the persecution of Romanists for many years past. Let us now turn to the history of these Churches. I have already noticed the early independence of the Church of Ireland, which continued from the time of St. Patrick, in the fifth century, till the twelfth century, when a papal legate was appointed in Ireland, and the archbishops of Ireland for the first time received the pall from Rome in 1152. This Church shared the fate of others; it became affected with the prevalent superstitions. Henry VIII. caused the papal jurisdiction to be abolished in 1537 by the parliament. The bishops and clergy generally assented, and several reforms took place during this and the next reign. In the time of Mary, five of the bishops favourable to the Reformation were irregularly expelled from their sees; and the laws made against the pope were repealed. When Elizabeth succeeded, the former laws were revived, the papal power again rejected, and the royal supremacy and the English ritual again introduced. These regulations were approved by seventeen out of nineteen Irish bishops in the parliament of 1560, and by the rest of the bishops and clergy, who took the oath of supremacy, and remained in the possession of their benefices. The people also generally acquiesced, and continued to attend on divine service for several years. Two bishops only, out of about twenty-six, refused to acquiesce in the Reformation, and were driven from their sees, into which they had been intruded in the time of Mary, while the rightful bishops were still living. It may be here added, that in 1615 the Church of Ireland framed a formulary closely resembling the Articles of the Church of England; which last, however, were adopted as the confession of the Church of Ireland in the synod of Dublin, 1634, where also a body of canons was enacted.

The pope, of course, regarded these proceedings

as highly sinful; and considering the Church of Ireland as schismatical, he resolved to induce the people to separate from it.   Accordingly, he ordained Creagh, who had shewn some diligence in exhorting the people to forsake the obedience of their bishops and the service of the Church, to the archbishopric of Armagh, although that see was already filled by the legitimate primate, Loftus. Creagh, who is styled by the Romish historians, "the principal propagator or restorer of the Catholic faith in Ireland," came over and perverted some of the people.   The pope sent some other emissaries, and, in conjunction with the King of Spain, to whom he had given the dominions of Queen Elizabeth, excited the Irish chieftains and people to insurrection.   In consequence, Ireland became the scene of war for thirty years, in which the bishops, Jesuits, and other priests sent by the pope, took a most active and leading part. In this war, numbers of the ignorant and savage people were exposed to the arts of the popish emissaries, and persuaded or forced to forsake the Church, in order to shew their hostility to the queen.   Let me mention a few facts in corroboration of these statements.   In 1575, Jaimus Geraldine, one of the Irish lords engaged in plotting an insurrection against his sovereign Queen Elizabeth, went to Philip II., king of Spain, on whom Pope Pius V. had conferred the dominions of the queen, and sought assistance from him for the Irish Romanists.   He then went to Rome, where, after some time, he obtained from the pope a pardon for all the bands of robbers who then infested Italy, on condition that they should undertake an expedition to Ireland for the exaltation of the see of Rome.   An army thus composed was headed by a titular popish bishop of Killaloe in Ireland, and by the Jesuit Sanders; and they landed in Ireland not long after, bringing a bull from Pope Gregory XIII., in which all who should unite in rebellion against Queen Elizabeth were promised a plenary pardon of their sins. This expedition, however, entirely failed; but the same titular bishop, a few years afterwards, is found introducing supplies of men, money, and arms from Spain for the relief of the insurgents. Another schismatic, assuming the title of Archbishop of Armagh, came with orders from the King of Spain that the Irish should revolt; and having excited a rebellion, he fell in battle with the royal troops. Ohely, called Archbishop of Tuam, was sent afterwards, by one of the Irish chieftains, to the King of Spain, whom he exhorted to invade and subdue Ireland. When the next insurrection broke out, we find Maceogan, a titular bishop and vicar of the Roman pontiff, issuing an excommunication against all who should give quarter to the prisoners taken from the queen's army. Maceogan caused all such persons to be put to death in his presence; and he himself at last fell in battle against the royal army, leading a troop of horse, with his sword in one hand, and his breviary and beads in the other!

The ignorance and superstition of the lower orders of the Irish at this time made them unhappily an easy prey to the emissaries of Rome, who came from Spain, Italy, and Flanders, and vehemently declaimed against the Churches of England and Ireland as heretical. Amongst the arguments used to delude this unhappy people, we find many lying wonders, visions, and miracles. It was said that on one occasion St. Columbkill took the form of a wolf, and carried a torch into the powder-magazine of a garrison of English "heretics," who were of course all destroyed. Another tale was, that a certain "heretic" converted a priest's vestment into a pair of trousers; but as soon as he had drawn them on, he took fire and was burnt to ashes. An English governor, very much hated by the popish party, was said to have been heard conversing with the devil; presently after, an explosion was heard, and he was found lying frightfully distorted and insane, and soon after died. By such arguments were the Irish taught to hate their pastors, and to separate from their national Church. But all would have been insufficient, if the country had remained in peaceable subjection to its sovereign; and therefore the Popes Pius V. and Gregory XIII. promoted insurrections in Ireland against the royal authority; and the people were compelled by their chiefs to forsake the communion of their legitimate bishops, and to become obedient to the usurpers whom the popes sent over to occupy their places. It was only by a long series of rebellions that the schism in Ireland was consolidated and became so widely extended. The reign of Queen Elizabeth, however, sufficed for this lamentable catastrophe.

King James I. wisely discouraged the Roman schism, and forbade the residence of its bishops, priests, and Jesuits, in his dominions; but under his successor, Charles I., a relaxation of this wholesome severity encouraged the schismatics in Ireland to insult and disturb the Church, and ultimately, in 1641, to massacre in cold blood a hundred and fifty thousand of its adherents, and to break into insurrection.

The Church was now dreadfully persecuted by the papists and by the English parliament; but on the return of Charles II. resumed its rights. Persecution was renewed under James II., in 1690, when the Romish party obtained power; and in the rebellion of 1798. From that period, the Romish party has acquired great political power, and the Church has been almost continually persecuted, especially within the last few years, in which the clergy have been reduced nearly to starvation; some have been murdered, and many placed in peril of their lives. To add to their afflictions, the government in 1833 suppressed ten of the bishoprics, on pretence of requiring their revenues for the support of ecclesiastical buildings; although the bishops of Ireland, in a body, protested against such an act, and offered to pay the amount required from the income of their sees, provided that so great an injury were not done to the cause of religion.

SCOTLAND had also become subject to the pope about the twelfth century; but the Reformation was not so soon or so happily introduced there as in England. There is room for censure of both parties in that country during the sixteenth century. The Romish party exercised cruelties on their opponents, which led to their own downfal. The reformed, headed by Knox, were turbulent and irregular in their proceedings. They at first, in 1560, adopted a temporary church-government, which in some degree resembled the episcopal, and in 1572 agreed that bishops should be constituted; but soon afterwards, under the influence of Melville, who had imbibed a taste for the Genevan discipline, they rejected episcopacy, and established presbyterianism. In the beginning of the following century, these disorders ceased; and in 1612 the Church of Scotland was provided with lawful bishops and pastors, who were consecrated in England.

In 1638 the presbyterian party again became predominant, and took an oath or covenant to exterminate episcopal government. When Charles II. was restored, in 1660, the Church again was protected by the state, and bishops were consecrated in England for all the vacant sees. A party of Covenanters, however, separated from the Church, esteeming episcopacy anti-Christian, and set up conventicles; and in 1690 the Scottish bishops having scrupled to take the oaths of allegiance to King William, this monarch caused the bishops to be expelled from their sees, and episcopacy to be abolished by act of parliament; and recognised the sectarians as the established Church. From this time the bishops, and the rest of the Scottish Church, were most sorely and cruelly persecuted by the Presbyterians, till 1788, when the penal laws were repealed; but during this period they had been much reduced in numbers.

A flourishing branch of the Catholic Church, derived from England, exists in AMERICA. When Virginia, and other provinces in North America, were settled by the English, early in the seventeenth century, the Church took root there, and for a long time was supported by the Society for Propagating the Gospel in Foreign Parts. Efforts were often made to obtain bishops for America, but they failed through the influence exerted by sectaries over the government. At length, after the United States had been declared independent, Dr. Seabury was ordained bishop of Connecticut, by the primus and bishops of Scotland; and other prelates were ordained for America, in England, in 1787 and 1790. The American Church is now governed by twenty bishops, and is rapidly increasing. Bishops have also been consecrated for many of the British possessions in India, North America, and the West Indies; and the limits of those Churches are continually enlarging. Many of the heathen have been converted by our missionaries in India and North America.

CHAPTER XXIII.

FRUITS OF FAITH IN THE BRITISH CHURCHES.

A.D. 1530-1839.

AMONGST that noble army of martyrs, who in the sixteenth century contended even to death for Christian truth against Roman errors and superstitions, none merits a more conspicuous place than NICHOLAS RIDLEY, bishop of London. He was born in Northumberland, in the beginning of the sixteenth century, and studied at the university of Cambridge, where he was distinguished for learning and piety. He afterwards pursued his studies in theology at Paris and Louvain; and returning back again, was senior proctor of the university of Cambridge in 1533, when the decree was made by that university, as well as by all the Church of England, "that the bishop of Rome has not, by the word of God, any jurisdiction in this realm." He also became a celebrated preacher, and was remarkable for his knowledge of Scripture and the fathers; so that in 1537 Thomas Cranmer, archbishop of Canterbury, appointed him one of his chaplains, and associated him with his family. Soon after, being made vicar of Herne, he diligently instructed his flock in the doctrines of the Gospel, and his preaching attracted multitudes of people from all the surrounding country. In 1540 he was elected master of Pembroke Hall, Cambridge, where he had been educated, and where he had been a most diligent student of the Scriptures, as we may collect from the following words of his farewell; where, apostrophising his college, he says, "In thy orchard (the walls, butts,

A A 2

and trees, if they could speak, would bear me witness), I learned without book almost all Paul's epistles, and the canonical epistles too, save only the Apocalypse; of which study, although in time a great part did depart from me, yet the sweet smell thereof I trust I shall carry with me into heaven; for the profit thereof I think I have' felt in all my life-time ever after."

About 1545 Ridley, by reading the book of Bertram, a presbyter of the ninth century, was induced to forsake the erroneous opinion of transubstantiation; and he was instrumental in bringing Archbishop Cranmer and Bishop Latimer to the same mind. In 1547 he was consecrated bishop of Rochester, and was most zealous in promoting the reformation of abuses; but he evinced great firmness in resisting such measures as he judged injurious to the cause of justice or religion. When he was appointed, without his knowledge, on a royal commission, for the suppression of Clare Hall at Cambridge, and found, on examination, that this society would not dissolve itself, he wrote to the lord protector, declaring that his conscience would not permit him to act further in the commission; and thus incurred the risk of offending most grievously the chief ruler of England. Such resolution was an earnest of that firmness and piety with which he afterwards faced death for his conscience towards God.

On the deposal of Bonner for contumacy, Ridley was installed bishop of London in his place. In this high station he behaved with great dignity, benevolence, mildness, and goodness. He was of a mortified spirit, given to prayer and contemplation, and useful and instructive to all his family. His day was divided between private prayers, family devotions, (in which he every day gave a lecture on the

New Testament, beginning with the Acts of the Apostles, and giving to every one who could read a copy of the Scriptures), the despatch of business, study in his private chamber, and useful discourse. He applied himself with all his power to reform the abuses in the disposal of Church-patronage by the crown, and others which arose from a spirit of covetousness.   Beholding with grief the distress of the poor in his city, who, in consequence of the suppression of monasteries, from which they had received much alms, were reduced to a state of sad destitution, he supplicated the king for a gift of the royal house at Bridewell as lodgings for these afflicted people, and succeeded in his application.

When that pious young king, Edward VI., was afflicted with his last illness, Bishop Ridley was appointed to preach before him one day; and in his sermon much recommended charity as a duty incumbent on all men, but especially on those who are in high place and dignity, as well in respect to their great abilities, as because they were bound to give examples of goodness to others.   The same day the king sent for him, caused him to sit in a chair beside him, and would not permit him to remain uncovered.   Then, after courteous thanks, he recapitulated the principal points of the sermon, and continued thus: "I took myself to be especially touched by your sermon, as well in regard to the abilities which God hath given me, as in regard of the example which of me he will require.   For as in the kingdom I am next under God, so must I most nearly approach him in goodness and mercy: for as our miseries stand most in need of help from him, so are we the greatest debtors, debtors to all that are miserable, and shall be the greatest accountants of our dispensation therein.   And therefore, my lord, as you have given me (I thank you) this general exhortation, so direct me, I entreat you, by what particular actions I may this way best discharge my duties." The bishop remained silent for some time; and then, weeping for joy, he besought his majesty for time to answer such a question; and having consulted the citizens of London, he returned again to the king, who gave the Greyfriars as an hospital for the support of infants, the aged, idiots, and cripples; St. Bartholomew's for wounded soldiers and sick persons; and Bridewell for the correction of idle and disorderly persons. These, with the hospital of St. Thomas, he richly endowed; and when he had signed the instrument to that effect, he, with reverent gesture and speech, thanked God for prolonging his life to finish that business.

Ridley's days of peace were now at an end. On the accession of Mary, he was expelled from his bishopric, and committed to the Tower, where he spent his time in pious exercises and conference with his fellow-prisoners, exhorting them to remain steadfast in maintaining the truth. "Resist the devil," he said, "and he will flee from you. Let us, therefore, resist him manfully; and, taking the cross upon our shoulders, let us follow our Captain Christ, who, by his own blood, hath dedicated and hallowed the way which leadeth unto the Father, that is, to the light which no man can attain,—the fountain of everlasting joys. Let us follow, I say, whither he calleth and allureth us, that after all these afflictions — which last but for a moment — whereby he trieth our faith as gold by the fire, we may everlastingly reign and triumph with him in the glory of his Father; and that through the same our Lord Jesus Christ, to whom with the Father and the Holy Ghost be all honour and glory now and for ever. Amen. Amen." Such were the resolutions and the hopes of this venerable martyr in the con-

templation of the sufferings which were preparing
for him.   His constancy was unshaken by any terrors, or by the instances of weakness which surrounded him.   One of his own chaplains, who then
fell away, wrote to Ridley with a view to shake his
resolution, and induce him to conform to the Romish errors.   His reply affords a noble example of
Christian faith and of apostolical admonition. " Sir,
how nigh the day of my dissolution and departure
out of this world is at hand, I cannot tell: the Lord's
will be fulfilled, how soon soever it shall come.   I
know the Lord's words must be verified in me, that
I shall appear before the incorrupt Judge, and be
accountable to him for all my former life.   And although the hope of his mercy is my sheet-anchor of
eternal salvation, yet am I persuaded that whosoever
wittingly neglecteth, and regardeth not to clear his
conscience, he cannot have peace with God, nor a
lively faith in his mercy.   Conscience, therefore,
moveth me, considering you were one of my family
and one of my household, of whom then I think I
had a special care; but, alas, now when the trial
doth separate the chaff from the corn, how small a
deal it is, God knoweth, which the wind doth not
blow away;—this conscience, I say, doth move me
to fear lest the lightness of my family should be laid
to my charge, for lack of more earnest and diligent
instruction which should have been done.   But
blessed be God, which hath given me grace to see
this my default, and to lament from the bottom of
my heart before my departing hence.   This conscience doth move me also now to require both you
and my friend Dr. Harvey to remember your promises made to me in times past, of the pure setting
forth and preaching of God's word and his truth.
These promises, although you shall not need to fear
to be charged with them of me hereafter before the

world, yet look for none other (I exhort you as my friends) but to be charged with them at God's hand. This conscience, and the love that I bear unto you, biddeth me now say unto you both, in God's name, ' Fear God, and love not the world;' for God is able to cast both body and soul into hell-fire; ' when his wrath shall suddenly be kindled, blessed are all they that put their trust in him.'   And the saying of St. John is true, ' All that is in the world, as the lust of the flesh, the lust of the eye, and the pride of life, is not of the Father, but of the world; and the world passeth away, and the lust thereof; but he that doeth the will of God abideth for ever.' "   This admonition, so calm, so solemn, so affecting, produced such a powerful effect on the unhappy person to whom it was addressed, that he pined away with grief and remorse, and soon after died.

Ridley had been removed to Oxford, with his venerable fellow-prisoners Bishops Cranmer and Latimer, before he wrote this letter.   In 1555 he and Latimer were examined by the papal delegates; and on their refusal to submit to the pope, were degraded from their orders; Ridley steadily refusing to move his cap, or shew the least sign of submission or reverence to the usurped authority of the papal delegates.   He, with Latimer, was then delivered to the temporal magistrates to be burnt to death.   The evening before his martyrdom, Ridley prepared himself for his departure with joy and triumph.   He washed himself, and invited his friends and relations to be present at his "marriage" in the morning.   His discourse melted into tears one of his most obdurate enemies who was present.   Ridley said, "You love me not now, I see well enough; for in that you weep, it doth appear you will not be at my marriage, neither be content therewith.   But quiet yourself; though my breakfast shall be somewhat sharp and painful, yet I am sure my supper shall be more pleasant and sweet."

In the morning he approached the place of execution arrayed in a handsome black gown; and as he passed the prison of Bocardo, he looked to the chamber where Archbishop Cranmer was imprisoned, hoping to have seen and spoken to him; but he was engaged in disputing with Friar Soto and others: but shortly behind him he saw and spoke to Latimer, who came clad in his shroud to be ready for the fire. When they came to the spot, he ran to Latimer with a joyful countenance, embraced and kissed him, and comforted him, saying, " Be of good heart, brother; for God will either assuage the fury of the flame, or else strengthen us to abide it." Then turning to the stake, he kissed it, and kneeling down, prayed earnestly, as did Latimer likewise. Then rising, they conferred together for a little while. Dr. Smith preached the sermon usual on such occasions, to which the martyrs besought permission to reply; but were informed, that unless they recanted, they should not speak. " Well," replied the illustrious martyr, " so long as the breath is in my body, I will never deny my Lord Christ and his known truth; God's will be done in me." He then said, with a loud voice, " I commit my cause to Almighty God, who will judge all indifferently."

They were then ordered to make ready for burning, which they mildly obeyed. Ridley gave away several small things to persons standing by, many of whom were weeping. Latimer now stood in his shroud; and he who before, in an old coat and cap, seemed a withered and crooked old man, now roused to play the man, stood upright, and appeared a venerable and comely person. Ridley, standing in his shirt at the stake, lifted up his hands toward heaven, and prayed, "O heavenly Father, I give unto thee most hearty thanks for that thou hast called me to be a professor of thee even unto death. I beseech thee, Lord God, take mercy upon the realm of England, and deliver the same from all her enemies." Then the smith fastened an iron chain round the bodies of both the martyrs, tying them to the stake. A faggot was now lighted and laid at Ridley's feet, when Latimer said, "Be of good comfort, master Ridley, and play the man. We shall this day light such a candle by God's grace in England, as, I trust, shall never be put out." When Ridley saw the fire flaming towards him, he cried with an exceeding loud voice, "Into thy hands, O Lord, I commend my spirit; O Lord, receive my spirit." Latimer, on the other side, exclaimed, "O Father of heaven, receive my soul." Then he received the flame as if he were embracing it, and soon died, with but little appearance of pain.

But Ridley had to undergo dreadful and lingering tortures; for the fire on his side was so smothered by the quantity of faggots, that his legs were slowly consumed, while he cried to his tormentors to "let the fire come at him." But in all his agony, he still called on God, "Lord, have mercy upon me." At length the faggots were removed by one of the by-standers; and when the tortured martyr saw the fire flaming up, he wrenched himself to that side. And when the flame reached a bag of gunpowder which hung round his neck, he was seen to stir no more, but burned on the other side; and either from the chain loosing, or by the overpoise of his body after his legs were consumed, he fell over the chain down at Latimer's feet.

Thus died this illustrious martyr—or rather, thus did he enter eternal life; and it may be said with truth, that never, since the days of the apostles, was there a nobler manifestation of Christian faith and heroism. It was worthy of the brightest days of the primitive Church; and not even Polycarp, in the amphitheatre of Smyrna, exceeded the glory of NICHOLAS RIDLEY.

Let us now pass to days when the righteous were no longer persecuted, and learning and piety were exposed to none but the ordinary trials.

RICHARD HOOKER (usually called "judicious Hooker") was born near Exeter, about 1553, of parents remarkable for virtue and industry. From his childhood he was grave, desirous of learning, modest, and of so sweet and serene a quietness and meekness of nature, that many believed him to have an inward and blessed divine light. The seeds of sincere piety which his parents early instilled into his mind were so continually watered with the dews of God's blessed Spirit, that his infant virtues grew into such holy habits, as made him daily more in favour both with God and man.

About 1567, when Dr. Jewel, that celebrated opponent of Romish errors, was bishop of Salisbury, the parents of Hooker being unable to defray the expense of an university education for their son, this learned bishop, being made acquainted with the circumstance, and having examined and observed the boy's knowledge and behaviour, procured for him a maintenance at Corpus Christi College, in the university of Oxford. Here he continued for several years, still increasing in learning and prudence, and so much in humility and piety, that he seemed to be filled with the Holy Ghost. In 1571 he experienced the loss of his kind friend and patron, Bishop Jewel, who died, as he had lived, in devout meditation and prayer; but soon after, Edwin Sandys, bishop of London, who had heard from Jewel of Hooker's great merits and learning, placed his son under his tuition. While Hooker was a student in the university, so great was his devotion, that in four years he was but twice absent from the chapel-prayers. His behaviour there was such as shewed an awful reverence of that God whom he there worshipped, giving all outward testimonies that his affections were set on heavenly things. He was never known to be angry, passionate, or extreme in his desires; never heard to repine or dispute with Providence; but by a quiet, gentle submission of his will to the wisdom of his Creator, bore the burden of the day with patience. He was never heard to utter an uncomely word; and by this, and his grave behaviour, he caused a reverence towards his person even from those that elsewhere cast off all strictness of behaviour. In 1577 he became a fellow of his college; and two years after was appointed by the chancellor of the university to read the Hebrew lecture. In 1584 he was appointed to the parsonage of Drayton Beauchamp, in Buckinghamshire; and in the next year, through the recommendation of his friend Sandys, archbishop of York, was made master of the Temple in London.

At this time the Church had been for some years exceedingly troubled by the schismatical proceedings of the Puritans, who declaimed against all her rites and ceremonies as popish and antichristian. Of this party was one Travers, who had been irregularly ordained abroad by some persons who were not of the degree of bishops, and who now ministered as lecturer of the Temple, though the law of the English Church prohibited such persons from acting as ministers. Travers, who had himself aspired to be master of the Temple, opposed Hooker's doctrines in the pulpit, and afterwards petitioned the privy council, charging him with many errors, especially for his charitable opinion, that many of our forefathers, who lived in the times of superstition, were saved; but Archbishop Whitgift, whom Queen Elizabeth entrusted with the entire management of ecclesiastical affairs, had such good testimonies of Hooker's principles, learning, and moderation, that all solicitations against him were of no effect.

Though Travers was obliged to leave the Temple, he had several supporters there, who rendered Hooker's position very uneasy. To bring them to a better mind, he resolved to write his celebrated books on the Laws of Ecclesiastical Polity; and finding that his situation did not afford sufficient leisure, he left it for the parish of Boscum, near Salisbury, where the first four books were written, and made public in 1594. Another book was published in 1597. It is recorded that when a part of this celebrated work had been translated for the pope, he said, "There is no learning that this man hath not searched into; nothing too hard for his understanding. This man indeed deserves the name of an author: his books will get reverence by age, for there are in them such seeds of eternity, that if the rest be like this, they shall last till the last fire shall consume all learning."

In 1595 he was appointed to the vicarage of Bishopsborne in Kent, in which place he continued his customary rules of mortification and self-denial, fasted often, was frequent in meditation and prayer, enjoying those blessed returns which only such men feel and know. Before long, his writings, and the innocency and sanctity of his life, became so remarkable, that many persons came from all parts to see him. His habit was usually coarse and mean; his appearance lowly, and accordant with the humility of his soul; his body was wasted, not with age, but with study and holy mortifications. He here forsook all the pleasures and allurements of the world, possessing his soul in a virtuous quietness, which he maintained by constant study, prayer, and meditation. He preached every Sunday morning, and in the evening catechised his parishioners. His sermons were not long, but delivered with a grave zeal; they were addressed to the reason, and abounded in apt illustrations. He fasted strictly in Ember-week, when he usually retired into the church for many hours, and did the same on most Fridays and other days of fasting. He was most diligent in visiting the sick, exhorting them to confession of their sins and repentance.

While Hooker was thus engaged in all the exercises of piety, and was also preparing the last books of his Ecclesiastical Polity, he fell into a long and sharp illness, and began to fail. A few days before his death, the pious Dr. Saravia, prebendary of Canterbury, who knew the very secrets of his soul, (for they were supposed to confess their sins to each other), came to him, and after a conference on the safety and benefit of the Church's absolution, it was resolved that Saravia should administer that and the holy eucharist the following day. When the time came, they retired for a short while from the company, and then returned, when Hooker received the blessed sacrament of the body and blood of Christ; which being performed, Saravia thought he saw a reverend gaiety and joy in his face; but it lasted not long, for his bodily infirmities returned with violence. The next day he found Hooker better in appearance, but deep in contemplation, and not inclined to converse. When he was asked the subject of his thoughts, he replied, "that he was meditating the number and nature of angels, and their blessed obedience and order, without which peace could not be in heaven; and O that it might be so on earth!" After which he said, "I have lived to see this world is made up of perturbations, and I have been long preparing to leave it, and gathering comfort for the dreadful hour of making my account with God, which I now apprehend to be near; and though I have, by his grace, loved him in my youth, and feared him in my age, and laboured to have a conscience void of offence to him and to all men, yet if thou, Lord, be extreme to mark what I have done amiss, who can abide it? And therefore, where I have failed, Lord, shew mercy unto me; for I plead not my righteousness, but the forgiveness of my unrighteousness, for His merits who died to purchase pardon for penitent sinners; and since I owe thee a death, Lord, let it not be terrible, and then take thine own time, I submit to it: let not mine, O Lord, but let thy will be done." He then fell into a dangerous slumber, and awaking once more said, "God hath heard my daily petitions, for I am at peace with all men, and he is at peace with me; and from that blessed assurance I feel that inward joy which this world can neither give nor take from me; my conscience beareth me this witness, and this witness makes the thoughts of death joyful. I could wish to live to do the Church more service, but cannot hope it; for my days are past, as a shadow that returns not." Thus speaking, his spirit failed, and the holy man slept in Jesus Christ.

NICHOLAS FERRAR, a holy deacon of the Church, was descended from an ancient and noble family, and was born in London in 1592. His parents educated him in the paths of piety and virtue, and his progress in learning was rapid. His disposition was grave, and he early shewed a dislike of any thing that savoured of worldly vanity. In his apparel he wished to be neat, but refused any thing that was not simple and plain. He was good-natured and tender-hearted in the highest degree, and so fearful of offending any one, that he would weep abundantly on the least apprehension of having done so. In his fourteenth year he went to study at the university of Cambridge, and was eminently distinguished there by his abilities and learning; so that his tutor used to say of him, " May God keep him in a right mind! for if he should turn schismatic or heretic, he would make work for all the world."

His health becoming much impaired, he was advised to travel, and in 1612 went abroad in the train of the Princess Elizabeth and the Palsgrave. He then studied at the universities of Leipsic and Padua. After visiting Rome and many parts of the continent, he returned to England in 1618; and soon after became actively engaged in the affairs of a great company for colonising Virginia in America, of which he was chosen deputy-governor; and in this situation he displayed the greatest ability in defending the company from the intrigues of Gondomar, the Spanish ambassador. While he was thus engaged, the excellence of his conduct induced an opulent merchant of London to offer him in marriage his only daughter, a young lady of great beauty and accomplishments, with a large fortune; but Ferrar replied with many thanks, declining so honourable an offer; "for if God," said he, "will give me grace to keep a resolution long since formed, I have determined to lead a single life; and after having discharged to the best of my ability my duty to the company and to my family as to worldly concerns, I seriously purpose to devote myself to God, and to go into a religious retirement."

On the dissolution of the Virginia company, he was elected a member of parliament, where he was highly distinguished for eloquence and ability, and was appointed to draw up the charge against the Earl of Middlesex, lord treasurer, for his conduct in the affairs of the Virginia company. Nicholas Ferrar was now at leisure to carry into execution his plan of a religious life.   He accordingly retired to Little Gidding, in Huntingdonshire, accompanied by his mother and brethren, whom he had persuaded to follow his example, and several friends to the number altogether of nearly forty. He was now twenty-seven years of age; and in order to carry on his religious plans by his own personal assistance, he resolved to become a deacon. This wish was communicated by a friend to Laud, bishop of St. David's, afterwards archbishop of Canterbury, who ordained him a deacon in 1626; after which he signed a vow, that since God had so often heard his most humble petitions, and delivered him out of many dangers, and in many desperate calamities had extended his mercy to him, he would therefore now give himself up continually to serve God to the utmost of his power in the office of a deacon, into which office he had that morning been regularly ordained; that he had long ago seen enough of the manners and of the vanities of the world, and that he did hold them all in so low esteem, that he was resolved to spend the remainder of his life in mortifications, in devotion and charity, and in a constant preparation for death.

Some high nobles at court, who knew his virtues, hearing that he had been ordained, immediately offered him some ecclesiastical benefices of great value; but these he refused with steadiness and humility, saying that he did not think himself worthy. He added, that his fixed determination was to rise no higher in the Church than the place and office which he now possessed, and which he had undertaken only with the view to be legally authorised to give spiritual assistance, according to his abilities, to his family and others with whom he might be concerned; that as to temporal affairs, he had now parted with all his worldly estate, and divided it amongst his family; that he earnestly besought his honoured friends to accept his sincere thanks for their good opinion of him, for whose prosperity, both in this world and a better, he would never cease to pray.

The parish church, which was close to the manor-house of Gidding, had fallen into decay, and divine service had been discontinued in consequence of the depopulation of the parish; it was now repaired and beautified at the expense of Ferrar's mother, a pious and holy woman. The house itself was very large, and Ferrar allotted one room as an oratory for the devotions of the whole family, besides two separate oratories for the men and women at night. His own lodgings were so contrived, that he could conveniently see that every thing was conducted with decency and order. He established a school close to the house, and provided masters for the free instruction of all the children who came from the neighbouring towns. He was very diligent in catechising the children of the neighbourhood, and caused them to learn the Psalter by heart. Every Sunday, after morning service, these children, more than one hundred in number, were hospitably entertained by the religious society at Gidding. Whilst dinner was serving, they sang a hymn to the organ; then grace was said by the clergyman of the parish; and during dinner a chapter in the Bible, together with some histories of the saints and martyrs, were read. After evening service, all the society went into their oratory, when select portions of the Psalms were repeated. After this, they were at liberty till eight o'clock, when the bell again summoned them to the oratory, where they sang a hymn to the organ, and went to prayers; and then all retired to their private apartments. On the first Sunday in every month they received the holy communion.

On week-days they rose at four in the morning; at five went to prayers in the oratory; at six said the Psalms of the hour,—for every hour had its appointed Psalm, with some portion of the Gospel; then they sang a hymn, repeated some passages of Scripture; and at half-past six went to church to matins. At seven they said the Psalms of the hour, sang a hymn, and went to breakfast. At ten they went to church to litany; at eleven to dinner, during which Scripture and pious books were read aloud. They went to evening prayers in the church at four; after which came supper and recreations till eight, at which time they prayed in their oratory. During the night there was a continual vigil or watching, in which several of the men and women, in their respective oratories, repeated the whole Psalter, together with prayers for the life of the king and his sons, from nine at night till one in the morning. The time of this watch being ended, they awoke Nicholas Ferrar, who constantly rose at one o'clock, and betook himself to religious meditation, according to these words, " At midnight will I rise and give thanks." Ferrar himself lay upon a skin stretched on the floor, arrayed in a loose frieze gown; and he watched in the oratory or the church three nights in the week. Several religious persons, both from the neighbourhood and from distant parts of the country, attended these vigils, and practised them elsewhere. The leisure-hours of this holy society were devoted to the instruction of the poor, the dispensation of alms and medicines to the sick, and the composition of a harmony of the Gospels. Ferrar himself wrote several valuable religious treatises, and compiled lives of saints.

In 1631, Dr. Williams, bishop of Lincoln, the diocesan, came to visit Ferrar, when he had an opportunity of seeing his way of serving God, and of examining the rules for watching, fasting, praying, psalmody, readings, almsgiving, and all other points established in this society; all of which he highly approved, and bade them in God's name to proceed. Some years after, he again visited Gidding; and, to honour the society, gave notice that he would preach in their church, where an immense multitude of people assembled to hear him. In his sermon he enlarged most on what it was to " die unto the world:" all tended to approve the dutiful and severe life of the Ferrars, and of the Church that was in their house.

King Charles I. held Nicholas Ferrar in great reverence, and came more than once to visit this religious society; and having perused the Harmony of the Gospels which they had compiled, he was so much pleased with it, that he requested them to prepare a copy for his own peculiar use.

In 1637 the strength of Ferrar began rapidly to fail; but he experienced no bodily pain. He conversed with his friends, exhorting them to persevere in the way he had pointed out to them; and after expressing his conviction that sad times were coming on the Church, and lamenting the sufferings which they would have to endure, he received the holy eucharist; and as the clock struck one at night, the hour at which for so many years he had constantly risen to worship God, he departed this life in a rapturous ecstacy of devotion. The society over which he had presided was persecuted and dispersed during the great rebellion, which shortly afterwards broke out, and in which the King and the Archbishop of

Canterbury, the friends of this holy man, were put to death by the Presbyterians and Independents.

HENRY HAMMOND was born in 1605, at Chertsey in Surrey; and was so early blessed with the grace of piety, that, even while he was a boy at Eton, he would retire from his playfellows into places of privacy to pray to God. He was remarkable for sweetness of disposition, and early proficiency in learning; so that when only thirteen years of age he was sent to the university of Oxford, where he became a fellow of Magdalen College, and studied thirteen hours a day. In a few years he had read most of the classic writers, fathers, councils, and schoolmen, besides the holy Scriptures. In 1629 he was elevated to the holy order of priesthood; and in 1633 he was appointed rector of Penshurst in Kent. He now devoted himself to his parochial duties, preaching diligently, offering up the daily sacrifice of prayer for his people, administering the sacraments, relieving the poor, keeping hospitality, reconciling differences among neighbours, visiting the sick, and catechising youth. He was also frequently called to preach at Paul's Cross in London; was a member of convocation, archdeacon of Chichester; and was engaged in every holy and good work of his ministry, when the rebellion broke out; and in 1643 an attempt having been made in favour of the king in that neighbourhood, which Hammond was supposed to have encouraged, he was obliged to escape to Oxford, where he lay concealed for some time, and wrote many excellent works in defence of true religion and the discipline of the Church, against the heresies and schisms then so prevalent. He afterwards disputed publicly against the sectarians, and was made canon of Christ Church, and chaplain to his majesty King Charles I. Hammond attended the king during his imprisonment until 1647, when all his majesty's attendants were removed from about his person. After this Hammond was himself cast into prison by the parliamentarians, where he commenced his Commentary on the New Testament, and his famous work in Defence of Episcopacy against Blondel.

He was never married, though he had some intentions of entering into that state ; but was deterred by the aspect of the times, and by recollecting the apostle's advice (1 Cor. vii. 26). His habits of chastity and modesty at all times were remarkable. His self-denial was so great, that he seldom eat more than once in twenty-four hours. He was perfectly indifferent as to the quality of his food. In sleep he was so temperate that he rarely slept more than four or five hours in the night. He was never idle, but always engaged in something useful. In devotion he has rarely been excelled : besides occasional and supernumerary addresses, his certain perpetual returns of prayer exceeded David's " seven times a day ;" and even the night was not without its office, the fifty-first Psalm being his designed midnight entertainment. In his prayers, his attention was not only fixed and steady, but his fervour was so great, that frequently his transport threw him prostrate upon the earth. His tears also would interrupt his words; and this not merely in his private prayers, but in the common service of the Church. So great was his spirit of forgiveness, that having been most cruelly and maliciously treated by some persons, he had a peculiar daily prayer purposely for them. From his friends he particularly sought to learn his faults and offences, and even his failings in discretion and wisdom. His alms, even when he was reduced to the greatest distress, were very abundant. He not only sought for the neighbouring poor, but assisted students at the universities, and the clergy who had been expelled from their parishes, or driven into exile, by the sectaries. Though he was very unwilling to be interrupted in his studies by any concerns of his own, he never kept any one waiting, but would immediately come to any visitor, more especially when he was informed that a poor man wished to speak to him.

After he was released from prison, he retired to Worcestershire, where he continued his labours in the cause of religion; and in 1660, when King Charles II. was restored to the throne of his ancestors, Hammond was designed to fill the vacant see of Worcester; but as he was on his way to London, he was seized with illness; and after suffering dreadful pains with all the patience, submission, and piety which might have been expected from so holy and useful a life, he departed to his eternal reward in the fifty-fifth year of his age.

Thomas Wilson, bishop of Sodor and Man, was born in Cheshire in 1663, and educated at the university of Dublin, where he intended to practise medicine, but was persuaded by a pious archdeacon to undertake the sacred ministry. In 1686 he was ordained deacon, and appointed to a curacy in Lancashire; and in 1689 he was raised to the priesthood, on which solemn occasion he again dedicated himself to the service of his Lord and Master, and formed the most solemn resolutions of living more than ever to the glory of that Saviour "who loved him, and gave himself for him." In conformity with these resolutions, he discharged his sacred duties with indefatigable zeal; "holiness to the Lord" was inscribed on every part of his conduct. The lustre of such a character could not long be concealed; and in 1692 he was selected by the Earl of Derby to be his chaplain and the preceptor of his

son.   After some time, observing with deep regret
the embarrassed state of his patron's affairs, caused
by habits of profusion and inattention to domestic
economy, he felt it his duty to remonstrate with
the earl on his conduct; and he so judiciously and
wisely managed this delicate affair, that ere long he
had the great satisfaction of seeing his noble friend
relieved from his embarrassments, and a train of
distressed tradesmen and dependents effectually relieved.

The bishopric of Sodor and Man had been vacant
from the year 1693, and Lord Derby, to whom the
appointment belonged as lord of the Isle of Man,
offered it to his chaplain.   He thankfully acknowledged the honour intended him, but declared himself
unworthy of so high an office, and incapable of so
arduous an undertaking; and it was only after the
see had been vacant for four years, and the metropolitan had complained to the king on the subject,
that Wilson was at last " forced into the see."   He
was consecrated in 1697.   Bishop Wilson now devoted himself most zealously to the duties of the
episcopate.   He felt that he had been called by
Divine appointment to this arduous station, and was
persuaded that every necessary help would be afforded
him.   He was frequent in prayer, and thence derived
the skill and grace which appeared in his ministry.
His life, indeed, was a life of prayer.   By his frequent intercourse with Heaven, he became heavenly
in his temper, his views, and his whole conversation.

The temporal and spiritual state of his diocese
called for most vigorous exertions.   He was obliged
to rebuild the episcopal mansion, which had fallen
into decay, and to effect many other expensive repairs.
He lamented that this forced him in some degree to
intermit his charity to the poor.   His attention was
directed to whatever could in any degree promote the

spiritual and temporal welfare of the country. He was seen in every quarter of his diocese, counselling, guiding, and directing. His charity was always most abundant. When he possessed, early in life, only 30*l.* per annum, he devoted one tenth of this income to the poor. As his income gradually increased, a greater share was distributed in alms. He always laid aside the proportion destined for the poor in a certain place. In this treasury, which he named "the poor's drawer," was deposited at first a tenth, then a fifth, afterwards a third, and at last half his income. Every deposit there was converted into an act both of charity and devotion; prayers and alms were incessantly united. At his house every kind of distress found relief. Whether the hungry or the naked applied, their claims were certain to be duly considered and liberally answered. In his barn was always a provision of corn and meal for the indigent; and the good bishop gave orders to his steward when corn was measured to the poor never to stroke it, as was usual, but to give heaped measure. His demesne contained several manufactories of different sorts, where artisans were engaged in preparing garments for the poor. The bishop attended even to the smallest circumstances which could benefit his people. He would purchase quantities of spectacles, and distribute them amongst the aged poor, that they might be enabled to read their Bibles.

Bishop Wilson was unwearied in his endeavours to improve the parochial schools. He was a constant and earnest preacher, and during the fifty-eight years of his episcopate he never failed every Sunday to preach or celebrate the holy rites of the Church, except when prevented by illness. Nothing could exceed his care and diligence in obtaining an effective and pious clergy. From the moment that any student declared his intention of entering the sacred ministry, the bishop formed a close connexion with him, watched over his conduct, and guided his studies and pursuits. After his entrance on the sacred ministry, the bishop made him reside with him for a whole year, that he might exercise a more minute inspection, and administer daily instruction and advice. He held many synods of the clergy, in which several wise constitutions and canons of discipline were made and enforced. He frequently addressed his clergy in pastoral letters full of piety and wisdom; and so great was the veneration in which they held him, that half a century after his decease, aged clergy have been heard to recount the virtues of Bishop Wilson with tears of affection trembling in their eyes. Bishop Wilson acquired a knowledge of the Manks language, into which he translated several pious books, and procured the Gospels and Acts of the Apostles to be translated into that language.

Bishop Wilson was a man of prayer. He not only prayed every morning at six o'clock with his family, and also in the evening, but he retired three times every day to his private devotions. Even in the night he might be heard engaged in prayer. Sometimes the words of the Psalmist were indistinctly heard by his attendants. " I will arise at midnight, and give thanks unto thee. Praise the Lord, O my soul; and all that is within me, praise his holy name." Sometimes parts of the *Te Deum* were recognised. Such were the nightly orisons of this holy man. Words of instruction and consolation were continually flowing from his lips; so that it was scarcely possible to enjoy his society even for a short time without growing wiser and better. His actions, however, spoke more forcibly than language; the beauty of holiness shone forth in all his conversation, irradiated his countenance, and gave a peculiar charm to every thing he said or did.

In 1722, the bishop, in the discharge of his duty as the guardian of the sacraments, forbade the governor's wife to approach the holy table, as a punishment for a very scandalous calumny which she had disseminated. A clergyman having disobeyed this injunction of the bishop, he was suspended; and the result was, that the bishop was illegally seized and imprisoned, with his two vicars-general. During this affliction, the bishop was occupied in prayer and meditation, and in plans for the advancement of his Master's kingdom. The poor were loud in their lamentations; and being indignant at the injustice practised towards their beloved pastor, they were about to level the governor's house to the ground, when they were restrained by the voice of their bishop, who spoke to them from his prison, and exhorted them to peace and submission. At length he was released on appeal to the king. The day of his release was one of universal rejoicing. The multitudes extended for three miles in length, scattering flowers beneath his feet, to the sound of music and loud rejoicings. Bishop Wilson's strictness in observing ecclesiastical discipline may be collected from the circumstances already alluded to.

At length he was to be called away to his reward in heaven. He beheld the approach of death with peace and calmness, but with the deepest humility. Shortly before his death, a crowd of poor people were assembled in the hall to receive his blessing and alms, when he was overheard saying, " God be merciful to me a sinner, a vile sinner, a miserable sinner !" He fell into delirium some weeks before his decease, but his dreams were filled with visions of angels. He died in 1755, in the ninety-third year of his age.

It would be easy to add many other instances of Christian piety from the records of the Church in the

period now before us. The learning and sanctity of
Usher, of Bedel, Andrewes, Beveridge, Bull, would
have done honour to the best days of Christianity.
In recent times, the spirit of missionary zeal has
again revived, and the venerable Societies for the
Propagation of the Gospel, and for Promoting Christian Knowledge, have enlarged the spheres of their
operations.   The foundation of these societies is
chiefly to be attributed to the pious zeal of Dr.
Thomas Bray, who, at the end of the seventeenth
century, was appointed by the Bishop of London as
his commissary in Maryland, America ; and who,
on his return, established in 1701 the Society for
the Propagation of the Gospel in Foreign Parts.
This excellent society has for a long series of years
devoted itself to the maintenance of Christian missions in North America, and other possessions of
the British crown.   The Society for Promoting
Christian Knowledge had been established in 1698 ;
and from that period to the present time it has laboured for the benefit of the Church, in circulating
the Scriptures and religious books, in contributing
to the assistance of distressed churches, and in maintaining missions to the heathen, especially in India.
Nor would it be just, in this place, to omit all mention of the Church Missionary Society, which has
been formed within the present century, and has contributed much to the spread of the Christian faith
amongst the heathen, especially in the islands of the
Southern Ocean.

———————

CHAPTER XXIV.

ON THE ROMAN CHURCHES.

A.D. 1517-1839.

THE Churches which, either voluntarily or by compulsion, remained under the papal jurisdiction and rejected the Reformation, were those of Italy, Spain, Austria, Poland, Hungary, Bohemia, France, and part of Germany and Switzerland. The pope's conduct toward the Lutheran and Reformed has already been noticed, as well as the assembling of the council of Trent. This famous synod, which in many of its sessions consisted of about forty or fifty bishops, had at last nearly two hundred. It closed in 1563, having decided in favour of purgatory, transubstantiation, and some other erroneous opinions, which it declared articles of faith; and approved of invocation of saints, honouring of relics, communion in one kind, the celibacy of the clergy, &c. Certain opinions, universally prevalent at that time in the Roman Churches, obliged their members to receive all the decrees of this synod implicitly and without any discussion or examination. One great party believed the pope infallible; the remainder held that a general council was infallible; consequently both agreed that a general council approved by a pope (as the council of Trent was) must be infallible, and that whoever differed from it must be a heretic. All this was widely different from the notions and the practice of primitive times, when the decrees of the councils were examined and judged by the universal Church, and derived their full authority only from *universal consent.* And hence it appears that the decrees of Trent were only those of the bishops assembled there, not the deliberate judgments of the whole Roman Church, and still less the judgments of the whole catholic or universal Church. Under the same erroneous opinions alluded to above, the Roman Churches refrained from communicating with the Reformed Churches and communities, and engaged in vehement controversies with them, which have not yet ceased. These controversies were for a long time chiefly managed by a learned and artful society, called the Jesuits, who were founded in 1537 by a Spaniard, named Ignatius Loyola, and who soon became the principal agents of the popes, and the chief support of their power.

The Roman Churches, soon after the council of Trent, became much divided amongst themselves on the questions of Divine grace, of the authority of councils compared with that of popes, and of the immaculate conception of the Virgin. In these disputes the different parties went so far as to charge their adversaries with heresy. It would occupy too large a space to detail these disputes and divisions; but the doctrines of Jansenius, bishop of Ipres, which were made public in 1640, led to infinite divisions and uneasiness in the Roman Churches. These doctrines, which approximated to those of Calvin, were assailed with vehemence by the Jesuits and the popes. But it was in vain that Urban VIII., Innocent X., Alexander VII., and Clement XI., fulminated censures, excommunications, bulls, rescripts, briefs, &c., against the Jansenists. In vain were subscriptions required to formularies condemning their doctrines, and every ingenious device put in force to get rid of this party. All was fruitless—the Jansenists continued to hold their benefices in the Roman Churches, and in the earlier half of last century a number of the French bishops were of that party. Jansenism has ever since more or less disturbed the Roman communion.

With Jansenism a reforming spirit rose, which produced a variety of innovations. In Germany, about 1760, many theologians decried the papal authority, which they wished to reduce within the narrowest limits; and taught that several of the common practices and opinions were superstitious. The Emperor Joseph II., who began to reign in 1781, acted on these principles, suppressed monasteries, forbade papal dispensations, regulated ceremonies, favoured the Jansenists, removed images from the churches, suppressed some episcopal sees, and assumed the patronage of all the bishoprics in Lombardy which had belonged to the popes. Pius VI. in vain opposed these proceedings; they became embodied in the laws of Austria; and the churches within that empire in Germany and Italy are more under the temporal power than under the pope. In various parts of Germany the Romish clergy condemn the celibacy of the clergy and communion in one kind, and celebrate divine service in German. The conduct of Joseph II. was imitated in Tuscany by the Archduke Leopold (who forbade all appeal to the popes), in Naples, Parma, Portugal. A number of monasteries were suppressed by the King of Sicily in 1776. In Holland the Jansenists have had bishops of their own since 1723, who claim to be members of the Roman Church, though the popes will not recognise them as such.

The most vehement opponents of the Jansenists were the Jesuists, already alluded to, who chiefly engaged in the defence of the Roman Church against its opponents, in the education of youth, and in the dissemination of Christianity in heathen lands. The leading members of this society were bound by an oath to go wherever the pope should think fit to send them. Their perfect internal discipline; their entire obedience to their general (thus the head of the order was termed); the art with which they adapted their instructions to every class of people; the consummate ability, learning, and judgment which they displayed; soon rendered them the most powerful and opulent of the monastic orders. They became the grand bulwark of the papacy, supporting all its claims with unwearied assiduity. The facility with which they relaxed the moral system of Christianity, and accommodated it to the propensities of mankind, rendered them exceedingly popular as spiritual advisers and confessors in the courts of princes, and amongst the wealthy and noble. They soon obtained exclusive dominion in these high places. For a century after the foundation of this society, all the most eminent theologians of the Roman communion were found amongst its members. The names of Salmeron, Lainez, Bellarmine, Vasquez, Petavius, and many others, might be mentioned in illustration of this.

The characteristics of the Jesuits were craft and subtilty. They were perfectly unscrupulous in the use of means for the accomplishment of their ends. Evasions, mental reservations, equivocations, were openly defended and unblushingly practised; even direct falsehood was employed, whenever it was imagined to be necessary for the interest of their cause. These dangerous principles and practices of Jesuitism were most ably exposed by the celebrated Pascal, in the *Provincial Letters*, about the middle of the seventeenth century. This powerful and wealthy society, however, was at last destined to fall.

About the year 1760, their evil practices and political intrigues having excited universal jealousy, the French parliament suppressed the order of Jesuits, in spite of the remonstrances of the pope and bishops. They were soon after suppressed by the civil power in Spain, Portugal, Italy, &c.; and, in fine, the order was extinguished by Pope Benedict XIV. This was a grievous blow to the papacy, of which the Jesuits were most devoted partisans. In the course of the present century, this dangerous order has been revived by Pope Pius VII., and is beginning again to trouble the Church.

A spirit of infidelity had long been spreading itself in France and other parts of the continent, under the influence of Voltaire, D'Alembert, and others. Many of these infidels were members, and even clergy, of the Roman Churches. In 1789 the French Revolution broke out, and led to the immediate suppression of monasteries, and the destruction of Church-property. The Gallican Church was then re-organised by the power of the republic; all the bishops were driven from their sees, in consequence of their refusing to acquiesce in this alteration, by which the number of bishoprics was reduced more than one-half, and the papal power suppressed. A body of new bishops was then appointed, and consecrated by Talleyrand, bishop of Autun. Before long, several of these Gallican bishops declared themselves atheists, and renounced the worship of God. All religion was then proscribed. When Buonaparte became first consul, he negotiated for the restoration of the Church with Pope Pius VII., who, in consequence, insisted on all the old royalist bishops and the constitutional prelates resigning their sees. Upon the refusal of many of the former, he declared their consent needless, annihilated 159 bishoprics, and created in their place sixty new ones. Buonaparte then enacted laws, placing the new Gallican Church entirely under the control of government, as it continues to be to the present day. The adherents of the deprived bishops declared these acts schismatical, and they form a distinct communion from the rest of the Roman Church. Some years afterwards, Buonaparte extinguished the temporal power of the pope; which, however, was restored again at the peace in 1814.

The monasteries were also suppressed in France, Italy, Germany; and in the course of the last few years, they have been suppressed in Spain and Portugal by the temporal rulers in those countries. The pope has now entirely lost that temporal power over the princes of Europe, which in the middle ages filled the world with confusion. The recent acts of the King of Prussia, in imprisoning some bishops who had violated the laws and their own engagements, with reference to marriages between persons of different communions, would a few centuries ago have been followed by his deposition from the throne, and the proclamation of a crusade against him.

The limits of the Roman Churches were much enlarged about the time of the Reformation by the conquests of the Portuguese and Spanish in the east and west. A great number of converts from heathenism in the east were made by the pious zeal of Francis Xavier, who in 1542 sailed for the Portuguese settlements in India, and in a very short time succeeded in spreading the Christian religion throughout that vast country and the adjoining islands. In 1549 he went to Japan, and established there numerous churches, which continued to flourish for many years, until they were brought into persecution, and destroyed by the intrigues of the Jesuits. He died in 1552, as he was about to attempt the conversion of the Chinese; but after his death,

Matthew Ricci, and other Jesuits, penetrated into that empire ; and having made themselves very acceptable to the emperor by their skill in science, they were permitted to instruct the people in the Christian religion ; and thus the foundation of the Church was laid amongst the Chinese, which still continues to exist, though under much persecution.   The Nestorians of St. Thomas were also forced to unite themselves with the Roman Church by Menezes, archbishop of Goa. Christianity, which was now introduced into South America by the Spanish and Portuguese, obtained numerous converts there, and took deep and permanent root.

The synod of Trent reformed some of the grosser abuses in discipline ; but its canons of discipline were not universally received. The controversies with the advocates of reformation led to some amelioration of doctrine amongst the well-informed members of the Roman Church. In the seventeenth century it became their object to represent their doctrines in the form which was most moderate, most conformable to Scripture, and most approximating to the tenets of the Reformation. One object in this new system of argument was to convict the Protestants of schism in voluntarily forsaking the communion of the Church, —an offence which was imputed to them by their antagonists, and too often admitted by themselves, in direct opposition to the facts of history. This mode of argument, however—in the hands of the celebrated Roman theologians Bossuet and Veron— had the effect of producing sounder and more moderate views on many subjects in the Romish Church itself, though it is unhappily but too certain that the great mass of that community are still involved in superstitions and errors very injurious to true religion. The notions and practices of the ignorant, and even of many of the better informed, are indeed, in several points, widely at variance with the theories which are put forward by some of the more enlightened members of the Roman communion. Amongst the practices to which we object is " the worship of saints." Some Romanists affirm that this " worship" is not what is commonly understood by the word ; that it merely signifies a certain degree of *honour* paid to the saints, " infinitely below the supreme worship which they pay to God." And yet it is certain that many persons do practically pay more honour to the saints than to God. Their private devotions consist *chiefly* of prayers and litanies to the Virgin Mary and other saints ; and in one of their most common offices, the Rosary, the blessed Virgin is addressed ten times more frequently than the Supreme Being. Such persons may imagine themselves free from the sin of idolatry, because they do not intend to worship the saints with the same high degree of honour which they would pay to God ; but these excuses will be of little avail when a " jealous God" shall require an account of their conduct, and they shall be obliged to acknowledge that their hours were devoted to the worship of created beings, in preference to that of the Author of " all good gifts." It is not an occasional prayer, or a general acknowledgment of supremacy, which God demands. He must be " all in all" to the Christian.

With reference to the " invocation of saints," we are informed by some Romanists that the intention is merely to ask for their *intercession* with God, and that they are not themselves believed to be " the authors or givers of divine grace." Nevertheless it is certain that they are frequently addressed in prayers which make no mention of intercession, but which evidently suppose them to be invested with the power of giving divine grace, and of bestowing blessings on those who pray to them. Such prayers are, in themselves, plainly idolatrous, and yet they are tolerated and excused by Romanists; and the ignorant are thus exposed to most grievous temptations to direct idolatry. The very practice, indeed, of calling on the saints, leads, not unnaturally, to the dangerous opinion that they can hear such addresses from all parts of the world; that they are in all places, like God himself, and are invested with supernatural powers.

As to images, again, we find many Romanists denying with indignation the notion that they worship the images of Christ or of the saints with divine honours. According to them, the honour paid to images is supposed to pass entirely to the person represented, and in no case is it considered lawful to worship the image itself with the honours due to God. Yet many of the writers most esteemed amongst them, such as Aquinas and Bellarmine, have maintained that the images of Christ, and the supposed relics of the true cross, ought *themselves* to be adored with latria, or the honour due to God; and this doctrine has never been censured or condemned amongst them; so that it may be lawfully held by any Romanist at the present day. There is indeed but too much reason to believe, that in many places images and relics receive a worship which is more or less idolatrous. Men put their confidence in the supposed miraculous powers of certain images or relics. They make pilgrimages and offer gifts to them, bowing down before them, and exhibiting every other sign of worship. Such persons evidently believe that some divine grace or power is present in the images or relics which they thus honour; and such a persuasion and consequent practice is admitted even by Bossuet himself to be idolatrous.

It would not be just to attribute such idolatries and superstitions to those Romanists who deny or reject them; but it is lamentable to observe that no effective measures have ever been taken by the Roman Church to remove these scandals. Aware, as some of its bishops and pastors are, of the gross superstitions which exist, they do not venture to oppose themselves to the mass of prevailing error. Fearful lest by so doing they might seem to acknowledge the necessity of the Reformation, and to justify those who were engaged in it; and impressed with dread of that cry of heresy, which would be assuredly raised against any vigorous measures; they deem themselves unequal to the task of purifying their Church, or are content with feeble and unavailing methods of checking the growth of superstition.

The principles of Christian morality have become much relaxed in the Roman Churches through the influence of the Jesuits. The modern practice with reference to confession and absolution has contributed to the same effect. It has been assiduously inculcated, that confession to a priest, with a proper degree of sorrow (which the Jesuits have reduced to a very low degree), and certain external works of satisfaction, such as fasting, almsgiving, pilgrimage, &c., are sufficient to atone for any sins, however enormous. Hence absolution is regarded as an infallible mode of removing sin; and less difficulty must be felt in the commission of sin which can be so easily pardoned. The doctrine of purgatory also, which supposes that a portion of the penance or repentance due for sins in this life is expiated by punishments in the next world, and that the remission of such punishments may be obtained by the prayers and offices of the living, is calculated in some degree to lead men to neglect the duty of repentance in this life, and to rely on

the prayers of others. It is also to be observed,
that the system of questioning adopted at confession must tend to disseminate vice, by presenting
unhallowed images to the minds of youth.

CHAPTER XXV.

FRUITS OF FAITH IN THE ROMAN CHURCHES.

A.D. 1530-1660.

HOWEVER deeply we may deplore the
abuses and corruptions which exist in
the Roman Churches, and however certain it be that many errors injurious
to Christian piety, and many offences
against Christian morality, are found in that communion, still it would argue a prejudiced and uncharitable mind to close our eyes on several bright examples of Christian holiness that have adorned the
Roman communion in later ages, and refuse to recognise the impress of Divine grace on lives adorned
by every virtue which can flow from a lively faith and
charity. The contemplation of such examples will
tend to remove any feelings of spiritual pride which
might arise from imagining that virtue and goodness are restrained to some particular branch of the
Church of Christ, while the great mass of Christendom is given over entirely to darkness and to sin.

FRANCIS XAVIER, the apostle of the Indies, was
born in 1506, in Navarre, of an illustrious family,
and was pursuing his studies at the university of
Paris, when he became the friend and ultimately
one of the disciples of Ignatius Loyola, the founder
of the order of Jesuits, a man of an enthusiastic turn
of mind, and of a piety which was deeply tinged with

superstition. In 1537 Xavier was ordained priest, and took the vows as a member of the new order. The following year, while Ignatius and his disciples were at Rome, whither they had gone to place themselves under the directions of the pope as to their future destination, an application was made by the King of Portugal for the assistance of some of these zealous men to preach the Gospel in the East Indies. In compliance with this request, Francis Xavier was sent to Portugal in 1540, whence, in the following year, he sailed for India, with various powers and recommendations from the pope. During the voyage he considered the crew of the vessel in which he sailed as entrusted to his peculiar care. He instructed the sailors in their catechism, preached every Sunday before the main-mast, visited the sick, converted his own cabin into an infirmary, while he himself lay on the deck ; and, with the ascetic spirit of his order at that time, subsisted entirely on charity, being possessed of nothing himself. In short, during the whole voyage he evinced a spirit of zeal and piety which afforded a pledge of the success of that great work which he was about to undertake.

In 1542 he landed at Goa ; and having obtained the sanction of the bishop, he commenced his mission. The state of religion amongst professing Christians in that place was most lamentable. The Portuguese inhabitants were full of revenge, ambition, avarice, and every description of wickedness ; all sentiments of religion seemed extinguished in them. The sacraments were neglected ; there were scarcely any preachers ; and the heathen, immersed in every sin, were neither led by precept nor example to forsake their errors and superstitions. Xavier beheld with grief the scandalous example of the nominal Christians around him ; and he resolved to labour for their conversion and reformation in the first instance.

He began by instructing them in the principles of religion, and by forming the youth in the practice of piety. Having spent the morning of each day in the hospitals and prisons, assisting and comforting the distressed, he walked through the streets of Goa, with a bell in his hand, summoning all masters, for the love of God, to send their children and slaves to be catechised. The children gathered in crowds around him; he led them to church, taught them the creed and practices of devotion, and impressed on them strong sentiments of piety and religion. The effect produced on the youth soon became manifest; the example began to spread; the whole town was influenced to turn from sin. After a time, Xavier preached in public, and visited the people in their houses; and a most extraordinary and universal reformation in their morals and habits ensued.

After six months spent in these successful labours, Xavier, hearing that many of the Paravas, a people on the eastern coast of India, near Cape Comorin, had some years before permitted themselves to be baptised, in order to gratify the Portuguese; and having gained some knowledge of their language, went thither with two young clergy who understood the language sufficiently well. Here Xavier preached the Gospel with such success, that these people were converted in thousands; and so great were the multitudes whom he baptised, that sometimes, from the fatigue of administering that sacrament, he could hardly move his arm. Xavier says, that on one occasion his prayers were blessed to the recovery of a sick person; and a belief in such signs, whether well or ill founded, seems to have had much influence in contributing to the extraordinary success of his ministry. His labours, indeed, were incredible: while he lived only on rice and water, like the very poorest of the people, he was able to devote his whole day and night, except *three* hours of sleep, to the exercise of his ministry and the duties of devotion.

Xavier had laboured for more than a year in the conversion of these people, when he was obliged to return to Goa for assistance. He came back in 1544 with several missionaries, some of whom he stationed in different towns, to continue the instruction of his converts; the others he brought with him to the adjoining kingdom of Travancore, where he baptised ten thousand Indians in one month; and in a very few months almost the whole kingdom of Travancore embraced Christianity. He afterwards visited several other parts of India, where he founded churches. Xavier then sailed to Malacca, a famous mart for merchandise, where he arrived in 1545; and by the irresistible ardour of his zeal reformed the Christians in that place, and converted many pagans and Mahommedans. He next preached in the Spice Islands, Amboyna, the Moluccas, and Ceylon, in all of which he brought great numbers to the faith. In this mission he experienced many sufferings and dangers; but his zeal for God caused him rather to rejoice in those things. "The dangers to which I am exposed," said he, "and the toils I undergo for the interest of God only, are an inexhaustible spring of spiritual joys, insomuch that these islands, bare as they are of all worldly necessaries, are the very places in the world for a man to lose his sight through the excess of weeping,—but they are tears of joy. I never remember to have tasted such inward delights; and these consolations of the soul are so pure, so exquisite, so constant, that they take from me all sense of my corporeal sufferings."

Having returned again to Goa, Xavier soon after

sailed on a mission to Japan, where he arrived in
1549, and was received favourably by the king, who
allowed him to preach the Gospel ; and he applied
himself with such extreme diligence to the study of
the language, that in a few weeks he was able to
translate the creed, and an exposition of it, together
with a life of our Saviour compiled from the Gospels, and to preach in public.   He made many converts, amongst whom he distributed the translations
he had made.   He continued to preach amongst the
islands with various success : at Fuceo vast multitudes of people desired to be instructed and baptised ; and the king himself was convinced of the
truth of the Gospel.   Having laid the foundations
of the Christian Church throughout Japan, he again
embarked for India in 1551; and after a short stay
there, was once more on his way to preach the Gospel in China, when, in 1552, it pleased God to call
away this great missionary, after ten years of labours and successes almost unparalleled since the
days of the apostles.

CHARLES BORROMEO, archbishop of Milan, and
cardinal of the Roman Church, was born of a noble
family in 1538, at Arona, in the duchy of Milan.
His father, a man of exemplary piety, gave him an
education proportioned to the great prospects of
promotion which his family connexions presented ;
and he gave early signs of a strong attachment to
literary pursuits.   His uncle, Pope Pius IV., on his
election to the Roman see, invited him to Rome,
and created him cardinal, and archbishop of Milan,
when he was only twenty-two years of age.   The
pope entrusted to him the chief management of
ecclesiastical affairs, in which he evinced an ability
and discretion which would have done credit to the
most experienced ecclesiastic.   The Romans were
remarkable for indolence and ignorance : to induce

them to aspire to a more honourable character, Borromeo instituted an academy, consisting of ecclesiastics and laymen, whom his munificence and example incited to study and animated to virtue. But in the midst of a luxurious court, the young cardinal was carried away by the torrent: his palace, furniture, equipage, and table, were splendid and sumptuous; and his uncle, in order to enable him to support such expenses, heaped on him a number of high and lucrative appointments, in addition to several rich abbeys and other benefices, of which he was possessed. In 1562 Borromeo's eldest brother died: and notwithstanding his high station in the Church, he was now urged by the pope, and by all his friends, to resign his ecclesiastical dignities, and marry, in order to support his family name; but he refused their solicitations, and was ordained priest the same year.

The council of Trent re-assembled about this time, and the reformation of the clergy became the subject of much discussion. Cardinal Borromeo was not content to urge that reformation on others; he adopted it himself. He dismissed at once above eighty officers of his household; laid aside his robes of silk; and submitted once in every week to a day of voluntary fasting on bread and water. In 1566, on the death of his uncle, he retired to Milan, and engaged earnestly in the reformation of his diocese. He began by the regulation of his own family, which consisted of about a hundred persons, chiefly clergy; considering that his task would be easier, when all he wished to prescribe to others was exemplified in his own house. He soon brought all his household to a most regular, orderly, and religious life. His own habits of piety and self-denial were very remarkable. He removed from his palace all the fine sculpture, paintings, hangings, and even

the armorial bearings of his family ; wore the coarsest
vestments under his robes ; and avoided, as much
as possible, being served or attended on by others.
In order to inspire his clergy with a contempt for
earthly possessions, he would severely reprove those
who discovered an interested or covetous spirit ;
even bishops were not exempt from his reproofs.
He himself exemplified most remarkably the virtues
of charity and disinterestedness.   When he came to
reside at Milan, he voluntarily resigned benefices
and estates to the value of 80,000 crowns per annum, reserving only an income of 20,000 crowns.
The principality of Oria, which had become his
property by the death of his brother, he sold for
40,000 crowns, which he commanded his almoners
to distribute among the poor and the hospitals.
When the list which the almoners shewed him for the
distribution amounted, by mistake, to 2000 crowns
more, Borromeo said the mistake was too much to
the advantage of the poor to be corrected, and the
whole was accordingly distributed in one day. When
his brother died, he also caused all the rich furniture and jewels of the family to be sold, and gave
the price, which amounted to 30,000 crowns, to the
poor. Several other cases of charity, on an equally
large scale, might be added. His chief almoner
was ordered to distribute among the poor of Milan,
of whom he kept an exact list, 200 crowns every
month. Borromeo would never permit any beggar
to be dismissed without some alms, whatever he was.

He was exceedingly hospitable and liberal in
entertaining princes, prelates, and strangers of all
ranks, but always without dainties or luxury ; and
he endeavoured as much as possible to conceal his
own abstemiousness. His religious foundations, repairs of churches, of the dwellings of the clergy,
and of the seminaries of learning, not only at Milan,

but at Bologna, Rome, and many other places, were on the most magnificent scale of liberality.

Borromeo found his diocese in the greatest disorder. The great truths of salvation were little known or understood; and religious practices were profaned by the grossest abuses, and disfigured by superstitions. The sacraments were neglected; the clergy seem scarcely to have known how to administer them, and were slothful, ignorant, and depraved: the monasteries were full of disorders. Borromeo instituted seminaries for the instruction of the clergy; appointed a number of vicars, or rural deans, who exercised a vigilant superintendence over every part of his diocese; and held many provincial and diocesan synods, in which the most excellent and judicious regulations were made, and enforced with inflexible firmness. In the course of his proceedings, he frequently encountered the most violent opposition from those who were unwilling to be corrected. The order of monks called Humiliati were particularly irritated by his labours for their reform, and excited against him one of their members, who actually fired a musket at the archbishop, as he was one evening at prayers with his family. Borromeo calmly finished his prayer, though the ball had struck his robe (happily without wounding him), and then, with truly Christian charity, forgave the assassin, and even solicited his pardon. But justice took its course, and the order was suppressed by the pope.

Borromeo divided the revenue of his see into three parts; one of which was appropriated to his household, another to the poor, and a third to the repairs of churches: and it was his custom to lay before the provincial councils the accounts of his revenues to the last farthing, saying that he was no more than an administrator or steward. He employed no clergy of his own kindred in the government of his diocese; nor did he resign to them any of the benefices which had been conferred on him.

It was one of his greatest pleasures to converse with and catechise the poor; and he would often visit them in the wildest and most mountainous parts of his diocese. On one occasion, while he was engaged in his visitation, the bishop of Ferrara coming to meet him, found him lying under a fit of the ague on a coarse bed, and in a very poor cottage. Borromeo, observing his surprise, remarked " that he was treated very well, and much better than he deserved." During the dreadful ravages of a pestilence, this excellent man encouraged his clergy to administer the consolations of religion to the sick and dying, and he was himself assiduous in the performance of this dangerous duty. On this occasion he sold all his furniture to procure medicine and nourishment for the unhappy sufferers. He was careful not to lose a moment of his time : even at table he listened to some pious book, or dictated letters or instructions. When he fasted on bread and water, and dined in private, he read at the same time, and on his knees when the Bible was before him. After dinner, instead of conversing, he gave audience to his rural deans and clergy. He allowed himself no time for recreation; finding in the different employments of his office both corporal exercise and relaxation of mind sufficient for maintaining the vigour of his mind and health of his body.

When he was put in mind of any fault, he expressed the most sincere gratitude; and he gave a commission to two prudent and religious clergy of his household to remind him of any thing they saw amiss in his actions; and he frequently requested the same favour of strangers. He was remarkable for sincerity; it appeared in all his words and actions, and his promises were inviolable. He delighted in prayer, to which he gave a large part of his time; and he never said any prayer, or performed any religious office, with precipitation, whatever business of importance might be on his hands, or however he might be pressed for time. In giving audience, and in the greatest hurry of business, his countenance, his modesty, and all his words, shewed that he was full of the recollection of God. His spirit of prayer, and the love of God which filled his heart, gave to him remarkably the power of exciting and encouraging others to religion. A short address, even a single word or action, sometimes produced the most powerful effects in animating his clergy to repentance and to virtue.

This great and good man died in 1584, in the forty-seventh year of his age; with the same piety and sanctity which adorned his short but admirable life.

FRANCIS DE SALES was born of noble parents in Savoy, and was remarkable for a spirit of piety and meekness from his earliest years. His mother taught him to venerate the Church and religion: she read to him the lives of holy men; brought him with her to visit the poor, and made him distribute her alms to them. Having studied theology and law at the universities of Paris and Padua, his parents intended that he should follow the legal profession, and they had already obtained a lucrative and important office from the Duke of Savoy for him; but Francis had resolved to devote himself to the sacred ministry, and declined so advantageous an establishment. Through the intervention and entreaties of a relative, his parents were at length, with much difficulty, persuaded to accede to his wishes, and he then was appointed to a dignity in the Church, and was ordained deacon. His diocesan, the bishop of Annecy, immediately employed him in preaching, in which he was eminently successful, as his sermons were always the result of fervent prayer. He was observed to decline whatever might gain the applause of the world; and he preferred resorting to the habitations of the poor, and to the rural districts, rather than preaching before the great and opulent. In 1591, the first year of his ministry, he instituted a society at Annecy, the associates of which were obliged to instruct the ignorant, to comfort and exhort the sick and prisoners, and to abstain from all lawsuits.

In 1594 the Duke of Savoy having conquered Geneva, and some of the adjoining parts of Switzerland, Francis de Sales was commissioned to preach in those parts to the reformed. Impressed, like the rest of his communion, with the mistaken notion that the Roman pontiff is, by Divine appointment, the centre of catholic unity, he of course viewed the reformed as separated from the true Church, and he laboured for their conversion for several years. He was much respected by Beza, and the rest of the reformed in Switzerland; and the excellence of his own character, and the piety and meekness which he always evinced, probably did much more for his cause than any other arguments by which it was sustained. The plague at one time raged violently in the place where he resided, but this did not deter him from assisting the sick in their last moments by day and night; and he was wonderfully preserved in the pestilence, which carried off several of the clergy who aided him. In 1599 he became coadjutor of the bishop of Annecy, with the right of succession to that see; and soon after was obliged to go to France, where he was received by all ranks and classes with the utmost distinction. He preached before the king, who endeavoured to detain him in France by promises of a large pension, and of the first vacant bishopric; but Francis de Sales declined all these offers; and returning to the poor bishopric of Annecy, was soon after, on the death of his predecessor, consecrated its pastor in 1602. He now laid down a plan of life, to which he ever after rigorously adhered. He resolved to wear no expensive clothing; to have no paintings except of a devotional character in his house; to possess no splendid furniture; to use no coach or carriage, but make his visitations on foot. His family was to consist of two priests, one to act as his chaplain, the other to superintend his servants and temporalities; his table to be plain and frugal. He resolved to be present at all religious and devotional meetings and festivals in the churches; to distribute abundant alms; to visit the sick and poor in person; to rise every day at four, meditate for an hour, read private service, then prayers with his family; then to read the Scripture; celebrate the holy eucharist; and afterwards apply to business till dinner. He then gave an hour to conversation, and spent the remainder of the afternoon in business and prayer. After supper he read a pious book to his family for an hour; then prayed with them, and retired to his private devotions and to rest. Such was the general mode of life of this excellent man.

Immediately after he became bishop, he applied himself to preaching, and to all the other duties of his station. He was very cautious in conferring holy orders, ordaining but few clergy, and only after a most rigid examination of their qualifications. He was also exceedingly diligent in promoting the instruction of the ignorant by catechising on Sundays and holydays; and his personal labours in this respect had a very great influence in persuading the clergy of his diocese to follow so good an example. He still continued to delight in preaching in small villages and to the poorest people, whom he regarded as the special objects of his care. He had a very wide correspondence on religious subjects; and composed several books full of piety and devotion, but of course not altogether free from the superstitions of his age and communion. His compassion was so excited by the unhappy condition of a poor deaf and dumb man, that he received him into his own family, taught him by signs, and instructed him in religion. He founded a new order of nuns, in which few bodily austerities were practised, and no great burdens of religious observances were imposed; his object being to render it suitable even for the sickly and weak.

The same disinterested spirit which he had early manifested always continued. When he was solicited by Henry IV., king of France, to accept an abbey of large income, he refused it, saying, "that he dreaded riches as much as others desired them; and that the less he had of them, the less he should have to answer for." The same prince offered to name him to the dignity of cardinal at the next promotion; but he replied, that though he did not despise the proffered dignity, he was persuaded that great titles did not suit him, and might raise new obstacles to his salvation. His conscientious firmness was also remarkable. On one occasion the parliament of Chambery in Savoy seized his temporalities for refusing, at its desire, to publish an ecclesiastical censure which he thought uncalled for by the circumstances of the case. When he heard of the seizure of his possessions, he said that he thanked God for teaching him by it, "that a bishop is altogether spiritual." He did not desist from preaching, or apply to the sovereign for redress;

but behaved in so kind and friendly a manner to those who had insulted him most grossly, that at length the parliament became ashamed of its proceedings, and restored his temporalities.

In 1619 he accompanied the Cardinal of Savoy to Paris, to demand the sister of King Louis XIII. in marriage for the prince of Piedmont. While he was in that city he preached a course of Lent sermons, which, aided by his conferences, the example of his holy life, and the sweetness of his discourse, most powerfully moved, not only the devout, but even libertines and atheists. He was entreated, for the sake of his health, not to preach twice in the day. He replied, with a smile, "that it cost him much less to preach a sermon than to find an excuse for himself when invited to perform that office. God had appointed him to be a pastor and a preacher, and ought not every one to follow his profession?" Amongst his common sayings was this, " That truth must be always charitable, for bitter zeal does harm rather than good. Reprehensions are a food of hard digestion, and ought to be dressed on a fire of burning charity so well, that all harshness be taken away; otherwise, like unripe fruit, they will only produce pains. Charity seeks not itself nor its own interests, but purely the honour and interests of God. Pride, vanity, and passion, cause bitterness and harshness. A remedy injudiciously applied may be a poison. A judicious silence is always better than a truth spoken without charity." On one occasion, seeing a vicious and scandalous priest thrown into prison, he fell at his feet, and, with tears, conjured him to have compassion on him his pastor, on religion which he scandalised, and on his own soul. The man was so deeply impressed by this conduct, that he was entirely converted, and became a virtuous man from that moment.

In 1622 this holy bishop fell into an apoplexy ; and as his illness slowly increased, he poured forth his soul in supplication to God, and in all those expressions of devotion and humility which might have been anticipated at the close of so Christian a life. He then peacefully expired, in the fifty-sixth year of his age.

VINCENT DE PAUL was born near the Pyrenees in France, of poor parentage, in 1576; and even from his childhood shewed a seriousness and a love of prayer remarkable for his years. His father was determined, by the strong inclinations of his child for piety and study, and by the quickness of his parts, to give him a school-education ; and for this purpose placed him at a monastery of Franciscan friars. He afterwards studied at the university of Toulouse, where he was admitted to the order of priesthood in 1600. Vincent was already endowed with many virtues ; but he was now to experience trials which were calculated to make the deepest demands on his self-denial, his humility, and his submission to the will of God. He was on a voyage from Narbonne to Marseilles, on some affairs, in 1605, when the vessel in which he was sailing was captured by pirates from Africa, who wounded him with an arrow, laid him in chains, and sailed for the coast of Barbary. At Tunis, Vincent was sold as a slave to a physician, who was a humane man, but who used his utmost efforts to induce his slave to embrace the Mahommedan law, promising, on that condition, to leave him all his riches, and communicate to him the secrets of his science. The result need scarcely be told. Vincent remained firm in his faith ; and on his master's death was sold to another Mahommedan, who treated him with extreme harshness and cruelty. He, however, learned to bear all his afflictions with comfort and joy, by remembering his blessed Redeemer, and studying to imitate his perfect meekness, patience, silence, and charity. At last he was sold again to a renegade (one who had apostatised from Christianity). This man had several Turkish wives, one of whom frequently went to the field where Vincent was digging, and, out of curiosity, would ask him to sing the praises of God. He used to sing to her, with tears in his eyes, the Psalm, "By the waters of Babylon we sat down and wept," and several Christian hymns. She gradually became so much captivated with the excellence of the Christian religion, though still unconverted and professing the Mahommedan creed, that she continually reproached her husband for his apostacy from so excellent a religion; and at length his conscience was so awakened, that he repented of his sin, and resolved to return to his country and his faith. In 1607 he made his escape to France, accompanied by Vincent de Paul. They afterwards went to Rome, where the renegade was received again into the Church.

On Vincent's return to Paris, he served as curate at a neighbouring village, and afterwards became preceptor and spiritual director in a noble family; and here his remarkable success in awakening the sleeping conscience of a dying sinner to a full sense of his guilt, led to his employment in the mission of preaching repentance; for which purpose he became the founder of a congregation or society of clergy, who were bound to devote themselves to the conversion of sinners, and the training up of clergy for the holy ministry. They traversed every part of France, and engaged in the sacred office wherever their assistance, in aid of the ordinary ministry, was particularly called for. Vincent lived to see this institution become very extensive, and highly approved by the Church and State.

He was also the founder of many other religious and charitable societies, especially of the Society of Charity, for attending on all the poor sick persons in each parish ; and of other societies for visiting the sick in hospitals, and for the education of girls. He also procured the foundation of many great hospitals. He instituted spiritual exercises for those who were about to receive holy orders, and ecclesiastical conferences on the duties of the clerical office. During the wars in Lorraine, hearing of the misery to which the people of that province were reduced, he collected alms amongst pious and charitable people at Paris to the amount of 100,000*l.* He was in the highest favour with King Louis XIII. and Queen Anne of Austria, who consulted him on all ecclesiastical affairs, and on the collation of benefices.

Amidst such a multiplicity of important affairs, his soul was always set on God. He was remarkable for self-denial, for profound humility, and for a spirit of prayer. He laid it down as a rule of humility, that, if possible, a man ought never to talk of his own concerns; such discourse usually proceeding from, and nourishing in the heart, the spirit of pride. At length, at the advanced age of eighty-four, this pious and profitable servant of God was called to his everlasting reward, amidst the veneration and love of all men. He died in 1660, and was buried in the church of St. Lazarus at Paris.

CHAPTER XXVI.

ON THE ORIENTAL CHURCHES.

A.D. 1517-1839.

HE faith and discipline of the eastern or Greek Churches in Russia, Turkey, Greece, Asia, Syria, and Egypt, have remained with scarcely any variation during the whole of this period. In the sixteenth century the Lutherans sought a union with the Constantinopolitan Church, but were prevented by various differences from accomplishing their wish. In the seventeenth century some intercourse took place between the Constantinopolitan and English Churches. Cyrillus Lucaris, patriarch of Constantinople, dedicated his work on the faith of the Eastern Church to King Charles I., and presented to him the celebrated Alexandrian manuscript of the Bible. And in 1653 Dr. Basire, archdeacon of Northumberland, when travelling in Greece, was invited twice by the metropolitan of Achaia to preach before the bishops and clergy; and he received from Païsius, patriarch of Jerusalem, his patriarchal seal, to express his desire of communion with the Church of England. The communion of our Churches and those of the East has not, however, yet been restored. In the seventeenth century, also, the doctrine of transubstantiation was first embraced by a portion of the Greek Church, though many persons still only make use of the term, without believing the Roman doctrine on this subject.

In the latter part of the sixteenth century the Russian Church, which had previously always been subject to the see of Constantinople, became independent; for, at the desire of the Russians, a patriarch of Moscow was created by the eastern patriarchs.   Peter the Great, in the last century, suppressed this office, and appointed a synod to conduct the affairs of the Russian Church. He also reformed several abuses and corruptions in that Church; but these improvements were not relished by some of the clergy and people, who were attached to the old superstitions and abuses, and who, like the Romanists in England and Ireland, separated from the Church, and are termed Roskolniks, or schismatics. Within the last few years the Church in the newly created kingdom of Greece has also been withdrawn from the jurisdiction of the see of Constantinople, and placed under the direction of a synod of bishops: but this has not led to any division in the eastern Church; for, unlike the popes, the patriarchs of Constantinople do not treat as heretics or schismatics every one who is not subject to their jurisdiction.   The Greek Church has also recently gained a considerable addition, by the reunion of those Churches in Poland who held the Greek rites, and which had been for some time obedient to the pope.

CHAPTER XXVII.

ON THE RISE AND PROGRESS OF INFIDELITY.

I HAVE already alluded to the spread of infidelity in the last century; but a circumstance so deeply affecting the Christian Church deserves a more detailed notice. It is fearful to contemplate the excess of wickedness to which God sometimes permits his enemies to proceed. One can hardly imagine that any human being in his senses, who was born in a Christian land, and who had been baptised and educated in a Christian Church, could be so far transported by his passions as to declare himself the enemy of Jesus Christ! The heart trembles at the very notion of such blasphemy. But that a man should, for nearly seventy years, devote himself to the extirpation of Christianity; to the destruction of that faith which alone consoles man amidst his afflictions and his fears; to the extinction of every principle of virtue and morality, and the inculcation of general depravity,—this opens to our view a deeper gulf of human guilt than even the records of Scripture supply, or the imagination could have conceived. Such was VOLTAIRE; a man whose private life was defiled by the grossest immorality, and whose heart burned with such a demoniacal hatred of HIM who came down from heaven and voluntarily sacrificed himself on the cross for the salvation of sinners, that he adopted as his watchword on all occasions those awful words, " Ecrasez l'infame !"—CRUSH THE WRETCH ! that is, " Crush Christ; crush the Christian religion !" Such was the language and the feeling of that organised band of infidels, who in the earlier part of last century associated in the impious attempt to subvert Christianity.

England had been already disgraced by the writings of some unbelievers ; but the works of Herbert and Bolingbroke, of Collins and Tindal, had produced little effect on the good sense and religious principles of the English nation. The clergy effectually exposed their errors, and they became the objects of popular hatred ; but they were unhappily destined to find a more congenial soil in France.

Voltaire was born in Paris in 1694, and lived to the age of eighty-four, dying in the year 1778. He was endowed with great natural abilities, quickness, versatility, wit; with a remarkable power of sarcasm ; and a pointed, easy, and fluent style, which was unrestrained by any principles of truth or decency. While he was at college, he manifested so sceptical a spirit, that his preceptor one day said to him, " Unfortunate young man, at some future time you will become the standard-bearer of infidelity." After he had left college, he associated only with persons of infamous morals ; and having published some infidel opinions, which gave offence to the ruling powers of France, he retired to England, where he became acquainted with several unbelievers like himself. Here he formed his resolution to destroy Christianity ; and on his return to Paris, in 1730, he made no secret of his design and his hopes. " I am weary," he would say, " of hearing people repeat that twelve men were sufficient to establish Christianity. I will prove that *one* may suffice to overthrow it."

In order to accomplish his design, Voltaire found it necessary to obtain the assistance of several coadjutors : of these D'Alembert was the chief. He was remarkable for his crafty cunning, which enabled him to insinuate infidelity in the most plausible and least offensive manner. His expressions were generally moderate; while Voltaire used to express his wish that he might "die on a heap of Christians immolated at his feet." Another associate was Frederick II., king of Prussia, a great general and statesman, but a shallow philosopher. He was in continual correspondence with Voltaire — complimented him on being the "scourge of religion"—and plotted for its destruction. Diderot was another coadjutor of Voltaire, who with D'Alembert devoted themselves even till death to the pursuit of their unhallowed design.

I have already spoken of the watchword of this association, the object of which was the overthrow of every altar where Christ was worshipped. It was not merely the Gallican or Roman doctrine which was marked out for destruction. In the latter part of his career, Voltaire exulted at the dissemination of Hume's infidel principles in England, and at the prospect of the fall of the Church of England, exclaiming with delight, that " in London Christ was *spurned.*" On another occasion, he rejoiced that " in Geneva, Calvin's own town," but few believers remained.

Voltaire invited men to forsake their religion by promising them liberty of thought. He declared, that " nothing was so contemptible and miserable in his eyes, as to see one man have recourse to another in matters of faith, or to ask what he ought to believe." Reason, liberty, and philosophy, were continually in the mouths of Voltaire and D'Alembert. Their adherents represented them as " devoutly waiting for those days when the sun should shine only on *free* men, acknowledging *no other master but their own reason.*" Voltaire had but little of

the spirit of martyrdom : his continual exhortation
to the conspirators was, to " strike, but *conceal* their
hands ; that is, to write anonymously. " The monster" (Christianity), he said, " must fall, pierced by
a hundred invisible hands ; yes, let it fall beneath a
thousand repeated blows."   In accordance with this
advice, the press swarmed with anonymous publications of the most impious character. The principal
mode of propagating infidelity was the publication
of the celebrated Encyclopedia, of which D'Alembert was the editor, and which was to contain so
perfect an assemblage of all the arts and sciences, as
to render all other books superfluous. The utmost
caution was used in insinuating infidel principles,
lest the design should be detected, and crushed by
the hand of power. All the principal articles on
religion were written in such a manner as to avoid
offence ; while by means of references at the conclusion of each, the reader was directed to places
where open infidelity was taught. Irreligion and
atheism were inculcated even in articles on chemis-
try, or other sciences, where their existence could
not be suspected.

When this work was completed, it obtained an
immense circulation. Numberless editions were
printed, in each of which, under pretence of correction, more impiety was introduced. In one of
these, a respectable and learned divine, M. Bergier,
was persuaded into writing the part which treated of
religion, lest it should fall into the hands of unbelievers ; but it was easy to foresee what actually
happened : his name conferred respectability on the
book, while all its other articles teemed with the
most dreadful impiety and blasphemy.

Infidelity now rapidly spread through France,
and through every part of the continent of Europe ;
several of the crowned heads were more or less fa-

vourable. The Empress of Russia, the Kings of Prussia, Denmark, Poland, Sweden, and all the princes of Germany, were either admirers of Voltaire or avowed infidels. The abominable licentiousness of the court of France assisted the conspiracy : the French ministry, tainted with infidelity, refused to put the laws in force for the suppression of blasphemous, infidel, and immoral publications, which now issued in a flood from the press. The most eminent scientific men, and the most popular writers of France, such as Buffon, Lalande, Marmontel, Rousseau, were unbelievers. It is awful to contemplate the excess of wickedness at which these men had arrived. The history of this time relates, that "above all the adepts did a fiend named Condorcet hate the Son of God. At the very name of the Deity the monster raged ! And it appeared as if he wished to revenge on Heaven the heart it had given him." Infidelity had widely spread among the higher orders ; it was now to be disseminated amongst the lowest. Infidel and blasphemous tracts were printed in myriads, and circulated profusely in all parts. Diderot and D'Alembert disputed on Christianity in the coffee-rooms of Paris ; and the pretended advocate of Christianity took care always to be defeated.

It is lamentable to add, that the clergy of the Roman communion were not universally to be found on the side of Christianity. The ecclesiastical patronage of the state, indeed, was too often exercised for the subversion of religion. The Abbé Barruel observes, with reference to France, that " the enemies of the Church possessed themselves of its avenues, to prevent the preferment of those whose virtues or learning they dreaded. When the bishops wished to repel an unworthy member, Choiseul, the infidel minister, replied, ' such are the men we want

and will have.'"   Cardinal de Brienne, archbishop
of Toulouse, was a friend of D'Alembert, and became an open apostate from religion.   He was followed by the bishops of Autun, Viviers, Orleans,
Lydda, Babylon, &c.   In the infidel association of
the "Illuminati" were many priests, and even a
high dignitary of the German Church.   The names
of the Abbés Raynal, De Prades, Condillac, De
Leire, Morrelet, Terray, Marsy, &c., are unhappily
but too well known as connected with infidelity.
Numbers of Jacobin and infidel priests were also
found in Italy, Spain, and other parts of the Continent.   The majority, however, of the Roman clergy
throughout Europe retained their faith, and, under
the most grievous afflictions and persecutions for
the name of Christ, evinced an increased measure
of zeal and piety.

Voltaire was received with a sort of popular triumph at Paris in 1778 ; but very shortly after, this
enemy of God and man expired in the most dreadful
torments of agony and remorse.   His associates did
not long survive him ; but the seed which they had
sown was soon to produce its bitter fruit.

All religious and all moral principle being now
extinguished, and every passion of man's nature
being left without control, human society perished
amidst the horrors of the FRENCH REVOLUTION of
1789.   Amidst rebellion, anarchy, plunder, desola-
tion, famine, massacre, and every imaginable evil,
the reign of infidelity commenced.   The worship
and ministry of Christianity were proscribed, and
God was no longer acknowledged.   Then was beheld the woful spectacle of bishops and priests has-
tening to the infidel assembly of France, casting
from them the ensigns of their ministry, and proclaiming themselves no longer believers in God.
The Roman Church, scourged for her sins, and

especially for that spirit of pride which resists all efforts for the removal of superstitions, beheld her pope despoiled of his territories, and the captive of Buonaparte; her revenues plundered in France and Italy; her monasteries suppressed; her bishops driven from their sees into exile, or dying beneath the guillotine; her clergy perishing by the hand of the executioner, or by more wholesale massacre. She beheld faith vanishing away, and a generation of men arising WITHOUT RELIGION.

Although the return of peace and order has been favourable to the restoration of Christianity, and though additional fervour may have been added to faith so sorely tried and afflicted, yet it is certain that the effects of the infidel conspiracy of last century have been deep and lasting. It is true, indeed, that Christianity has for many years past been less directly assailed; that infidelity may have been less industriously propagated; but still an infidel and perverse generation lives without God in the world; and in France, more especially, the prevalence of this deadly evil is so great, that an eloquent ecclesiastic of that nation (La Mennais) some years since declared, that "the state to which we are approaching is one of the signs by which will be recognised that last war announced by Jesus Christ: 'nevertheless, when the Son of man cometh, shall he find faith on the earth?'" "What," said he, "do you perceive every where but a profound indifference as to duties and creeds, with an unbridled love of pleasure and of gold, by means of which any thing can be obtained? All is bought, for all is sold; conscience, honour, religion, opinions, dignities, power, consideration, even respect: a vast shipwreck of all truths and all virtues." Indifference, total indifference to religion; the uttermost neglect and contempt of Christianity, as a thing unworthy of examination, are the characteristics of modern infidelity in France.

In Germany the spirit of unbelief assumes the name of Rationalism, and pretends to respect the character of Christ; while, under the guise of Christianity, it boldly subjects the revelation of God to the judgment and criticisms of man's reason, rejects all that is incomprehensible by our limited faculties, deprives the Gospel of all its peculiar and divinely revealed doctrines, tramples in contempt on the universal belief of all Christians from the beginning, arraigns the Scriptures themselves of falsehood and folly; and leaves the mind at last without one particle of Christian faith or hope. This destructive system arose among the Protestants of Germany after the middle of the last century. It has unhappily become almost universally prevalent amongst them.

Though England has, through the infinite mercy of God, been comparatively unvisited by the scourges which have so terribly afflicted the nations of the Continent, and though open infidelity has been always met, confronted, and subdued by the energy of religious zeal, it cannot but inspire alarm to behold the wide dissemination of principles which tend, by a very short descent, to the overthrow of all faith. Such appears to be the character of that most erroneous notion, that sincerity is the only test of religion; so that he who persuades himself that he is right in his faith, believes all that is necessary for his salvation; for if this be true, it cannot be necessary to believe any particular doctrine of Christianity; it cannot be necessary to prefer Christ to Mahomet; and belief in Christ cannot be (as the Gospel says it is) the condition on which men shall be saved. How true is it that the Evil one clothes himself as an angel of light! In the last century

infidelity appeared under the specious garb of philosophy and freedom of thought : it is now insinuating itself under the disguise of charity, kindness,
and liberality.   All modes of faith are treated with
impartial favour, all are regarded as equally true ;
and the hour may be at hand, when the necessary
conclusion will be drawn, that they are all equally
false.   There is much in the spirit of the age to
threaten such lamentable results ;—a spirit of insa-
tiable inquiry, not always accompanied by modesty
or patience ; a thirst for novelty ; a superficial information ; the adoration of intellect and of knowledge; and the exclusive devotion of men to sciences
which relate to merely material objects.   All com-
bine to shew the danger to which belief is exposed ;
and to warn the Church of God that renewed watchfulness, and humility, and zeal, are more than ever
imperatively called for.

<hr>

CHAPTER XXVIII.

CONCLUSION.

E have now briefly traced the progress of
the Church of Christ through eighteen
centuries of its varied existence. In the
midst of temptations and dangers, the
ark of eternal truth has still been preserved by an Almighty hand.   That " city set on an
hill," that " ensign" which was once " set up to the
Gentiles," has never been concealed.   The Church
has always continued to preach " Christ crucified"
as the Saviour of the world, and to urge the necessity of believing and obeying his words ; and amidst
the existing diversities of religious doctrine, it will
be found, that all those Churches which have not

arisen from schism or voluntary separation from the universal Church, agree to a very great extent in their belief. In proof of this, it may be observed, that the three creeds, called the Apostles', the Nicene, and the Athanasian, are accepted and approved equally by the Greek or Oriental, the British, and the Roman Churches, as well as by the relics of the foreign reformation. The same doctrines which were universally received in the second century are still so in the nineteenth. All Churches believe, and with one mouth confess, one God, who created the world by his only begotten Son, our Lord Jesus Christ, who being co-eternal with the Father, and of equal glory, and power, and majesty, came down from heaven and became man for our salvation, and in his human nature suffered death on the cross, and ascended into heaven, making an eternal and all-sufficient atonement and intercession for us. All believe that the condition of man by nature is such, that he is unable without the aid of Divine grace to turn to God and become pleasing and acceptable to him; that to sinful man Divine grace is given by the free and unmerited mercy of God; and that he is enabled by the sanctifying influences of the eternal Spirit of God, the third person in the most blessed Trinity, to triumph over the sins and infirmities of his nature, and to become sanctified by faith and the love of God, bringing forth the fruits of obedience. All believe that we shall give an account of our works at the last judgment, when the righteous shall be rewarded with life eternal, and the wicked consigned to everlasting fire. The holy Scriptures of the Old and New Testament are universally acknowledged to be the word of God, given by inspiration of the Holy Ghost. The sacraments instituted by Christ are celebrated amongst all nations; and the same Christian ministry has descended by successive ordinations of bishops from the time of the apostles to the present day. Such is the substantial and real agreement in doctrine which exists between Churches which are in some respects dissentient from each other. Their differences turn chiefly on doctrines and practices not taught by our Lord, but which some men in later ages have imagined to be deducible from revelation, or to be allowable and justifiable. Questions as to the truth and lawfulness of such doctrines and practices divide the Christian Churches; but it will probably be found that no article of the faith, no doctrine clearly and distinctly revealed by our Lord, is denied by any of these Churches.

It may be added, that many even of the sectaries or schismatics, who have voluntarily forsaken the Church, still maintain the great mass of Christian doctrine, however destitute they may be of Christian charity.

The union of the Christian Church, flowing from a common faith, and hope, and charity, was indeed enjoined and urged by our blessed Lord' and Saviour; but no promise was given that the Church should at all times be actually united in external communion. The divisions which have for a long time existed arose chiefly, if not entirely, from the mistaken notions of the papal authority entertained by the popes and their adherents during the eleventh and following centuries. If it should please God to open the eyes of Romanists to their error on this point, we might have some reason to hope for the approach of those happy days predicted in holy Scripture, when "Ephraim shall not envy Judah, and Judah shall not vex Ephraim." On the doctrine of the papal supremacy the whole mass of superstitions which we deplore to see in the Roman communion essentially depends. It is this doctrine

which leads Romanists to view the Oriental and
British Churches as separated from the true Church;
and which renders it equally impossible for those
Churches to expect the restoration of general harmony and union.

And while we lament the disunion of the Christian Church, we have also to deplore the multitude
of abuses and errors which in many parts of the
world choke the good seed and make it unfruitful.
Superstitions which arose "while men slept," still
continue, almost unchecked and unresisted, to prevail.   The ignorant are in many Churches left exposed to the danger of honouring the creature instead of the Creator, by the worship of images, and
the invocation of saints.   But on all sides there is
much of infirmity, of imperfection, and of sin.   Every
Church and every age has its temptations and its
faults.   At one period there may be a tendency to
superstition; at another, a tendency to self-confi-
dence, spiritual pride, or irreverence.   Those who
are ready to reject all usurped authority in religion,
may not be altogether free from a spirit of pride,
and a disposition to resist even legitimate rule.   A
fear of bigotry and enthusiasm may sometimes be
found united with slothfulness and indifference.   To
every Church and every individual, the apostolic
precept, "Be not high-minded, but fear," should
be the subject of continual meditation and prayer.
It is only in this spirit that we should ever dwell
on the faults of others, or on the blessings which
the mercy of God has vouchsafed to bestow on ourselves.

But, amidst our sorrows for the numerous evils
with which the sin and infirmity of human nature
have afflicted the Church, we are consoled by the
perpetuity of the Church itself, and by the many
examples of Christian sanctity which have in every

age adorned our holy faith. Nothing can more powerfully prove to us the presence of God with his Church, than the lives of those men whom Divine grace has transformed into the image of Christ. There is in true religion a REALITY which comes home to the heart of every one; which stimulates the feeblest faith, and animates the most languid charity.

Series of Bishops

FROM THE APOSTLES TO THE PRESENT PRIMATE OF
ALL ENGLAND.

		A.D.
1	St: Peter and St. Paul.	
2	Linus bishop of Rome	58
3	Cletus	68
4	Clement	93
5	Evaristus	100
6	Alexander	109
7	Xystus or Sixtus	116
8	Telesphorus	129
9	Hyginus	138
10	Pius	142
11	Anicetus	156
12	Soter	168
13	Eleutherius	177
14	Victor	192
15	Zephyrinus	201
16	Calixtus	219
17	Urbanus	224
18	Pontianus	231
19	Anterus	235
20	Fabianus	236
21	Cornelius	250
22	Lucius	252
23	Stephen	253

		A.D.
24	Sixtus II.	257
25	Dionysius	258
26	Felix	271
27	Eutychianus	276
28	Caius	283
29	Marcellinus	296
30	Marcellus	304
31	Eusebius	309
32	Melchiades	311
33	Sylvester	313
34	Mark	335
35	Julius	336
36	Liberius	352
37	Felix II.	359
38	Damasus	366
39	Siricius	384
40	Anastasius	398
41	Innocentius	402
42	Zozimus	417
43	Boniface	418
44	Celestinus	423
45	Sixtus III.	432
46	Leo the Great	440
47	Hilary	461
48	Simplicius	467
49	Felix III.	483
50	Gelasius	492
51	Anastasius	496
52	Symmachus	498
53	Hormisdas	514
54	John	523
55	Felix IV.	526
56	Boniface II.	530
57	John II.	532

		A.D.
58	Agapetus	535
59	Sylverius	536
60	Vigilius	540
61	Pelagius	555
62	John III.	560
63	Benedict	574
64	Pelagius II.	578
65	Gregory the Great, who sent .	590
66	Augustine, first Archbp. of Canterbury	596
67	Laurentius	604
68	Mellitus	617
69	Justus	622
70	Honorius	626
71	Adeodatus	654
	A vacancy of four years.	
72	Theodore	668
73	Brithwald	692
74	Tatwin	731
75	Nothelm	735
76	Cuthbert	740
77	Bregwin	758
78	Lambert	764
79	Athelard	793
80	Wulfred	806
81	Theogild	832
82	Ceolnoth	832
83	Athelred	872
84	Plegmund	889
85	Athelm	915
86	Wulfhelm	924
87	Odo	934
88	Dunstan	959
89	Ethelgar	988
90	Siricius	989

		A.D.
91	Alfric	993
92	Elphege	1009
93	Livingus	1013
94	Agelnoth	1020
95	Eadsinus	1038
96	Robert	1050
97	Stigand	1052
98	Lanfranc	1070
	A vacancy.	
99	Anselm	1093
100	Ralph	1114
101	William Corbeil	1122
102	Theobald	1138
103	Thomas à Becket	1162
104	Richard	1171
105	Baldwin	1184
106	Reginald Fitz-Jocelin	1191
107	Hubert Walter	1193
108	Stephen Langton	1206
109	Richard Wethershed	1229
110	Edmund	1234
111	Boniface of Savoy	1244
112	Robert Kilwarby	1272
113	John Peckham	1278
114	Robert Winchelsey	1293
115	Walter Reynolds	1313
116	Simon Mepham	1327
117	John Stratford	1333
118	John De Ufford	1348
119	Thomas Bradwardin	1349
120	Simon Islip	1349
121	Simon Langham	1366
122	William Wittlesey	1369
123	Simon Sudbury	1375

		A.D.
124	William Courtenay . . .	1381
125	Thomas Arundel	1396
126	Henry Chicheley. . . .	1414
127	John Stafford	1443
128	John Kemp	1452
129	Thomas Bourchier . . .	1454
130	John Morton	1486
131	Henry Deane	1501
132	William Warham . . .	1504
133	Thomas Cranmer . . .	1533
	Vacancy. Reginald Pole intruded	1555
134	Matthew Parker	1559
135	Edmund Grindal	1575
136	John Whitgift	1583
137	Richard Bancroft	1604
138	George Abbot	1611
139	William Laud	1633
	A vacancy.	
140	William Juxon	1660
141	Gilbert Sheldon	1663
142	William Sancroft	1678
143	John Tillotson	1691
144	Thomas Tenison	1694
145	William Wake	1715
146	John Potter	1737
147	Thomas Herring	1747
148	Matthew Hutton	1757
149	Thomas Secker	1758
150	Frederick Cornwallis . . .	1768
151	John Moore	1783
152	Charles Manners Sutton . .	1805
153	WILLIAM HOWLEY, present Archbp.	1828

Series of Bishops

FROM THE APOSTLES TO THE PRESENT PRIMATE OF IRELAND.

		A.D.
1	St. Peter and St. Paul.	
2	Linus, bishop of Rome	58
3	Cletus	68
4	Clement	93
5	Evaristus	100
6	Alexander	109
7	Xystus or Sixtus	116
8	Telesphorus	129
9	Hyginus	138
10	Pius	142
11	Anicetus	156
12	Soter	168
13	Eleutherius	177
14	Victor	192
15	Zephyrinus	201
16	Calixtus	219
17	Urbanus	224
18	Pontianus	231
19	Anterus	235
20	Fabianus	236
21	Cornelius	250
22	Lucius	252
23	Stephen	253
24	Sixtus II.	257
25	Dionysius	258
26	Felix	271
27	Eutychianus	276
28	Caius	283

A.D.

29 Marcellinus 296
30 Marcellus 304
31 Eusebius 309
32 Melchiades 311
33 Sylvester 313
34 Mark 335
35 Julius 336
36 Liberius 352
37 Felix II. 359
38 Damasus 366
39 Siricius 384
40 Anastasius 398
41 Innocentius 402
42 Zozimus 417
43 Boniface 418
44 Celestinus, who sent . . . 423
45 Patrick, first Archbishop of Armagh 432
46 Benignus 455
47 Jarlath 465
48 Cormac 482
49 Dubtachus 497
50 Ailildus 513
51 Ailildus II. 526
52 Dubtachus II. 536
53 David 548
54 Feidlimidus 551
55 Cairlanus 578
56 Eochaid 588
57 Senachus 598
58 Mac Laisirius 610
59 Tomianus 619
60 Segenius 661
61 Flan-Febla 688
62 Suibneus 715

		A.D.
63	Cognusa	730
64	Cele-Petrus	750
65	Ferdachrius	758
66	Foendelachus	774
67	Dubdalethus	778
68	Affiatus	793
69	Cudiniscus	794
70	Conmachus	798
71	Torbachus	807
72	Nuadus	808
73	Mac Loingle	812
74	Artrigius	822
75	Faranan	834
76	Diermot	848
77	Factua	852
78	Ainmire	874
79	Catasach	875
80	Moelcob	883
81	Moel-Brigid	885
82	Joseph	927
83	Moel-Patrick	936
84	Catasach II.	937
85	Muredach	957
86	Dubdalethy	966
87	Murechan	998
88	Moelmury	1001
89	Amalgaid	1021
90	Dubdalethy II.	1050
91	Cumasach	1065
92	Moelisa	1065
93	Donald Mac Amalgaid	1092
94	Celsus	1106
95	Maurice	1129
96	Malachi	1134

		A.D.
97	Gelasius	1137
98	Cornelius	1174
99	Gilbert Ocaran	1175
100	Moelisa Ocarrol	1184
101	Amlave Omurid	1184
102	Thomas Oconnor	1185
103	Eugene Macgillivider	1206
104	Luke Netterville	1220
105	Donatus Ofidabra	1227
106	Albert of Cologn	1240
107	Reiner	1247
108	Abraham Oconellan	1257
109	Patrick Oscanlan	1261
110	Nicholas Macmolissa	1272
111	John Taaf	1305
112	Walter de Jorse	1306
113	Roland Jorse	1311
114	Stephen Segrave	1322
115	David Ohiraghty	1334
116	Richard Fitz-Ralph	1347
117	Milo Sweetman	1361
118	John Colton	1382
119	Nicholas Fleming	1404
120	John Swayn	1417
121	John Prene	1439
122	John Mey	1444
123	John Bole	1457
124	John Foxalls	1475
125	Edmund Counesburgh	1477
126	Octavian de Palatio	1480
127	John Kite	1513
128	George Cromer	1522
129	George Dowdal	1543
130	Hugh Goodacre	1552

		A.D.
131	Adam Loftus	1562
132	Thomas Lancaster	1568
133	John Long	1584
134	John Garvey	1589
135	Henry Usher	1595
136	Christopher Hampton	1613
137	James Usher	1624
138	John Bramhall	1660
139	James Margetson	1663
140	Michael Boyle	1678
141	Hugh Boulter	1702
142	Narcissus Marsh	1702
143	Thomas Lindsay	1713
144	John Hoadley	1742
145	George Stone	1747
146	Richard Robinson	1765
147	William Newcome	1795
148	William Stuart	1800
149	JOHN GEORGE BERESFORD, the present Archbishop	1822

Explanation of Words.

Alb, a vestment of the clergy.

Almoner, a person who distributes alms.

Amphitheatre, a place for public amusements.

Anathema, excommunication, — the severest censure of the Church.

Ascetics, devout persons, given up to a life of religion.

Asiarch, the principal heathen priest of Asia Minor.

Baptistery, a place for administering baptism.

Canons, ecclesiastical laws made by synods, also certain of the clergy.

Catholic, universal, or universally received.

Convocation, an assembly of the clergy.

Council, an assembly of bishops.

Heresy, an obstinate denial or perversion of some article of the faith.

Iconoclasts, image-breakers.

Irenarch, a magistrate who watched over the public peace.

Matins, morning service.

Metropolitan, a bishop who has the chief authority amongst the bishops of a province.

Oratory, a private chapel.

Œcumenical Synod, an assembly of bishops from all parts of the world.

Orisons, prayers.

Pall, an ornament worn originally by patriarchs, afterwards by metropolitans.

Patriarch, a bishop who has authority over metropolitans.

Proconsul, a Roman governor.

Schism, a criminal division in the Church, or a voluntary separation from it.

Synod, an assembly of bishops.

Temporalities, the property of the Church.

Vigil, watching at night with prayer.

Index.

FINIS

www.ingramcontent.com/pod-product-compliance
Lightning Source LLC
Chambersburg PA
CBHW051259130726
47987CB00004B/1583